Library Technology
and Digital Resources

LIBRARY SUPPORT STAFF HANDBOOKS

The Library Support Staff Handbook series is designed to meet the learning needs of both students in library support staff programs and library support staff working in libraries who want to increase their knowledge and skills.

The series was designed and is edited by Hali R. Keeler and Marie Shaw, both of whom teach in support staff programs and have managed libraries.

The content of each volume aligns to the competencies of the required and elective courses of the American Library Association–Allied Professional Association (ALA-APA) Library Support Staff Certification (LSSC) program. These books are both textbooks for library instructional programs and current resources for working library staff. Each book is available in both print and e-book versions.

Published books in the series include:

1. *Foundations of Library Services: An Introduction for Support Staff*
2. *Library Technology and Digital Resources: An Introduction for Support Staff*

Upcoming titles include:

3. *Cataloging and Classification: An Introduction for Support Staff*
4. *Collections: An Introduction for Support Staff*

Library Technology and Digital Resources

An Introduction for Support Staff

Marie Keen Shaw

Library Support Staff Handbooks, No. 2

ROWMAN & LITTLEFIELD
Lanham • Boulder • New York • London

Published by Rowman & Littlefield
A wholly owned subsidiary of The Rowman & Littlefield Publishing Group, Inc.
4501 Forbes Boulevard, Suite 200, Lanham, Maryland 20706
www.rowman.com

Unit A, Whitacre Mews, 26-34 Stannary Street, London SE11 4AB

British Library Cataloguing in Publication Information Available

Library of Congress Cataloging-in-Publication Data Available

ISBN 978-1-4422-5643-9 (cloth : alk. paper)
ISBN 978-1-4422-5644-6 (pbk. : alk. paper)
ISBN 978-1-4422-5645-3 (ebook)

♾™ The paper used in this publication meets the minimum requirements of American National Standard for Information Sciences—Permanence of Paper for Printed Library Materials, ANSI/NISO Z39.48-1992.

Printed in the United States of America

To my sister, Elaine,
a gifted writer who will forever be a dear friend.

Contents

.

PART III: NEW DIRECTIONS

Figures

Tables and Textboxes

TABLES

TEXTBOXES

Preface

Library Technology and Digital Resources: An Introduction for Support Staff is intended to provide practical information and guidance about digital resources and library technologies for those who work or intend to work in libraries. The chapters are aligned with the American Library Association Library Support Staff Certification (LSSC) program competencies for technology. The content addresses the competency expectations and provides fundamental explanations about the current technology found in academic, public, and school libraries today.

This book is for anyone who works or intends to work in a library. Library Support Staff (LSS) are most likely to be called upon by patrons who seek help with technology issues. This important handbook is geared toward improving the reader's knowledge and skills of library technology. Each chapter is broken down into short subheadings to make complex topics easy to find, read, and understand. Tables and illustrations are abundantly used throughout the text to present key ideas simply and clearly.

The text is written for three intended audiences: working LSS, instructors, and students in library certificate or degree programs. LSS are known by many names and have various levels of responsibility. LSS may be called library assistants, library technicians, library technical assistants, library associates, school library assistants, or library aides. No matter the type of library, today LSS are expected to have a working knowledge of many kinds of technology and to be proficient in the use of digital resources. Readers will find throughout this text basic explanations and helpful suggestions to use library technology and databases more effectively.

Instructors in library technology certificate or associate degree programs will be able to use this book as a primary instructional resource. Discussion questions, learning activities, and practice opportunities are found in each chapter. With extensive chapter bibliographies, this book can serve as a textbook for courses with curriculum on fundamentals of library technology, digitization, Internet searching, digital resources and collections, e-books, databases, metadata, and future trends or directions LSS should be prepared to work with. Students will find this a useful text because the information is presented in clear, non-technical language. There is an abundance of tables and figures which make concepts easier to understand. Suggested websites and readings at the end of each chapter can further students' knowledge of topics that are introduced in the book. Many references are from academic journals that are cited for further reading.

The scope of this book is to provide LSS with an introduction to the many databases and other digital resources libraries depend upon today and to offer practical ideas on how to use innovative technologies that are rapidly changing traditional library service. Sequenced in three parts, the book explains:

- *Digital Resources*: How to find and use important digital resources that are either available on the Internet or purchased as subscription databases;
- *Library Technologies*: How to use library technologies to improve or enhance patrons' reading, viewing, and research experiences; and
- *New Directions and Future Trends*: How LSS can prepare to be technology leaders in their libraries.

Part I begins with the introduction where we learn that digital resources are as equally important to patrons as traditional library services. By knowing the rudiments of how computers work in a binary system, LSS can better understand the power of digital resources for research, information, and the personal needs of patrons. The reader discovers digital resources found in global, national, state, and local collections are available today because of the efforts of fine global, national, and state libraries that are committed to scanning, preserving, and providing digital access to artifacts, data, and many other types of information sources. The reader also learns the important role of local libraries that preserve and digitize their own primary sources and artifacts making them accessible through online collections. In Part I, the challenges of online reading and viewing on a computer are discussed and ways are presented for LSS to help patrons become more digitally and visually literate. Finally in Part I the unique benefits of library subscription databases and the steps of how to plan, evaluate, acquire, budget, and fund databases from quality providers are all clearly presented.

Part II continues with practical explanations and suggestions on how to use the content of subscription databases such as journals, magazines, newspapers, and other media. The Internet is a primary source of information, but many do not know how to search effectively and efficiently for the best results. Advanced shortcuts and other techniques are clearly presented for LSS to use to increase their proficiency as Internet users. The world of e-books is explored, and useful suggestions are shared about devices, content, and file management. LSS who are confident and comfortable with using many different platforms, devices, and content providers will be of invaluable help to patrons. Part II continues with a chapter on digital copyright, acceptable use, and LSS responsibilities for confidentiality and security of digital data. Finally, the last chapter in Part II delves into computers and other equipment found in libraries, software, and network infrastructure. This practical chapter gives LSS the information they need to troubleshoot and solve many technology problems and tells how to communicate with providers in times of crisis.

Part III concludes the book with a coda. This part's one chapter covers new directions and the future where social media, Makerspaces, digital publishing, and other innovative ways to reach and expand the library community through technology and digital resources are explored.

Each chapter begins with *Key Terms* that are important to the content. The key terms are defined in the context of both their importance to technology, but also how that technology relates to library services, and why LSS should be familiar with them. Each chapter has an introduction where the upcoming topics and content are foreshadowed. Background knowledge, practical examples, and many step-by-step instructions abound in every chapter. The aim of this book is to describe library technology in clear and direct ways so that the reader has both a basic understanding and the immediate knowledge of how to use technology with confidence. This book has broad appeal because of its topic coverage and practical suggestions. The reader can immediately put into practice many of the ideas gleaned from each chapter.

Library Technology and Digital Resources: An Introduction for Support Staff covers new ground with its content aligned with the technology competencies established by the American Library Association Library Support Staff Certification Program (ALA-LSSC) (http://ala-apa.org/lssc). Each chapter addresses one or more of the technology competencies in ways so that the reader can understand each competency in real and practical applications and examples. The technology competencies are turned into examples of library practices which LSS find on the job each day.

This text provides a different perspective from most books or materials written for library professionals. Simply put, the majority of library literature is aimed for professional or Master of Library Science (MLS) graduate level librarians. Works are often highly theoretical and not practical. Other books on this topic of digital resources or library technology are written at a level that is aimed for professional librarians and not support staff. However, 85 percent of library support staff does not hold professional degrees. Written in clear language, this book ensures that readers can become effective users of digital resources. This book will provide many ways and examples of how support staff can use databases and technology to meet most patrons' needs. LSS are expected to work with a high level of technology but often do not have the formal training in library technology or digital resources.

There are many examples of how this book can help LSS to become more proficient and confident using digital resources and library technology. At the end of each chapter are discussion questions that are written to refocus the reader to the more important or salient parts of the chapter. There is also one, often two, learning activities at the end of each chapter that either an instructor can use with a class or the LSS can work through independently or with other staff to gain experience or additional practice with ideas or process described in the text.

Just a few examples of how the information in this book helps people are in the chapter 9 directories on Internet searching. By using the simple techniques shared in this chapter, LSS can streamline and target their searching process to find exact fields of information that once may have been elusive. Another example of how this book can help people is in chapter 11 on equipment, software, and networks. There are tables in this chapter on how to troubleshoot to solve common problems LSS face with technology. There is a checklist on how to evaluate technology in the library, tables with common network devices and what they do, and the types of Internet connectivity found in libraries today and the benefits of each. The goal of this book is to provide hands-on, real experiences of learning for LSS who can either refer to the book for specific topics or read it in its entirety for a thorough and practical understanding of library technology and digital resources.

This book is needed because there is a shortage of books written for library support staff on the topics of digital resources and technology. Library support staff are often required in their work to have practical knowledge of databases and websites that they can apply to effectively help patrons with their questions or needs. This book was developed around both the ALA-LSSC competencies for technology and the course curriculum of digital resources taught at Three Rivers Community College that has been approved by the American Library Association as an accredited course that meets the LSSC standards. Because of the lack of textbooks for LTA programs in technology, the author developed the content from her own research and teaching of digital resources and technology. The author also has practical experiences with technology having managed a large high school library media center with over 250 computers and other digital devices.

Upon reading this book, it is the intention of the author that the reader will be more confident in his or her approach to being a library technology leader. By this, the author means that the LSS will have the confidence to expand their use of technology in ways that help patrons find information or conduct research more effectively and efficiently using digital resources that either the library has acquired via subscription databases or because of the knowledge gleaned from this book. The author wrote this book to instill confidence in LSS who are often on the front line when a computer process is not working or a patron has an urgent need to make technology work. Approaching the vast and ever-changing world of technology takes a level head and a framework for categorizing similar situations or issues so that connections can be made between them. When LSS have the supports to be adventurous and explore technology, their learning will undoubtedly soar. This book is intended as a support for all LSS and LSS students so that they, in turn, will be able to confidently and smartly use technology to enhance their patrons' library experiences.

Acknowledgments

I am grateful for my collaboration of Hali Keeler. Hali, you provided me steady support throughout my writing of this book. Thank you for including me in this endeavor with our publisher, and for being both a colleague and a friend.

I thank my editor, Charles Harmon, for your confidence in me as a writer and for your constant encouragement and helpful suggestions.

With special appreciation I acknowledge my Editorial Advisory Board who provided important feedback during many stages of this book. You made thoughtful suggestions and shared ideas from the proposal phase thorough the final copy. Your hard work and book endorsements mean much to me.

To my parents, Mildred and Harry Keen, and my seven sisters and brothers, you have provided me with a lifetime of love and inspiration to achieve that which sometimes seems out of reach. My children and grandchildren, Joe, Jiayi, AJ, Alyssa, Ken, Sarah, and Nora, thank you for your ongoing interest and encouragement which sustains my writing.

I would not have begun—or completed—this book without the love and support of my husband, AJ. You enthusiastically expressed confidence in me, and you supported me throughout my writing process. Thank you for always being there for me.

Finally, I could not have written this book without my experiences of working with so many wonderful Library Support Staff. I thank each of you for always being hardworking, caring, and dedicated to providing the highest level of library service to patrons no matter what the challenges may be.

Editorial Advisory Board

PART I

Digital Resources

CHAPTER 1

Introduction

Library Support Staff (LSS) know the general trends and developments in technology applications for library functions and services. (ALA-LSSC Technology Competency #1)

Topics Covered in This Chapter:

- Digital Resources: Changing the Role for Library Support Staff
  - Collections
  - Digital Libraries
- Analog and Digital
  - Analog
  - The Digital Environment
  - Bits and Bytes
- Libraries Acquire Digital Resources
  - Enhanced Searching
- Preservation and Access through Digitization
- The Digital Library Federation

Key Terms:

Analog: Tape was the type of media libraries circulated for many years. Examples are audio and video cassettes, VHS tapes, 16 mm film, and phonograph records. Recorded in a continuous line with a beginning and end, to search a certain frame or location, one had to play or fast forward from the beginning of the tape. Libraries preserve important analog collections or convert them to digital.

Digital: This standard of today's technology uses binary code to create, store, and process data. Computers read data that is either expressed as "on"(1) or "off"(0). Alphabets and numbers are converted into binary code. Searching and other functions are much more efficient with digital than analog. Understanding how digital works is important for library staff who work with it every day.

Digital Collections: These are files of data whose content has a common theme, subject, time period, or other logical grouping. Types of data in digital collections can be text, sound, images, video, or combinations of each. Library staff creates digital collections for preserving and sharing local history, genealogy, research, special interests, or programs.

Digitization: Digitization is the process of scanning and converting text and pictures into a digital format. Library staff can learn how to digitize text, pictures, photographs, and other physical items in order to share them with patrons in an online format.

Electronic Resources: This is another name for digital resources. E-book comes from the term "electronic book." Library staff will find the term "electronic" or "electronic resources" in some of our literature or on library products.

Preservation: Libraries often are the keepers of local history and artifacts. The act is to maintain something in its original state. Library staff often accept unique or important items into the library collections to maintain and keep for future generations.

DIGITAL RESOURCES: CHANGING THE ROLE FOR LIBRARY SUPPORT STAFF

Digital resources have changed how Library Support Staff (LSS) work. Not long ago they mainly checked out books and managed other aspects of circulating materials. Today patrons may self-checkout their own materials while library staff help patrons download novels from the library e-book collection onto e-readers or create digital resources of text, images, music, or video.

LSS use digital resources daily in their work. They may interact with others both within and outside of the library community. Using their technology skills LSS may participate in shared projects among libraries and other educational or government institutions. Library staff may work with their local historical societies or museums to create online collections by scanning and classifying objects or researching the importance of each item. They may also support public television by creating programming and announcements to market or broadcast library and other nonprofit events. These are just two of many examples of how LSS use technology to better library services.

There are many kinds or types of library digital resources (see table 1.1). What is common to all is that they are used with or dependent upon computers. They may also be called **electronic resources** or "e" resources, such as electronic journals (e-journals), electronic books (e-books), or electronic subscriptions (e-subscriptions).

Digital resources may also refer to the hardware for viewing the Internet and databases: computers, tablets, mobile devices, Wi-Fi, network components, DVD and MP3 players, smart or whiteboards or even gaming systems. As technology advances so does the variety of devices libraries make available to their patrons. A

Table 1.1. Examples of Library Digital Resources

Internet Websites	Subscription and Non-Subscription Databases	E-books
Electronic Journals	Social Media	MP3 or Other Sound Files
DVD	Digital Video	HD Television
Digital Photography	Streaming Video	Computer Programs and Applications
Interviews	Scans of Original Text	PDF Documents

digital resource my library has for Young Adult (YA) programs (and at times for older patrons) is a Wii sports system.

Collections

A collection contains multiple resources linked around a specific subject, theme, or genre. Libraries traditionally are built upon a structure of collections whereby like books were grouped together. Traditional library book collections are in the areas of reference, fiction, nonfiction, biography, young adult, and children's or juvenile. Mysteries, science fiction, or romance books are often culled from the fiction collection and given special shelf space for ease of browsing. Collections can be subdivided further into media type, such as the DVD collection. Collections can also be small and specific. In my library I kept a special collection of *Life* magazines from 1939 to 1952 that students used for researching World War II topics. LSS often have firsthand knowledge of the reading choices, interests, and information needs of the patrons. Their knowledge is invaluable for building purposeful collections within the library that patrons will seek and use.

In a similar way, collections are made of many digital resources. For example, an e-book is a digital resource. My library's selection of over seventy-five e-books on historical fiction is a digital collection. Collections can be made of any purposeful combination of online of text, media, sound, and images. These **digital collections** often help users find resources on a specific time period, person, or event, such as scanned local newspaper articles that are inaccessible to patrons in their original print format (see table 1.2). Searchable by key word, locally made digital collections are found on small school library websites to the largest academic and public libraries sites.

Digital Libraries

A digital library is a website enriched with multiple digital collections. The digital library does not offer analog or print resources nor does it offer physical access to patrons. Digital libraries are created and hosted at the institution, state, national, and international levels.

Digital resources have transformed traditional library services. Today librarians provide both traditional and digital services. Many patrons use their library for computer access and digital resources. Because of remote access to digital resources, many patrons do not have to come to the library to find e-books or magazine and newspaper articles. We will visit some digital libraries in later chapters.

Table 1.2.   Examples of Digital Collections

Digital Collections Library of Congress[1]	Scanned or converted to digital format, these are significant collections of music, photographs, government documents, newspapers, media, and other formats preserved by the Library of Congress.
The New York Public Library Henry Wadsworth Longfellow Collection[2]	Portraits of Henry Wadsworth Longfellow taken throughout his life from his childhood to his late years.
Duke University Libraries Caribbean Sea Migration Slide Collection[3]	Documents in digital photographs of Dominicans, Cubans, Haitians, and others who fled their countries in small boats in the late twentieth century for freedom in America. Many of these photographs are of the US Coast Guard intercepting migrants in their treacherous passage.
Nashville Public Library Veterans History Project Collection[4]	Primarily oral histories of Nashville veterans from World War I to the war in Afghanistan. Also contains such items as letters, memoirs, photographs, scrapbooks, maps, and other materials which tell the stories of individual veterans through firsthand sources.

1 "Digital Collections & Services," Digital Collections, last modified 2015, accessed February 10, 2015, http://loc.gov/library/libarch-digital.html.

2 "Henry Wadsworth Longfellow," New York Public Library Digital Collections, last modified 2015, accessed February 10, 2015, http://digitalcollections.nypl.org/search/index?utf8=%E2%9C%93&keywords=digital+collections#/?scroll=6.

3 "Caribbean Sea Migration Collection," Duke University Libraries Catalog, last modified 2015, accessed February 10, 2015, http://search.library.duke.edu/search?source=duke&Ntk=Keyword&Nr=OR%28210969%2cOR%28206474%29%29&Ne=2+200043+206474+210899+210956&N=210959+200076.

4 "Veterans History Project Collection," Nashville Public Library Digital Collections, last modified 2015, accessed February 10, 2015, http://digital.library.nashville.org/cdm/search/collection//searchterm/Veterans%20History%20Project/field/relati/mode/exact/conn/and/display/200/order/nosort/ad/asc.

ANALOG AND DIGITAL

Analog

Library collections traditionally were comprised of print and analog resources. Print resources are paper books, newspapers, magazines, pictures, photographs, brochures, and other items created from tree pulp. Analog resources are media made of film or tape. "The word '**analog**' refers to data that is recorded linearly in a continuum,"[1] such as a sound cassette recording or a film on a VHS tape. The first analog resources began to appear in libraries in the late nineteenth century. Thomas Edison is credited for recording the first sound on a phonograph record in 1877. We can listen to his original sound by accessing the American Memories archive at the Library of Congress (see figure 1.1).[2]

Another early analog resource is silent film that soon evolved into "talkies." "The first projected sequential proto-movie was made by Eadweard Muybridge some time between 1877 and 1880."[3]

Figure 1.1.   The Library of Congress American Memory. *Library of Congress*

Analog media have a distinct beginning and ending. Because analog resources are a continuous line, it is difficult to locate specific information on them. Analog is also cumbersome and challenging to search, edit, or merge with other media.

Sound advanced from phonographs to reel-to-reel to audio cassette. Cassettes became lendable resources to library patrons when the tape was contained in a small carrier and cost of playback equipment became affordable. By the mid-1980s it was expected that public and school libraries would lend VHS tapes from their analog film collections.

The Digital Environment

School librarians and support staff in the early 1980s began to acquire and provide educational software digital resources for teachers and students. Personal computers such as the Apple IIE and TRS-80s (see figure 1.2) were often located in the school library for shared access and instructional support. Teachers found early math and literacy software useful for practice or reinforcement with their students.[4] Computers were used mostly for writing, calculations, or drill and practice.

Bits and Bytes

It may be helpful for LSS to understand the basics of computer data. The word *digital* refers to data that is expressed and stored in binary code or the two digits 0 and 1. Each 0 or 1 is called a bit. Either the bit is "on" signified by the number "1" or "off" signified by the number "0." Bytes, on the other hand, are a group or string of eight bits. The eight bits in each byte are coded to be turned on or off.[5]

Figure 1.2. First Desktop Computers

BASICS OF HOW BINARY CODE WORKS (BITS AND BYTES)

Bytes are represented by the following sequence of numbers that are doubled beginning with the number one:

128   64   32   16   8   4   2   1

In coding the programmer turns bytes on (with 1) or off (with 0). In order for a computer to read the number 175 the byte would look like this:

1   0   1   0   1   1   1   1

whereby bytes 128 + 32 + 8 + 4 + 2 +1 are turned "on" to equal 175. Bytes 64 and 16 are turned "off" because if added, they would exceed the number 175.

Go ahead and see for yourself how this works. Choose any number. Turn off or on the "bytes" of 1 through 128 that add up to your chosen number with the binary numbers of 0 and 1.

Alphabets, on the other hand, are converted into bits. Computers can only understand numbers, so letters of the alphabet have to be converted to a number representation. This representation is called ASCII, which stands for American Standard Code for Information Interchange (http://www.asciitable.com). The ASCII system converts our English alphabet into numbers. Words are recognized by the computer obtaining the right number for each letter by turning off the 0s and turning on the 1s just as we did above. The computer interprets each bit (or number) into a specific letter to form words. The ASCII code numerical representation of the upper case letter "A" is 65. Lower case "a" is 97.[6] Some other ASCII letter codes are shown in table 1.3.

Why should bits and bytes be important to LSS? By understanding what goes on with bits and bytes at a basic level, we see how it is possible for the computer to search out words. When the computer matches the correct sequence of bytes to our search words or terms, data or information in the form of a website or document that is indexed will be offered to the user.[7]

A limiting factor of digital, however, when compared to analog, is the quality of film. The digitization process creates an estimate of the image while analog film captures the true picture. The digitized image is very acceptable in most instances, but to the artistic eye, analog film is superior and has a following in the film industry.[8] This distinction is important for library staff to know who may have patrons where film quality is of utmost importance.

LIBRARIES ACQUIRE DIGITAL RESOURCES

The laser videodisc was the first digital disc I worked with. Laser videodiscs became available just before DVD technology. They were very large but functioned much like DVDs in that one could search and track digital images in a nonlinear fashion. A drawback of laser video discs was the expense. My library could only afford one player and only a few discs because of the prohibitive cost. I believe because they were not affordable they never had market share and fizzled.

Most public libraries did not create collections of circulating digital resources until the price of compact disc and DVD hardware became affordable for personal use. Patrons came to the public library seeking compact discs and DVDs for their new home devices. However, because educational licensing was more favorable, school libraries focused on acquiring and lending teachers and students learning software and educational games. Most public libraries could not lend software to patrons but rather built digital collections of media that were desirable for home use.

Enhanced Searching

In addition to collection development, the evolution to digital resources greatly enhanced the process of information searching. With an analog VHS tape one has to often rewind and play back to find a particular spot or frame of the film. With digital resources bytes of information that convert to words are easily searched and retrieved.

Table 1.3. Example of Spelling "Library" in ASCII

Letter	ASCII Code	Converted into a Bit (Add numbers on second line in each box)								
		128	64	32	16	8	4	2	1	
L	76	0	1	0	0	1	1	0	0	= 76
I	73	0	1	0	0	1	0	0	1	= 73
B	66	0	1	0	0	0	0	1	0	= 66
R	82	0	1	0	1	0	0	1	0	= 82
A	64	0	1	0	0	0	0	0	0	= 64
R	82	0	1	0	1	0	0	1	0	= 82
Y	89	0	1	0	1	1	0	0	1	= 89

This means the ability of LSS to find or help patrons find information is also greatly enhanced with digital resources. Indexing, searching, and locating information, which once could be a time consuming and arduous task, is now taken for granted. Having background knowledge of how digital searching works is helpful for the LSS both to support the creation of local library websites and databases as well as accessing information from a wide variety of digital resources.

PRESERVATION AND ACCESS THROUGH DIGITIZATION

Digitization is a process of preserving artifacts by means of scanning. The scanned image can be converted into a web-friendly file format such as jpeg, pdf, or html. Digitization enhances research because metadata of key words and important facts are associated with the artifact in a searchable and retrievable way. Scanning technology has advanced so that multi-dimensional images of artifacts can be authentically displayed and accessed across diverse platforms. Digitized artifacts provide patrons firsthand knowledge about events, objects, or people that can spur their own thinking and depth of research into areas that once they could only read about.

Preservation of digital resources not only provides accessibility for patrons; it also invites libraries to create local digital archives. Archives are places or collections in libraries and museums with restricted access where unique artifacts are stored and only retrieved under special circumstances. Scanned artifacts found in digital resources are stored on servers that are large capacity computers that may be accessed via the Internet. Storage servers are often referred to as "the cloud." Clouds of servers are located offsite and back up digital files and content. Clouds are managed by database experts who run processes of backup, storage, and data retrieval. "The word 'cloud' often refers to the Internet and more precisely to some datacenter full of servers that is connected to the Internet."[9]

THE DIGITAL LIBRARY FEDERATION

The Digital Library Federation (http://www.diglib.org) is a program of the Council of Libraries and Information Resources. The Council on Libraries and Information Resources (see figure 1.3) is an "independent, nonprofit organization that forges strategies to enhance research, teaching, and learning environments in collaboration with libraries, cultural institutions, and communities of higher learning."[10] The Digital Library Federation "is a community of practitioners who advance research, teaching, and learning through the application of digital library research, technology, and services. DLF serves as a resource and catalyst for collaboration among digital library developers, project managers, and all who are invested in digital library issues."[11]

The membership of the Digital Library Federation is predominantly large and renowned universities in the United States. Key government institutions including the National Archives, National Library of Medicine, the Library of Congress, and the Smithsonian Libraries are a few of the other type of important members. The Digital Library Federation members set standards for creating and sharing their most prized digital resources. The Digital Library Federation has also developed procedures and

Figure 1.3. The Council on Libraries and Information Resources. *The Council on Libraries and Information Resources, Digital Library Federation*

processes for creating digital resources and encourages the development of collections and archives by all libraries. By sharing their best practices, the Digital Library Federation helps those working in both large and small libraries and museums to learn how to create, share, and preserve artifacts from their own unique collections, classifying digital resources by content, chronology, or other thematic organizations. The archives created by the members of the Digital Library Federation have a growing following of users who are interested in primary research of historic documents, events, places, and people.

Librarians and LSS can learn much about creating local digital resources and collections by delving into the practices of the Digital Library Federation. While their collections are top notch, our own development of local digital resources can be spurred by their example. Lacking an archive or purposeful collection of school athletic history, students worked with me to create a sports digital resource. The library held in its periodical archive original local newspapers from decades before that were decaying. The newspaper had gone defunct and out of business. By scanning and digitizing articles about past school athletes, we began to create a digital resource of school athletic history. Not unlike the Digital Library Federation, we used scanning technology and brief metadata to create a digital resource that could be accessed via the Internet by the school community.

CHAPTER SUMMARY

A key concept of this chapter is that digital resources are as equally important to patrons as traditional library services in school, public, and academic libraries. LSS are seen by others as technologists who are required to know the general trends and developments in technology applications for library functions and services. LSS can learn from experts in national and academic libraries how to use digitization technologies to preserve local artifacts and create collections of databases to give patrons web access to important information ordinarily in closed archives. By knowing the rudiments of how computers work in a binary system, LSS can better understand the power of digital resources for research, information, and the personal needs of patrons.

DISCUSSION QUESTIONS AND ACTIVITIES

Discussion Questions

1. Name three of the most popular digital resources in your library and discuss why patrons seek them over other library materials.
2. Describe one main difference between analog and digital resources that LSS should know about.
3. How does digitization support preservation and sharing of special library materials?
4. What is the Digital Library Federation and in what ways can it be a helpful resource to library staff and patrons?
5. Discuss ways libraries have changed because of technology and digital resources from just ten or twenty years ago.

Activity

Explore the Digital Library Federation

You may engage others, such as colleagues or friends, with this activity. Invite them to join you on your favorite social media or e-mail to discuss the results of your exploration of the DLF.

Go to the DLF Website: http://www.diglib.org/members/

Task: You are to investigate several of the digital resources of the Digital Library Federation collections. As you explore find a collection in (1) literature, (2) science, and (3) history that appeals or is of interest to you.

Spend time exploring each collection you select so that you become familiar with what it has to offer in terms of content and historical value.

You are then to post to a friend or colleague on social media or e-mail. Be specific as you:

1. Describe the site.
2. Tell them why you think it would be important for a librarian to know about each of the collections. Why should a librarian be familiar with it? Who may it interest? What is the content? When is the time period of the collection?

Once you have made three postings, respond to one of your colleagues' postings—is there something else you can add to the description or reason why librarians should know about it?

NOTES

1. "What Is the Difference between Analog and Digital Technology?" PC Net, accessed September 15, 2014, http://pc.net/helpcenter/answers/difference_between_analog_and_digital.

2. "Thomas Edison and the First Phonograph August 12, 1877," American Memory, accessed September 15, 2014, http://www.americaslibrary.gov/jb/recon/jb_recon_phongrph_1.html.

3. "Silent Film," accessed September 15, 2014, https://www.princeton.edu/~achaney/tmve/wiki100k/docs/Silent_film.html.

4. "Calendar | Visit | Connect | Support | Membership | Press Room You Are Here Home › About › International Center for the History of Electronic Games International Center for the History of Electronic Games," The Strong National Museum of Play, last modified 2014, accessed September 15, 2014, http://www.museumofplay.org/about/icheg.

5. "Computer Tutorial: How Binary Codes Work," YouTube, last modified 2009, accessed September 15, 2014, https://www.youtube.com/watch?v=EDxZI_T1Jpg.

6. "ASCII Table and Description," AsciiTable- ASCII Character Code, last modified 2015, accessed February 10, 2015, http://www.asciitable.com/.

7. "Ascii Codes Explained," accessed September 16, 2014, http://www.tntbasic.com/learn/help/guides/asciicodesexplained.htm.

8. Ben Fritz, "Movie Film, at Death's Door, Gets a Reprieve," *Wall Street Journal*, July 29, 2014.

9. "Definition Of: Cloud," PC, last modified 2014, accessed September 15, 2014, http://www.pcmag.com/encyclopedia/term/39847/cloud.

10. "Council of Libraries and Information Resources," Council of Libraries and Information Resources, last modified 2014, accessed September 15, 2014, http://www.clir.org/.

11. "The Digital Library Federation," last modified 2014, accessed September 15, 2013, http://www.clir.org/dlf.

REFERENCES, SUGGESTED READINGS, AND WEBSITES

"Ascii Codes Explained." Accessed September 16, 2014. http://www.tntbasic.com/learn/help/guides/asciicodesexplained.htm.

Asciitable.com. "ASCII Table and Description." AsciiTable-ASCII Character Code. Last modified 2015. Accessed February 10, 2015. http://www.asciitable.com/.

"Calendar | Visit | Connect | Support | Membership | Press Room You Are Here Home › About › International Center for the History of Electronic Games International Center for the History of Electronic Games." The Strong National Museum of Play. Last modified 2014. Accessed September 15, 2014. http://www.museumofplay.org/about/icheg.

"Computer Tutorial: How Binary Codes Work." YouTube. Last modified 2009. Accessed September 15, 2014. https://www.youtube.com/watch?v=EDxZI_T1Jpg.

"Council of Libraries and Information Resources." Council of Libraries and Information Resources. Last modified 2014. Accessed September 15, 2014. http://www.clir.org/.

"Definition Of: Cloud." PC. Last modified 2014. Accessed September 15, 2014. http://www.pcmag.com/encyclopedia/term/39847/cloud.

"The Digital Library Federation." Last modified 2014. Accessed September 15, 2013. http://www.clir.org/dlf.

Duke University. "Caribbean Sea Migration Collection." Duke University Libraries Catalog. Last modified 2015. Accessed February 10, 2015. http://search.library.duke.edu/search?source=duke&Ntk=Keyword&Nr=OR%28210969%2cOR%28206474%29%29&Ne=2+200043+206474+210899+210956&N=210959+200076.

Fritz, Ben. "Movie Film, at Death's Door, Gets a Reprieve." *Wall Street Journal,* July 29, 2014.

Library of Congress. "Digital Collections & Services." Digital Collections. Last modified 2015. Accessed February 10, 2015. http://loc.gov/library/libarch-digital.html.

Nashville Public Library. "Veterans History Project Collection." Nashville Public Library Digital Collections. Last modified 2015. Accessed February 10, 2015. http://digital.library .nashville.org/cdm/search/collection//searchterm/Veterans%20History%20Project/field/ relati/mode/exact/conn/and/display/200/order/nosort/ad/asc.

New York Public Library. "Henry Wadsworth Longfellow." New York Public Library Digital Collections. Last modified 2015. Accessed February 10, 2015. http://digitalcollections .nypl.org/search/index?utf8=%E2%9C%93&keywords=digital+collections#/?scroll=6.

"Silent Film." Accessed September 15, 2014. https://www.princeton.edu/~achaney/tmve/ wiki100k/docs/Silent_film.html.

"Thomas Edison and the First Phonograph August 12, 1877." American Memory. Accessed September 15, 2014. http://www.americaslibrary.gov/jb/recon/jb_recon_phongrph_1 .html.

"What Is the Difference between Analog and Digital Technology?" PC Net. Accessed September 15, 2014. http://pc.net/helpcenter/answers/difference_between_analog_and_digital.

CHAPTER 2

Digital and Visual Literacies

LSS know the role and responsibility of libraries for introducing relevant applications of technology, including digital literacy, to the public. (ALA-LSSC Technology Competency #2)

Topics Covered in This Chapter:

- Digital Literacy
  - Standards and Research
  - Paper vs. Screen
  - Reading
  - Writing
  - LSS Support Digital Literacy
- Visual Literacy
  - Computer Graphics
  - Improve Your Visual Literacy Skills

Key Terms:

JPEG: An abbreviation for *Joint Photographic Experts Group*, and pronounced *jay-peg*. This file format compresses a color image to about 5 percent of its normal size with only slight loss of quality. Because the JPEG file size is so small, download speed is faster and less storage space is needed. JPEG is the accepted file format for Internet images.

Literacy: The ability and skills of a person to read, write, and perform mathematics. The term also defines having knowledge and expertise in a particular field of study.

Nonlinear Text: Words or sentences that are not in consecutive order nor follow a left-to-right, line-by-line arrangement. Nonlinear text may be words in any vertical or horizontal manner and may not appear connected to each other.

Technology Standards: Clear expectations of outcomes that define what students should know how to do with technology and be able to do using technology to support their learning. Standards set goals for student achievement.

Do you read differently on a computer screen than you do from a traditional paper book? How so? Do you really understand and fully interpret information conveyed in the thousands of images you view online each day? How has your ability to read text and view pictures changed with technology?

The goal of this chapter is to answer these questions for ourselves so that we, in turn, can support our patrons who seek information from digital resources. Our world is digital, and libraries have dramatically changed their collections and services to keep current with new technology. In this chapter we will examine the implications of technology and how it has changed how people read, write, and view digital resources from their libraries.

DIGITAL LITERACY

Digital literacy is a relatively new term. Below are four statements that define digital literacy. This chapter will focus on the first definition, the ability to read and write with technology tods. Other chapters of this book address the other three important definitions.

If **literacy** is the ability for a person to be able to read and write in traditional ways with paper and pencil, then digital literacy is the ability to read and write using computer technology. The concept of literacy is used to separate the educated from the uneducated. A literate person goes to school and learns how to read and write. An illiterate person either drops out of school or is otherwise uneducated and cannot read or write. A digitally literate person successfully uses computer technology to read, write, and effectively communicate information. A digitally illiterate person struggles with technology standards.[1]

DIGITAL LITERACY

1. The ability to read and write with technology tools.
2. The ability to find, evaluate, utilize, share, and create content using information technologies and the Internet. (Cornell University[a])
3. The ability to use and manage technology proficiently.
4. The ability to comply with ethical and legal technology use.

[a] *http://digitalliteracy.cornell.edu*

In addition to using technology to read, write, and communicate, a digitally literate person also has expertise in the field of technology. He or she is able to operate and use technology for research, problem solving, and innovation, and adheres to all legal and ethical requirements. Cornell University defines digital literacy as "the ability to find, evaluate, utilize, share, and create content using information technologies and the Internet."[2] The University of Illinois advocates that a digital literate person is able to use technologies, regardless of platform or format, to support all means of communication, research, and tasks and to apply technology to interpret and evaluate media and information.

The transfer of our traditional literacy skills is not automatic, and we have to work to achieve digital literacy proficiency. We who have traditional reading and writing skills may struggle until we learn to be proficient with technology. We will now look at some of the research and standards that support digital literacy and libraries.

Standards and Research

The Internet has been available now for personal use for more than two decades, and we have adopted it into our lives. Technology has become more compact and easier to use, such as with cell phones, our portable computing and communication device. However, being able to push a button does not make someone digitally literate.

UNIVERSITY OF ILLINOIS'S DEFINITION OF DIGITAL LITERACY[a]

- The ability to use digital technology, communication tools, or networks to locate, evaluate, use, and create information.[b]
- The ability to understand and use information in multiple formats from a wide range of sources when it is presented via computers.[c]
- A person's ability to perform tasks effectively in a digital environment....Literacy includes the ability to read and interpret media, to reproduce data and images through digital manipulation, and to evaluate and apply new knowledge gained from digital environments.[d]

[a] *"What is Digital Literacy?" Digital Literacy Definition and Resources, accessed April 18, 2015, http://www.library.illinois.edu/diglit/definition.html.*

[b] *Paul Gilster, Digital Literacy (New York: Wiley and Computer Publishing, 1997), 1.*

[c] *Barbara R. Jones-Kavalier and Suzanne L. Flannigan, Connecting the Digital Dots: Literacy of the 21st Century, http://connect.educause.edu/Library/EDUCAUSE+Quarterly/Connecting theDigitalDotsL/39969.*

[d] *Digital Strategy Glossary of Key Terms, http://www.digitalstrategy.govt.nz/Media-Centre/Glossary-of-Key-Terms, accessed August 21, 2008.*

Schools today are doing much to teach students digital literacy, but not all teachers grew up with technology nor are they comfortable and proficient with it. Library media specialists and library support staff in schools are expected to be technology experts who assist students and teachers. The International Society for Technology Education (ISTE) has established **technology standards** for students, teachers, and school administrators[3] that set expectations on how those in schools use technology to communicate, solve problems, conduct research, and effectively enhance teaching and learning. Library staff that know the technology standards of students and teachers may also apply those standards to themselves as they continue to learn how to use technology with patrons.

There is much research available on the ongoing issues and concerns surrounding digital literacy. "Internet and American Life" is an ongoing project by the Pew Center for Research[4] that aims to regularly identify, analyze, and help us understand how technology impacts our culture. In the Pew report "Teaching Research Skills in Today's Digital Environment"[5] we learn being able to use technology to conduct and understand research also defines digital literacy. In a recent survey the majority of teachers described their middle or high school students as "fair" or "poor" when it comes to:

- using multiple sources effectively to support an argument;
- assessing the quality and accuracy of information they find online; and
- recognizing bias in online content.[6]

Ideally all teachers should be able to teach these research skills in their courses, but some teachers said they do not feel qualified to do so. Participants said librarians are a key resource in teaching students how to use the Internet for research.[7]

The American Library Association found in its study on "Public Library Funding & Technology Access"[8] that public library staff have an active role in boosting patrons' digital literacy skills. The study reported:

- 90.2 percent of public libraries offer some type of formal or informal technology training;
- 44 percent of non-urban public libraries and 63.2 percent of urban public libraries offer formal technology classes;
- 34.8 percent of public libraries provide one-on-one training by appointment; and
- 82.7 percent of public libraries offer informal point-of-use technology training assistance.

Librarians report in this study that there are large numbers of patrons who struggle with technology. They may not have computers at home and rely on the public library staff to help them obtain digital literacy skills. When LSS are themselves proficient with technology, they can do much help improve individual patron's digital literacy skills. An LSS at my college library recently told me, "It seems I help a student at least once a day who has difficulty connecting a laptop to the college network or other problems with using his or her computer. Even though I may not be familiar with the device, I am pretty confident that if I try a few of the things I know from my own experience about networks and computers, I can usually help them out. I also learn something new when I help others." This LSS uses and improves his digital literacy skills as he assists patrons.

Paper vs. Screen

Prior to personal computers which began to appear in our homes and at work in the mid-1990s, people primarily read only from two-dimensional paper books, journals, or other texts. Occasionally we would read a message on a TV or movie screen, but the text was often in very large print and the message was a short sentence or two. With the onset of computers, there was an assumption reading skills would automatically transfer to technology. Users were not told that reading would be different on the computer.

As a high school library media specialist with over 250 computers in the library, my observation was many students labored to read text on the computer screen. Ordinarily solid readers had difficulty reading online when the format, alignment of words, and other variables were very different than reading from a book. If printing was available, students opted to print the full text so that they could read in a traditional manner. If printing was not available, they often would give up trying to read long articles on the computer. Managing printing with limited resources was a challenge (we defaulted our printing to draft quality, double-sided paper). Providing students with a free paper copy of the website was the right thing to do because otherwise they had difficulty comprehending the information online. Most school and public libraries rarely can afford to provide free copies of text for patrons and must charge for printing. Print management software[9] streamlines the process of collecting money (e.g., special accounts connected to the integrated library system or the other methods of credit). While the need to control printing is understood, it also limits patrons' ability to fully read, understand, and use information found online.

Reading

The relationship between the act of reading and the work of the human brain is complex. The Dartmouth College Reading Brains Lab suggests many processes have to be in place and work together for one to read:[10]

- orthographic processing that involves the visual look of a word or string of letters;
- phonological processing that involves the sounds of language;
- morphological processing such as knowing the difference between "cat" and "cats";
- semantic processing involves the meaning of words; and
- syntactic processing involves the order and arrangement of words in phrases and sentences.

Syntactic processing, how sentences are understood, relates to some of the issues of reading on a screen. We learn to read in a linear or line-by-line way. When we read linear sentences, we are able to comprehend more from the text. In reading linear text our eyes focus on a larger amount of text and subtly we can pre-read ahead and re-read behind to get deeper meaning and context from the paragraphs. Reading on a computer is often **nonlinear** because sentences appear in unpredictable places all over the screen. Neuroscience has found we use different parts of the brain when reading from a piece of paper or from a screen.[11] We skim and jump among sentences on a screen. A problem could be is if you don't use the deep reading part of your brain, you will lose the ability to do so. Therefore, the more we read online, the more likely we will lose—or for young people never develop—the ability to comprehend deep and complex text.[12]

Our brains recognize and distinguish between physical objects such as a car and a truck.[13] Text is a physical object which our brain is quick to recognize as not only letters and words but also its linear order and predictable arrangement. Before we even begin to read the words, our brain is working to perceive the text in its entirety, forming a mental representation of the sentences. Similar to a map, by using the mental representation our brains support all types of reading, including deep reading. However, on a screen words and sentences do not fall into linear, predictable mental representations that the brain is comfortable and familiar with. Instead, our brains have to work harder for less depth of understanding. The speed of our reading complex text decreases dramatically on a screen. Working harder bogs and slows down the reader. It may also explain why people are more likely to read Twitter feeds and short news or magazine articles online but have a much harder time (and often give up!) reading long passages of nonfiction and complex text on a screen. When our brains have to work very hard to figure out what is going on with the unfamiliar layout of the screen or where only a small amount of text is viewable, sustained reading is often interrupted by sudden bursts of our flipping between screens to pre-read and re-read sentences.

It is important for library staff to understand that the more people read online, the less likely they may or may be able to read nonfiction text that is rich in innovative and complex ideas. As those who are in the position to suggest materials to patrons, it appears important from the growing research on screen reading that we encourage patrons to also read from books in order to sustain and promote deep reading (see table 2.1). We also should keep in mind the research about digital literacy as libraries convert more and more resources that contain deep text into digital resources and learn ways to support patrons' screen reading.

Writing

Digital literacy is also defined by the ability to write using technology. While LSS do not typically get involved with the writing process of patrons, it is interesting to note here that research shows, similar to the reading process, different centers of the brain are activated when we write by hand with a pen than when we type on a computer. Writing by hand activates multiple regions of the brain associated with processing and remembering information more than pressing keys.[14] Yet there is efficiency in using computers to write, and elementary schools are almost completely abandoning teaching cursive writing to teach keyboarding. At a younger

Table 2.1. Partnership for Twenty-First-Century Skills, ISTE Student K–12 Technology Standards

1	Creativity and innovation
	Students demonstrate creative thinking, construct knowledge, and develop innovative products and processes using technology.
2	Communication and collaboration
	Students use digital media and environments to communicate and work collaboratively, including at a distance, to support individual learning and contribute to the learning of others.
3	Research and information fluency
	Students apply digital tools to gather, evaluate, and use information.
4	Critical thinking, problem solving, and decision making
	Students use critical thinking skills to plan and conduct research, manage projects, solve problems, and make informed decisions using appropriate digital tools and resources.
5	Digital citizenship
	Students understand human, cultural, and societal issues related to technology and practice legal and ethical behavior.
6	Technology operations and concepts
	Students demonstrate a sound understanding of technology concepts, systems, and operations.

and younger age, children learn typing skills to enhance communication, computer performance, and to take state and national online assessments.[15]

The major benefit of handwriting over keyboarding is the retrieval of information. The engagement of the brain during handwriting results in better recall of the information. You may try handwriting rather than using a computer during library planning, staff, or other meetings because the process of writing critical information may affect how well you remember and use it later.

Self-Test Activity

Compare your or a friend's reading ability on paper vs. screen (see table 2.2). My college students were convinced the brain works differently on paper vs. screen after they took the self-test.

LSS Support Digital Literacy

One way LSS can help patrons improve their digital literacy is for themselves to keep current with new research of how technology may both support and inhibit reading. There is still much to be known about how we read and the different functions of the brain reading from paper or reading on a computer. All reading is not alike. Reading for quick news or entertainment is very different than reading for understanding and learning.

Table 2.2. Self-Test

Step	Action
1	Create two T-charts. Make each T-chart by simply writing a very large letter "T" on a full piece of paper. The vertical line of the "T" divides your paper into two columns. On the top line of the "T" write "Positives" on the left side of the page and "Negatives" on the right side of the top of the page.
2	Go to the Pew Research Internet Project found at http://www.pewinternet.org/.
3	Select two of the current reports on Internet and technology that are about equal in length. One report you will read on the screen; the other report you are to print and read on paper.
4	As you read each report, list five positive ideas that you found in the article on the left side of the T-chart. On the right side of your T-chart list five negative ideas from the article. By doing this you are going to have to read deeply.
5	Get a timer and read each article and fill in T-chart. What were your results?

Below are ways LSS support digital literacy for patrons:

1. Become familiar with how you read both traditionally and on screen. Take the self-test several times. Figure out ways that you can augment reading on the screen. You may find that it benefits you to pre-read or skim ahead if the screen is small or if your font size is large and leaves less room for more words. By analyzing the differences between your reading on paper and reading on a screen, you can provide firsthand experiences that may be helpful to others.

2. Support the research process. Use techniques we learned in chapter 9 on Internet searching to help patrons locate authoritative and valid websites. Share with them the Google shortcuts for effective searching. Help patrons locate and select appropriate articles and other fine resources from digital resources sponsored by national, state, and local governments and other digital resources discussed in this book.

3. Well-constructed and authored digital resources are more likely to be created in ways that will support reading on a screen. Share websites that offer clean representations of linear text over those that may be harder to navigate.

4. Provide print copies to patrons whenever possible, especially if they are doing research.

5. If you create or contribute to making library web pages, think about creating linear text in appropriate places. A crowded and unorganized web page is not helpful to the reader. Do not make your readers skim and jump to multiple places when they could read text in a recognizable representation of a paragraph.

6. Likewise, if you create digital resources or collections, plan and discuss with others the issues of digital literacy to improve the reading experiences of future users.

7. Nonfiction more likely requires deep reading than fiction. Newspaper and popular magazine articles are easier to read than academic or research journal articles. As you help patrons find digital or electronic resources, guide them to use screens for lighter, less intense reading. In other words, suggest patrons use

their devices or screens for fiction or popular reading and paper for research or deep reading.

8. Practice will improve reading on screens and awareness of the work the brain must do will help readers sustain their efforts for the hard work of reading online.

VISUAL LITERACY

We need to have both digital and visual literacy skills to evaluate, use, and create digital resources. LSS need to be practiced in digital and visual literacy because libraries provide text, images, and media for online reading and viewing. Being able to read screens with deeper understanding and to interpret meaning from pictures enables us to make educated judgments about what we find online. LSS who are trained in these skills can help and support patrons who use digital resources.

Visual literacy is the ability to draw information and inferences from photographs, pictures, or illustrations, whether they are still or moving. Visual literacy is an important idea to share in this chapter because so many library digital resources are pictures. Libraries today create digital collections by scanning primary source documents, artifacts, and other treasures not typically available to patrons. Images are now readily available to patrons in the format of computer files with JPEG being the most versatile and familiar to us. If we are not trained in visual literacy, important information can be skipped or overlooked. LSS can assist patrons with finding the details in images when they themselves know what to look for.

A more thorough definition of visual literacy comes from the Association of College and Research Libraries. It goes beyond the examination of a photograph or illustration to challenging the viewer to look deeply to understand the cultural, ethical, aesthetic, and technical pieces of visual materials and media.

> Visual literacy is a set of abilities that enables an individual to effectively find, interpret, evaluate, use, and create images and visual media. Visual literacy skills equip a learner to understand and analyze the contextual, cultural, ethical, aesthetic, intellectual, and technical components involved in the production and use of visual materials. A visually literate individual is both a critical consumer of visual media and a competent contributor to a body of shared knowledge and culture. [16]

Background research may be required to get full meaning from an image. We need to understand the context, setting, time period, or purpose of people in a

---

VISUAL LITERACY

1. The ability to focus on important details in a photograph or picture which provides rich or historical context or setting.
2. The ability to draw information from photographs, pictures, or illustrations.
3. The ability to extract a greater sense of meaning or purpose than text provides from a picture or photograph.

photograph. Clothing, styles, man-made innovations, location, and other things, such as cultural cues, can help reference the information of a photograph. How does the LSS research a photo?

There are ways to think about looking at a photograph that can help guide LSS who may create digital images for library collections or guide patrons in their use. Kaplan and Mifflin[17] suggest there are three levels of awareness of visual literacy (see table 2.3).

1. Superficial awareness: This is our first glance or look at a photograph, film, or other media. We ask ourselves what is the picture "of"? Most of our viewing is done at the superficial level as images confront us constantly in our lives. We often take in just enough information from the picture that we need to get by.
2. Concrete awareness: What is the picture "about"? At this second level of awareness we focus on details of the photograph or media. Here we determine things such as setting, time period, faces, actions that occur, and other information that gives us a frame of reference about what is going on.
3. Abstract awareness: What is the context? What did the creator intend to evoke in his or her audience with this picture? Is there deeper meaning or inferences that can be made from the image? At this level we study the picture and make connections with our own base of knowledge or experience. As with deep reading, at the abstract awareness level we need to think hard about the intended message in a more meaningful context that concrete awareness. At the abstract level the creator of the photograph or media wants to convey to the viewer a subtle but important message.

Computer Graphics

It is highly desirable for LSS today to have training and practice in computer graphics for many reasons. Libraries must market themselves, but they do not have budgets for commercial advertising. Staff who can help in this effort with visual and digital communications skills are very valuable. **JPEG** (http://users.wfu.edu/mat thews/misc/graphics/formats/formats.html) or image files are commonly used by libraries to market programs, communicate with patrons, and enhance the library website and many other media applications. An LSS in our library had studied communications and graphic arts. She brought creative and new ideas for promoting library services. LSS who have computer graphic knowledge and experience may also be highly valued for their skills to create digital resources. Another LSS who had a deep interest in local history is now the library archivist. She has honed her computer graphic skills and creates digital collections from the local history materials kept in the library history room. Her role and responsibilities are ever-expanding because of the work she does to promote and share local history through the library digital collections and website.

Anne Morgan Spalter[18] in her discussion of digital visual literacy warns us of *fauxtography* or the ease with which digital images can be altered. It is not at all difficult today with the fine programs such as Adobe's Illustrator and Photoshop (http://www.adobe.com/products/catalog.html) for an amateur to change the intent and information of a JPEG or other type of photograph through computer

Table 2.3. Levels of Visual Awareness

Figure 2.1. Levels of Visual Awareness. *US Department of Interior*

Superficial Awareness:

I see an airplane in a field with some items near the door and men near the front. It appears to be a nice day.

Figure 2.2. Levels of Visual Awareness Details. *US Department of Interior*

Concrete Awareness:

Details of the picture emerge such as men loading the front of the plane with supplies. There are canisters that look like they may hold liquid. The boxes indicate they have twelve meals in each. There is also a pile of shovels that indicates they may be needed for digging and axes for chopping wood. The plane has its propellers on the top of the wings which suggests it does not need a lot of runway to land.

Figure 2.1. Levels of Visual Awareness. *US Department of Interior*

Abstract Awareness:

Intuitively something is going on here that suggests working with trees, digging dirt, and needing food in isolation for long periods of time. Zooming in on the two men in the front shows they are passing sandbags to each other. Axes, shovels, and sandbags are used for fighting forest fires. The canisters are holding something liquid. The men have crew cuts suggesting a 1950s or early 1960s time period.

This is a picture of loading supplies to fight a large forest fire in 1963 in the Alaskan wilderness. Photograph from the US Department of the Interior[1]

1. Workers load a plane to fight a fire in Alaska (1963). Photograph. Department of the Interior, Bureau of Land Management. June 20, 2008. Accessed December 9, 2014. http://www.blm.gov/wo/st/en/bpd.html.

manipulation. These skills are valued in commercial enterprises for advertising and marketing. However, when it comes to maintaining authenticity and accuracy, one has to be aware and vigilant. This is not to say LSS should not use these programs to enhance photographs. These and other photo imaging computer graphic programs can be used to zoom in on details, correct brightness, enhance color, and other attributes or elements that would improve concrete and abstract awareness in viewing and "reading" a historic photograph.

We will conclude this section on visual literacy with ways LSS can learn to improve their own visual literacy skills in order to help patrons gain full information from pictures and media.

Improve Your Visual Literacy Skills

Digital and visual literacies have become common to how we communicate with others. Today in schools children learn digital and visual literacy as part of their

---

FROM "READING AND RESEARCHING PHOTOGRAPHS,"[a] BY HELENA ZINKHAM

Read Photograph:

1. Note first impressions.
2. Name everything you see.
3. Look again at picture.
4. Write description about meaning.
   - Read accompanying text.
   - Describe what it shows.
   - Assumptions?

Research Photograph:

1. Confirm your caption information:
   - Where to verify original and additional info?
   - What do colleagues see that you missed?
2. Study photo, housing, and written information.
3. Describe details for research of place and time.
4. What events led to photo's creation?
5. The image's style, form, and genre.
6. Physical features to research for image processes, formats, sizes, color/b&w.
7. The types of image mounts used; and image bases – film, glass, metal, paper?

a. Helena Zinkham, "Reading and Researching Photographs," *Archival Outlook*, January/February 2007, 6–7. Accessed November 12, 2014. http://files.archivists.org/periodicals/Archival-Outlook/Back-Issues/2007-1-AO.pdf.

lives, like a language. Kindergarten students learn to pre-read and view online. Most elementary and middle schools offer curriculum in art and basic computer graphics, classes where students' visual literacy skills to create and view are developed. In high school students may specialize by taking advanced courses in these areas.

Today a visual literate person can:

- communicate information in a variety of forms;
- create, modify, and reproduce images in multiple ways; and
- create new images and shape the reality of their and others' worlds.

We want to improve our digital literacy skills so that we can think more critically about what we view and help others to do the same. How do we improve our visual literacy skills? Helena Zinkham suggests ways to read and research photographs.

LSS who practice these skills for improving their visual literacy will be able to help patrons find and interpret information more accurately from both print and digital photographs of historical value from local library collections.

CHAPTER SUMMARY

Digital and visual literacies have become common to how we read and view information and communicate with others. Digital and visual literacies help us interpret what we experience, analyze what we are exposed to, and make conclusions using our critical thinking skills. By practicing how to read on screens and evaluating the experience, LSS will become better able to help patrons do the same. Also LSS who are aware of ways to view digital images more carefully and critically can help support the role and responsibility of libraries for introducing relevant applications of technology, including digital literacy, to the public.

DISCUSSION QUESTIONS AND ACTIVITIES

There are many ways LSS can extend their learning of digital and visual literacy. We will now practice visual literacy by looking carefully and asking ourselves questions. Both of these activities can help you achieve a higher level of visual literacy.

Discussion Questions

Visual Literacy Questions
The following questions are designed to help readers make sense of images they encounter in various contexts.
Ask the Following Questions:

1. Why are we looking at this?
2. Is this image in its original state (i.e., no manipulation or "doctoring")?
3. What are the different components in this image?
4. How are they related to each other?

5. What is the main idea or argument the image expresses?
6. In what context or under what conditions was this image originally created? Displayed?
7. Who created it?
8. Can you find any tension or examples of conflict within the image? If so, what are they? What is their source? How are they represented?
9. Is there a larger context of which this image is a part?
10. What is the place in the image to which your attention is most immediately drawn?
11. What is the smallest detail that says the most?
12. What do we need to know to read the image successfully?
13. If this image was altered, who did it and why?
14. What information do I need to ask to read this image successfully?

Activity

Visual Literacy: Photographic Investigation and Interpretation
Photographs reveal multiple pieces of information. Select five photographs from the collection of the George Eastman House International Museum of Photography and Film collection that convey contextual or subtle information. The collection is found at http://www.geh.org/taschen/htmlsrc10/index.html.

Copy each of the five photos you select into a cell on the table below. In the cell to the right of the photo describe at least three "hidden" or subtle parts of the photo which tells the viewer more about either the time period, working conditions, climate, and so forth. In other words, identify pieces of visual information that go beyond the surface value of the picture. Use the questions in table 2.4 to help your visual literacy skills.

For example, if you select a photo of the Chrysler Building, what pieces of the photo tell us about the economy of the time when it was built?

Table 2.4.   Activity Table

Copy and paste photograph here from GEH Collection (resize photo to be about 2–3 inches square)	Copy the name of the photo and describe at least three "hidden" or subtle parts of the photo here.

NOTES

1. http://www.iste.org/docs/pdfs/20-14_ISTE_Standards-S_PDF.pdf.
2. http://digitalliteracy.cornell.edu/.
3. http://www.iste.org/docs/pdfs/20-14_ISTE_Standards-S_PDF.pdf.
4. http://www.pewinternet.org/.
5. http://www.pewinternet.org/2012/11/01/part-iv-teaching-research-skills-in-todays-digital-environment/.
6. Ibid.
7. Ibid.
8. http://www.ala.org/research/initiatives/plftas.
9. https://www.techsoupforlibraries.org/files/CB2_Meal%20Plan%20Six.pdf.
10. http://www.dartmouth.edu/~readingbrains/ResearchFiles/reading.html.
11. http://www.pri.org/stories/2014-09-18/your-paper-brain-and-your-kindle-brain-arent-same-thing.
12. Ibid.
13. Jabr, Ferris. "The Reading Brain in the Digital Age: The Science of Paper versus Screens," *Scientific American*, http://www.scientificamerican.com/article/reading-paper-screens/.
14. http://msa.medicine.iu.edu/msa-newsletters/20130404/typing-or-writing.
15. Kinmberly Drelich, "It's never too soon to learn about technology in Lyme and Old Lyme," *The Day* (New London, CT), October 6, 2014.
16. "Visual Literacy Defined," ACRL Visual Literacy Competency Standards for Higher Education, accessed April 18, 2015, http://www.ala.org/acrl/standards/visualliteracy.
17. Elisabeth Kaplan and Jeffrey Mifflin, "Mind and Sight: Visual Literacy and the Archivist," *Archives & Social Studies: A Journal of Interdisciplinary Research* 1, no. 0 (2007): 135–37. http://archivo.cartagena.es/files/36-167-DOC_FICHERO1/09-kaplanmifflin_mind.pdf.
18. Anne Morgan Spalter, "Digital Visual Literacy," *Theory Into Practice* 47, no. 2 (March 2008): 94. Accessed December 8, 2014. https://search.ebscohost.com/login.aspx?direct=true&db=aph&AN=31657180&site=ehost-live&scope=site.

REFERENCES, SUGGESTED READINGS, AND WEBSITES

American Library Association. "Public Library Funding & Technology Access Study." Project Overview. Last modified 2012. Accessed December 5, 2014. http://www.ala.org/research/initiatives/plftas.

———. "Visual Literacy Defined." ACRL Visual Literacy Competency Standards for Higher Education. Accessed April 18, 2015. http://www.ala.org/acrl/standards/visualliteracy.

Dartmouth College. "Reading Brains Lab: Reading Development." Last modified 2014. Accessed December 5, 2014. http://www.dartmouth.edu/~readingbrains/ResearchFiles/reading.html.

"Digital Literacy Is. . . ." Cornell University Digital Literacy Resource. Last modified 2014. Accessed December 6, 2014. http://digitalliteracy.cornell.edu/.

Drelich, Kinmberly. "It's Never Too Soon to Learn About Technology in Lyme and Old Lyme." *The Day* (New London, CT), October 6, 2014.

International Society for Technology Education. "ISTE Standards Students." ISTE Standards. Last modified 2014. Accessed December 5, 2014. http://www.iste.org/docs/pdfs/20-14_ISTE_Standards-S_PDF.pdf.

Jabr, Ferris. "The Reading Brain in the Digital Age: The Science of Paper versus Screens." Scientific American 309, no. 5 (April 2013). Accessed April 11, 2013. http://www.scientifi-camerican.com/article/reading-paper-screens/.

Jones-Kavalier, Barbara, and Suzanne Flannigan. "Connecting the Digital Dots: Literacy of the 21st Century Literacy today depends on understanding the multiple media that make up our high-tech reality and developing the skills to use them effectively." Educause Quarterly 2 (2006). Accessed December 4, 2014. https://net.educause.edu/ir/library/pdf/eqm0621.pdf.

Kaplan, Elisabeth, and Jeffrey Mifflin. "Mind and Sight: Visual Literacy and the Archivist." *Archives & Social Studies: A Journal of Interdisciplinary Research* 1, no. 0 (2007): 125–66. Accessed December 9, 2014. http://archivo.cartagena.es/files/36-167-DOC_FICHERO1/09-kaplanmifflin_mind.pdf.

Keefe, Mary-Elizabeth. "The Prism of Visual Literacy for Archivists: A Course Prototype." School of Library and Information Science. Last modified January 30, 2009. Accessed October 10, 2014. http://www.google.com/url?sa=t&rct=j&q=&esrc=s&source=web&cd=4&ved=0CCoQFjAD&url=http%3A%2F%2Flis.cua.edu%2Fres%2Fdocs%2Fsymposium%2F2009-symposium%2Fkeefethe-prism-of-visual-literacy1208.ppt&ei=v_aGVJ6rPM6ryASmjILgCw&usg=AFQjCNGMwQRWqTp3uNB7i5moueStuwsFyQ&sig2=y1_18xWThWlDjRpJOhjuOQ.

Peters, Chris. *The Joy of Computing—Recipes for a 5-Star Library.* San Francisco, CA: MaintainIT Project of TechSoup, 2014. Accessed December 5, 2014. https://www.techsoupforlibraries.org/files/CB2_Meal%20Plan%20Six.pdf.

Pew Research Center. "Pew Research Center's Internet Project." Pew Research Center. Last modified 2014. Accessed December 5, 2014. http://www.pewinternet.org/.

Purcell, Kristen, Lee Rainie, and Alan Heaps. "How Teens Do Research in a Digital World: Part IV: Teaching Research Skills in Today's Digital Environment." Pew Internet and Tech. Last modified November 1, 2012. Accessed December 5, 2014. http://www.pewinternet.org/2012/11/01/part-iv-teaching-research-skills-in-todays-digital-environment/.

Raphael, T. J., ed. "Your paper brain and your Kindle brain aren't the same thing." PRI—Public Radio International. Last modified September 18, 2014. Accessed December 6, 2014. http://www.pri.org/stories/2014-09-18/your-paper-brain-and-your-kindle-brain-arent-same-thing.

Spalter, Anne Morgan. "Digital Visual Literacy." *Theory Into Practice* 47, no. 2 (March 2008): 93–101. Accessed December 8, 2014. https://search.ebscohost.com/login.aspx?direct=true&db=aph&AN=31657180&site=ehost-live&scope=site.

University of Illinois. "What is Digital Literacy?" Digital Literacy Definition and Resources. Accessed April 18, 2015. http://www.library.illinois.edu/diglit/definition.html.

Wade, Patricia Ann. "Do Students Learn Better by Typing on a Keyboard or Writing with a Pen?" Indiana University School of Medicine. Last modified April 4, 2013. Accessed December 5, 2014. http://msa.medicine.iu.edu/msa-newsletters/20130404/typing-or-writing.

Workers load a plane to fight a fire in Alaska (1963). Photograph. Department of the Interior, Bureau of Land Management. June 20, 2008. Accessed December 9, 2014. http://www.blmv.gov/wo/st/en/bpd.html.

Zinkham, Helena. "Reading and Researching Photographs." *Archival Outlook,* January/February 2007, 6–7. Accessed November 12, 2014. http://files.archivists.org/periodicals/Archival-Outlook/Back-Issues/2007-1-AO.pdf.

CHAPTER 3

Primary Sources and Digital Collections

LSS know the role and responsibility of libraries for introducing relevant applications of technology, including digital literacy, to the public. (ALA-LSSC Technology Competency #2)

LSS demonstrate flexibility in adapting to new technology. (ALA-LSSC Technology Competency #5)

Topics Covered in This Chapter:

- Primary Sources
  - Local Libraries and Primary Sources
  - Artifacts
  - Secondary Sources
  - Locate Primary Sources
  - Primary Sources and Student Research
  - Common Core
- LSS Create Digital Collections
  - Digitize Primary Resources
  - Digital Enhancement

Key Terms:

Archive: This term has two meanings for library staff. As a verb, it is the act of acquiring, preserving, and maintaining special resources or materials that have a high value to researchers and others. As a noun, it is a special location in a library where the unique materials are preserved and housed with restricted access. Libraries are increasingly scanning archived materials in large numbers for Internet patron access.

Artifacts: These are two- or three-dimensional objects that have artistic, cultural, personal, or historic value. Libraries and museums preserve these objects in special collections for future generations with care because of their irreplaceable value. Most are original to the time period or event and are not circulated. Libraries today can create and share online digital collections of images of valuable objects from their special collections.

Memoir: This is a first-person account of the author about how his or her life was impacted by a change in attitude, beliefs, or even a philosophical enlightenment. While autobiographies typically chronicle an author's lifespan, a memoir focuses on what made the author have significant emotional or mindset changes. Library staff create or support the making of digital collections of memoirs for the library collection. Memoirs can be of elderly who saw or participated in events, people who contributed to town government, or others whose stories and perspectives are important to preserve.

OCR: This is an acronym for optical character recognition. The software converts scanned documents into word processing text that can be edited and changed on a computer. Library staff who are familiar with OCR can scan paper documents for later editing with a word processing program.

Scan: The act of creating file images using imaging technology. Libraries offer scanning technology to patrons to make digital copies of print documents. Library staff may use scanning technology to preserve documents, post copies of print items online, or communicate or archive other important information. Most scanners convert images of the page to the PDF computer file format that is efficient in storage space and commonly accepted for personal and business use.

Libraries are often the **archive** of local materials and **artifacts** where patrons glean new learning about the past. Libraries preserve and maintain books and objects for current and future use. Because library staff have expertise in classifying, preserving, and maintaining many collection types, libraries are often the designated keepers of local historical materials to be preserved and passed on to future generations.

Historic items are valued because they give us a true sense of the past. There are many kinds of historic materials libraries naturally preserve such as original town charters and documents or first editions of local newspapers published years ago. The library may have been chosen as the repository for these full sets of papers. However, sometimes archives are made by librarians around a theme or event whereby they go out and find related artifacts. In this case library staff collect and compile individual items that may come from many diverse places around a topic of local history. An example of such a collection is the Rhode Island Image Collection created by staff at the Providence Public Library from pictures in their library collections and other places in the state. Using Flickr as a hosting service, staff created albums of images from historic whaling logs, Newport America's Cup, Rhode Island mills, aerial views of mansions, and other historic themes. All of these items together give us a better picture around a time period or event in Rhode Island history (see figure 3.1).

Figure 3.1. Rhode Island Image Collection. *Providence Public Library, Rhode Island Image Collection*

Library Support Staff (LSS) can help digitize artifacts and photographs to create a digital collection of local history. The first step after locating, identifying, and determining its authenticity is deciding whether it is a primary or secondary source.

PRIMARY SOURCES

Primary sources are original to the person, time period, or event, such as a personal narrative, legal document, or artifact. A primary source may also be a creation, such as an original piece of art or the first invention of its kind.[1] Witnesses or recorders who experienced the event provide firsthand testimony or direct evidence of the topic.[2] One of the key elements of a primary source is the firsthand relationship to the speaker, author, or creator. When an author writes his memoir, he is sharing with his readers how his life was significantly impacted or his attitudes, beliefs, or mindset changed because of a series of events or life experiences.[3] Documents,

Table 3.1. Examples of Primary Sources

Letters and Correspondence	Original Documents	Photographs
Autobiographies	Personal Accounts or Narratives	Documentary Film
Diaries	Speeches	Artifacts
Original Books, Magazines, Newspapers, Pamphlets	Music	Original Creative Works (Art, Novels, Plays, etc.)
Memoirs	Oral Histories	Government Documents
Original Manuscripts	Maps	Dissertations
Interviews	Published Materials Written at the Time of the Event	Records
Genealogy	Court Proceedings	Census Data

photographs, artifacts, letters, plays, and artwork are just a few examples of primary sources. See table 3.1 for other examples of primary sources.

Often we relate primary sources to history, such as armaments from a battle or an important speech of a world leader. But primary sources are equally found in science, literature, cultural heritages, medicine, mathematics, technology, and the arts. Primary sources are not restricted to a certain discipline, time, or place. In some instances, published materials can also be viewed as primary materials for the period in which they were written. The Library of Congress defines primary sources as "actual records that have survived from the past, such as letters, photographs, articles of clothing."[4]

Local Libraries and Primary Sources

Library collections are treasure troves of primary sources (see figures 3.2 and 3.3). Original writing and spoken words permeate fiction and nonfiction. Libraries circulate unlimited primary sources found in books and media. Photographs taken at the event, songs that were written and sung for a cause, and actions that were captured on film are all part of the resources of the library. LSS can find primary sources throughout the book collections. Original novels are primary sources. So are parts of a book like when the author enhances his or her research with original quotations and photographs. The same primary source may be found in multiple libraries, such as a popular autobiography that has thousands of copies in print

Figure 3.2. Example of a Library Primary Source. *Postcard (front) of the Baptist Church on Iron Street from the History Collection, Bill Library, Ledyard, CT*

Figure 3.3. Example of a Library Primary Source. *Postcard (back) of the Baptist Church on Iron Street from the History Collection, Bill Library, Ledyard, CT*

and is circulated by many libraries. Original town documents may be preserved and archived solely by the library. Primary sources that are also artifacts should be handled with extreme care and restricted by library staff from circulation or handling by the public.

Artifacts

Some primary sources in libraries are artifacts. Artifacts are unique objects that were created by a person from a particular place, event, or time period. Artifacts may have artistic, cultural, historic, or other significance. Artifacts also are limited in number as unique as one or just a small number of copies that were created by people at the same time and are considered original to the event.

Libraries have all kinds of artifacts, yet no two libraries have the same. Below are three examples of artifacts that required special handling and security in my library:

- one of three copies of the benefactor's will that bequeathed funding to establish the library;
- an original sculpture made years ago by a local artist that represented learning and knowledge; and
- the dedication plaque that established the name and mission of the library.

With digitization technologies, library staff now have the potential to share with others artifacts that would not normally circulate or even be displayed to the public from their special collections. They also have the ability to create digital resources around a theme or topic by gathering or borrowing pieces or units to create a digital collection from primary sources that are not housed in one place, such as the Rhode Island Image Collection.

Secondary Sources

There is a distinction between primary and secondary sources. We learned that primary sources are created by people during a specific time or event. Think of primary sources as being "firsthand." Secondary sources are once removed from the creator or the time or event (see table 3.2). Secondary sources interpret, paraphrase, or translate information. Secondary sources also help us think about and analyze what the person said, why the event occurred, and what may have been going on that had an influence during the time period. We use secondary sources to critically examine elements to form our opinions and guide our thinking. Secondary sources involve us in reading, hearing, viewing, or communicating about the event or person because we were not there. Often nonfiction books present information about a primary source to help us understand the topic in a cultural or historic context. Secondary materials, such as textbooks, synthesize and interpret primary materials and are accounts of the past created by people writing about events sometime after they happened.[5] It is common for many secondary source textbooks to contain some primary source materials such as photographs, speeches, or copies of original degrees or other documents written during the event. Secondary sources may provide background information by someone removed from the actual event, such as a scholar or expert studying a particular field who offers a credible interpretation that can broaden perspectives and research.[6]

It is important to question the authority of a secondary source. Library staff can rely on book reviews from professional sources such as *Library Journal, Booklist*, the *New York Times*, and others that annotate and rate an author's work. Reviewers have delved into the background of the author and the content of the book to examine reliability and accuracy. LSS can also research the author's credentials and the sources he or she uses in their writing. Question how the author is interpreting the event. Research how extensive the author's experience and expertise is of the topic.[7]

LSS work with primary and secondary sources found in every library collection. It is important we know the differences in order to provide the best support to patrons' selection of information.

Locate Primary Sources

LSS can help patrons search and locate primary sources (see table 3.3). There are extensive efforts being made in libraries at the national, state, and local levels to digitize primary sources for shared research experiences. Many other institutions, typically higher education, government agencies, and museums, also convert important primary source materials to digital format that can be found on the Internet. One way LSS can find and introduce primary sources to patrons is to use the Google shortcuts.

Table 3.2. Examples of Secondary Sources

Textbooks	Biographies	Histories
Encyclopedias	Reference Books	News Reports
Magazine and Journal Articles Examining a Topic	Chronologies	Abstracts
Genealogy Data	Handbooks	Interpretations and Translations

Table 3.3.   Use Google Shortcuts to Locate Primary Sources at Universities

Step	Action
1	Access Google at http://www.google.com.
2	Select a topic you want to find primary sources about. In my example below I have selected the topic of US Civil Rights.
3	Construct the search query by typing: *site:edu primary sources U.S. Civil Rights*
4	Some of the search results lead to primary sources on US Civil Rights from Tufts University, Princeton, and the Universities of Maryland, Washington, and Virginia.
5	Repeat these steps substituting *site:gov* in the search query for US government primary sources on the topic.

There are other ways to quickly find primary sources using databases we have already been introduced to. Similar to above, you can find websites with primary source material on the topic by using the directory Internet Public Library.[8] Type "primary sources" site:edu primary sources US Civil Rights in the search box along with your topic to retrieve appropriate sites. Some vendors offer databases, such as the History Reference Center by EBSCO, that offer a link to retrieving primary sources as a material type in advanced search. This option usually exists for history databases as primary sources are often associated with this discipline.

In the next chapter we will look at two government websites that preserve both original works for our country and create digital images for their websites. The Library of Congress has a database named American Memory that is dedicated to sharing our country's culture. The National Archives preserves documents and images. Both sites are instrumental to our ability to locate primary materials from and about life in the United States.

Primary Sources and Student Research

Teachers often require students to have one or two primary sources embedded in their papers. This could be a quote from a famous person or a few lines from an important speech. In the past a handful of reference books were all a librarian needed to satisfy the requirement. Two events in education increased the importance of the library primary sources dramatically. One event occurred about fifteen years ago when schools adapted block scheduling. Block scheduling is when a school day has fewer classes but class periods are for longer periods of time. With having the time for sustained library research embedded into the class period, teachers require students to look deeper into a topic or area of study. No longer does research consist of students seeking quick facts but rather they use primary source information so that they can analyze and synthesize ideas into new meaning and understanding.[9]

Common Core

A second reason school libraries need primary sources for student research are the state and national changes in public school curriculum. Students today are required to use source materials that enhance their critical thinking skills. Local state and national Common Core State Standards set the requirements that students use primary sources. For example, Common Core State Standard CCSS.ELA-Literacy. RH.11-12.1 states students are to be able to "cite specific textual evidence to support analysis of primary and secondary sources, connecting insights gained from specific details to an understanding of the text as a whole."[10] In order to achieve this and other reading and writing standards students across the country must be able to analyze primary sources. Thus the need is great for libraries to provide these materials on a wide range of subjects across time periods and locations.

LSS CREATE DIGITAL COLLECTIONS

LSS are often asked to help students find sources for their homework or research assignments. Teachers challenge students to learn through the interpretation and experience of primary sources. Traditional classroom textbooks do not often support authentic learning. In some California schools students were challenged to increase their content knowledge by creating a digital textbook of primary sources.[11] Students were more engaged in learning about war when they located, scanned, and created a digital textbook of firsthand accounts and visuals of soldiers and communities in the state of war.

In a similar way LSS can help make research experiences authentic to patrons who are interested in a topic that may be found in secondary sources. Library staff help patrons find and locate appropriate information in books and other texts. They can assist the patron to **scan** photographs, personal narratives, maps, letters, and other primary sources into digital format. Where once we only showed patrons the paper photocopier, libraries can obtain **OCR** or optical character recognition software inexpensively that enables patrons to view, read, and edit scanned content on e-readers or computing devices. LSS can support the creation of thematic collections—large or small—of primary sources into digital content.

These collections are not only for historic content. Teachers in all disciplines now encourage students to seek primary sources to encourage learning, questioning, and critical thinking.[12] In the digital collections of the Smithsonian and the Library of Congress there are a wealth of digitized primary sources that spur thinking about so many subjects including science, technology, health, and our environment. LSS will learn about some of these exemplary collections in the following chapters. However, in our own local collections of nonfiction primary and secondary sources, there is a lot of material that can be collected and digitized for patrons to support their interests and learning through collections of authentic artifacts, images, and documents grouped around a theme or topic of study.

Digitize Primary Sources

LSS can support and create digitized collections of primary sources to enhance research and learning experiences of patrons. An excellent guide, *Digitization Project: Easy as 1, 2, 3*, which steps library staff through the process of digitization is published by the Connecticut State Library (CSL) and Library Connection.[13] The guide was published to help library staff start digitizing important items in their

Table 3.4. Steps Suggested by the Connecticut State Library and Library Connection[a] for Digitization

Step	Action
1	Identify if the item is published, unpublished, and in the public domain.
2	Identify the value of the item.
3	Examine copyright or legal issues.
4	Determine viability of digitization (can the item be physically handled)?
5	Identify format and use appropriate scanning guidelines for photographs, text, manuscripts, and maps.
6	Review image once scanned.
7	Name and save TIFF and JPEG files using established nomenclature.
8	Create metadata or cataloging data using required fields.

[a] Ibid.

collections for preservation or sharing via the web. I recommend any LSS who will be working on a digitization project to download this guide for its important information that is clearly written and easy to follow. The major steps of the digitization process are shown in table 3.4.

All of these steps require time, support, or research. Start the digitization process slowly with one or two items that you have clear information about (see figure 3.4).

Figure 3.4. Digitization Process—Scanning Primary Sources. *Staff at Bill Library, Ledyard CT digitizing primary sources*

As the project grows, expect it will take more time to fully research each item so that it can be classified and cataloged appropriately before it is uploaded to the library website or database. Step 6 is very important in that you review the scanned image to be sure that it is not blurry and best shows the item or artifact. Practice scanning and be patient with the results as you will learn much about placement of items on the scanner and things like scanner and computer settings to enhance the image. The image saved as a JPEG file can always be sized or improved upon with editing software Photoshop.[14]

Digital Enhancement

With digital technology the content and visuals of primary sources no longer need to remain hidden from the public in library archives or special reserves. As we read in chapter 1, the process of digitization enables libraries to share with patrons collections of rich materials that are unavailable for circulation. Digitization also makes it possible for library staff to create new collections of materials around a theme or topic by associating images of items on a topic that are disperse and not classified or located together.

Often primary sources are handwritten in a script that may be faded or hard to read. The value of the source is limited because of this. There also may be other important elements that cannot be seen or absorbed by the regular eye. Adobe Photoshop is very powerful as it lets the editor zoom and enlarge an illegible text or image to a magnification that the researcher can now interpret. Contrast features of Photoshop may also help with this process so that the full integrity of the primary source is revealed. LSS who learn how to use Photoshop or other editing software can be very useful not only in the digitization process of primary sources but also in creating related images of difficult to read text that now can be seen in the enhancements. Using technology to enhance scans of rare or unique books increases the value of digital objects to researchers.[15] Examples of the kinds of primary resources found in library collections LSS can help decipher and share with researchers through scanning and digitization are: rare books, handwritten diaries, speeches, or letters, interviews, historic photographs, maps, and oral histories. Genealogical information that may be contained in town records and other handwritten documents can also be digitized and enhanced. Researchers will be able to better understand and interpret the rich content of family records and first account observations. In the following chapters we will look at national and state projects and initiatives that have the goal to preserve history through the digitization of primary sources.

CHAPTER SUMMARY

LSS can support the use of primary sources in many ways. They can locate firsthand information for patrons and create scanned images of texts, photographs, and artifacts for local library digital collections. With advancements in scanning technology and the Internet, items that were once in reserve collections and not for circulation can now be shared with patrons through the library website. LSS can support the role and responsibility of the library by using relevant applications of technology to locate and create primary sources. LSS who are knowledgeable and competent in the use of technology can apply their skills to create digital collections of local primary sources for patrons to access that they otherwise would not be able to view or use.

DISCUSSION QUESTIONS AND ACTIVITIES

Discussion Questions

1. Name three differences between primary sources and secondary sources.
2. What are some examples of primary sources that libraries may typically have in their collections?
3. What are some examples of secondary sources that libraries may typically have in their collections?
4. Why is optical character recognition (OCR) an important feature of scanning library staff should know about and be able to use with patrons or in their own work?
5. Name key steps in digitizing a primary source for a library collection.

Activities

Activity 1: Locate Primary Sources and Artifacts on a Topic or Theme
This activity is to help you gain practice identifying and locating primary sources in your library that could become a digital collection on a topic or theme.

1. Chose a topic that is well represented in your library such as local history or a historic event that took place nearby. In my hometown the first submarine to travel under the Arctic, the USS *Nautilus* is preserved. My project for this assignment would be to locate primary sources and artifacts in my public library about the USS *Nautilus*.
2. Locate a minimum of five primary sources in your library on your topic looking through books, photographs, and other collections. Talk with the reference librarians to ask if there are artifacts the public does not typically have access to on your topic. Be sure to select at least one three-dimensional artifact.
3. Create a detailed chart of the five primary sources on your topic with the information in table 3.5.

Table 3.5. Activity Table

Title	Source and Location	Description and Format	Relevant Information

The chart logs the information you need to begin a digital collection on your topic.

The second activity will provide practice with digitizing one primary source and one artifact.

Activity 2: Scan or Digitize Primary Sources
This activity requires you to use a scanner and a digital camera.
Select one document primary source from Activity 1 that can be scanned.

1. Place the item on scanner and save it to the JPEG format. If the scanner only scans in .PDF, download the free version of Photoshop, or use Paint or another free editing program to covert the file from .PDF to JPEG.
2. Once the image is scanned into a JPEG, name it and save it in a file folder on your computer.
3. Open the file with the editing software and adjust its size, density, etc. to authenticate its image.
4. Rename the image and save it in the folder.

Select one artifact from Activity 1 to be photographed.

1. Set the artifact on a table or stand on a solid color cloth. Remove any other items from the foreground or background.
2. Using a digital camera, take several pictures of the object from different angles and positions.
3. Download all images and save them in a computer folder.
4. Using the editing software, adjust size, density, color, etc. for best clarity and authentic representation.

Organize and arrange images in a folder labeled "Demonstration Folder." You may consider completing a small digital collection for the library. If so, share images with library staff as part of your proposal. I am sure you will receive great interest and reception for your work!

NOTES

1. "What Is a Primary Source," What is a Primary Source, last modified 2014, accessed November 14, 2014, http://www.princeton.edu/~refdesk/primary2.html.
2. "What Are Primary Sources?," Primary Sources at Yale, last modified 2008, accessed November 15, 2014, http://www.yale.edu/collections_collaborative/primarysources/primarysources.html.
3. "Autobiography, Biography and Memoirs," Life Writing, last modified February 13, 2015, accessed March 1, 2015, http://libguides.southernct.edu/biography.
4. "What Are Primary Sources?," UCLA Institute on Primary Resources, last modified 1999, accessed November 15, 2014, http://ipr.ues.gseis.ucla.edu/info/definition.html.
5. Ibid.
6. "Guide to Finding Secondary Sources," Finding Secondary Sources, last modified February 2, 2013, accessed November 15, 2014, http://www.library.illinois.edu/ugl/howdoi/secondarysources.html.

7. Ibid.

8. "Search ipl2," ipl2: Information You Can Trust, last modified 2014, accessed December 5, 2014, http://www.ipl.org/.

9. Marie Keen Shaw, *Block Scheduling and Its Impact on the School Library Media Center*, Greenwood Professional Guides in School Librarianship (Westport, CT: Greenwood Press, 1999).

10. "English Language Arts Standards » History/Social Studies » Grade 11–12," Common Core State Standards Initiative, last modified 2014, accessed November 13, 2013, http://www.corestandards.org/ELA-Literacy/RH/11-12/.

11. Laura Moorhead, "What War Looks Like: Students Present Moments of Historical Crisis Using Primary Sources and Digital Textbooks. Be Careful What You Ask For," *Interdisciplinary Humanities* 31, no. 1 (Spring 2014), accessed November 13, 2014, http://search.ebscohost.com/login.aspx?direct=true&db=aph&AN=97938645&site=ehost-live&scope=site.

12. Mary Alice Anderson, "Not Just for History: Primary Sources in the Science and Health Classroom," *Internet Schools* 21, no. 1 (January/February 2014), accessed November 13, 2014, http://search.ebscohost.com/login.aspx?direct=true&db=aph&AN=94849627&site=ehost-live&scope=site.

13. Connecticut State Library and Library Connection, *Digitization Project: Easy as 1, 2, 3* (Hartford, CT: Connecticut State Library, 2009), accessed November 15, 2014, http://www.libraryconnection.info/pdfs/digitization123Aug2009.pdf.

14. Adobe Photoshop, last modified 2015, accessed March 1, 2015, http://www.photoshop.com/.

15. Maura Valentino, "Adding Value to the University of Oklahoma Libraries History of Science Collection through Digital Enhancement," *Information Technology & Libraries* 33, no. 1 (March 2014), accessed November 14, 2014, http://search.ebscohost.com/login.aspx?direct=true&db=aph&AN=95317932&site=ehost-live&scope=site.

REFERENCES, SUGGESTED READINGS, AND WEBSITES

Adobe Photoshop. Last modified 2015. Accessed March 1, 2015. http://www.photoshop.com/.

Anderson, Mary Alice. "Not Just for History: Primary Sources in the Science and Health Classroom." *Internet Schools* 21, no. 1 (January/February 2014): 1–3. Accessed November 13, 2014. http://search.ebscohost.com/login.aspx?direct=true&db=aph&AN=94849627&site=ehost-live&scope=site.

Common Core State Standards Initiative. "English Language Arts Standards » History/Social Studies » Grade 11–12." Common Core State Standards Initiative. Last modified 2014. Accessed November 13, 2013. http://www.corestandards.org/ELA-Literacy/RH/11-12/.

Connecticut State Library and Library Connection. *Digitization Project: Easy as 1, 2, 3*. Hartford, CT: Connecticut State Library, 2009. Accessed November 15, 2014. http://www.libraryconnection.info/pdfs/digitization123Aug2009.pdf.

Moorhead, Laura. "What War Looks Like: Students Present Moments of Historical Crisis Using Primary Sources and Digital Textbooks: Be Careful What You Ask for." *Interdisciplinary Humanities 31*, no. 1 (Spring 2014): 54–71. Accessed November 13, 2014. http://search.ebscohost.com/login.aspx?direct=true&db=aph&AN=97938645&site=ehost-live&scope=site.

Princeton University. "What Is a Primary Source." What is a Primary Source. Last modified 2014. Accessed November 14, 2014. http://www.princeton.edu/~refdesk/primary2.html.

"Rhode Island Images." Providence Library. Last modified 2014. Accessed November 13, 2014. https://www.flickr.com/photos/ppl_ri_images/sets/72157622205329114/.

"Search ipl2." ipl2: Information You Can Trust. Last modified 2014. Accessed December 5, 2014. http://www.ipl.org/.

Shaw, Marie Keen. *Block Scheduling and Its Impact on the School Library Media Center.* Greenwood Professional Guides in School Librarianship. Westport, CT: Greenwood Press, 1999.

Southern Connecticut State University. "Autobiography, Biography and Memoirs." Life Writing. Last modified February 13, 2015. Accessed March 1, 2015. http://libguides.southernct.edu/biography.

University of California - Los Angeles. "What Are Primary Sources?" UCLA Institute on Primary Resources. Last modified 1999. Accessed November 15, 2014. http://ipr.ues.gseis.ucla.edu/info/definition.html.

University of Illinois Library. "Guide to Finding Secondary Sources." Finding Secondary Sources. Last modified February 2, 2013. Accessed November 15, 2014. http://www.library.illinois.edu/ugl/howdoi/secondarysources.html.

US Government. "National Archives." The National Archives and Records Administration. Last modified 2014. Accessed November 10, 2014. http://www.archives.gov/index.html.

Valentino, Maura. "Adding Value to the University of Oklahoma Libraries History of Science Collection through Digital Enhancement." *Information Technology & Libraries* 33, no. 1 (March 2014). Accessed November 14, 2014. http://search.ebscohost.com/login.aspx?direct=true&db=aph&AN=95317932&site=ehost-live&scope=site.

Yale University. "What Are Primary Sources?" Primary Sources at Yale. Last modified 2008. Accessed November 15, 2014. http://www.yale.edu/collections_collaborative/primarysources/primarysources.html.

CHAPTER 4

National and Global Collections

LSS know the role of technology in creating, identifying, retrieving, and accessing information resources and demonstrate facility with appropriate information discovery tools. (ALA-LSSC Technology Competency #7)

Topics Covered in This Chapter:

LC

- Digital Library Federation ➤ *universities, academic members, ALA*
- Digital Public Library of America
  - ○ Metadata
  - ○ Searching the Digital Public Library of America
- World Digital Library
- The Library of Congress
- The National Archives and Records Administration
  - ○ US Census

Key Terms:

Apps: A common abbreviation for computer software applications. Examples of application software used by library staff and patrons are database programs, word processors, spreadsheets, online catalogs, social media, quick access newspapers, journals, magazines, and many other programs used for education, literacy, or research.

Census: A survey typically conducted by the state or federal government which gathers information about people. The survey typically provides descriptive demographic data about each household and its members. Library staff who know how to find census data can help patrons research social issues, the economy, health, and many other aspects of life and culture.

Enumeration District: A census taker is also called an enumerator, someone who counts or quantifies information. His or her assigned geographic area, which could be as small as a city block or as large as a county, is called an enumeration district (ED). Census data is collected and displayed by ED. Library staff should become familiar with how to identify enumeration districts to effectively help patrons search the US Census online.

Metadata: In cataloging, these are additional elements or pieces of information data that describe an object beyond its basic description. Examples of the elements are the names of those who contributed to the creation or preservation of the object or what materials the object is made of. Library staff use these additional elements in descriptive cataloging for artifacts and objects. Library staff apply metadata elements to conduct more effective searching of digital objects of online museum and library collections.

Portal Interface: This is a starting point or gateway for searchers to locate a large number of websites on a topic at once. Library staff who are familiar with specific portals can help patrons find information from many sources simultaneously on a topic or theme.

Here we begin to learn about digital libraries and other institutions that share rich online collections of primary source text, pictures, and media with the public. This chapter will focus on the growing archives of important global and national historic or cultural materials that are now available on the web that are part of special digital resource collections of leading libraries.

DIGITAL LIBRARY FEDERATION

Chapter 1 introduced us to the Digital Library Federation (DLF). The DLF was one of the first national efforts to set common standards for digitization of collections among universities and libraries. The DLF began in the mid-1990s when personal computers and the Internet were still very new to most people. Started by a small group of university librarians, the DLF began by talking about this new digital technology and what it could do for libraries. University libraries had special collections that ordinarily would not be seen by the public. At about the same time, the Library of Congress announced its intention to create a national digital library. The Library of Congress soon joined the academic librarians and became a member of DLF. Because DLF members have a long history of establishing and updating universal standards for digitization, that include file format and **metadata**, we can seamlessly locate and use items no matter what kind of computing devices we have or where the items are stored.

The DLF, however, does not have its own unique search engine for its members' collections. There is a list of members on the DLF site. While it is engaging and very interesting to browse individual members' collections, such as Purdue University in West Lafayette, Indiana, LSS should know that to use only the DLF with patrons, they must have invested time in learning about the holdings of its members'

Table 4.1. Search Purdue Libraries Digital Collections for Amelia Earhart

Step	Action
1	Go to Purdue University and find the academic library link at http://www.purdue.edu/purdue/ academics/index.html. *→ Academics → library → Find → Repositories*
2	Locate and click on e-Archives. *→ e Archive collections*
3	Click "Collections."
4	Type "Amelia Earhart."

collections by conducting many searches. Here are steps to follow to search Purdue University Libraries' collection to find excellent research on Amelia Earhart (see table 4.1).

You will see wonderful digital images of Amelia Earhart's letters, handwritten notes, telegrams, journals, and so many intriguing pictures and other documents (see figure 4.3). It did take four clicks to reach this special collection on Amelia Earhart. Amelia Earhart had a special relationship with Purdue University as a visiting professor in the Aeronautics Department in 1935. Her husband, George Palmer Putnam, donated Amelia's papers to Purdue University Libraries. Purdue is home to the world's largest compilation of Earhart-related papers, memorabilia, and artifacts, which also is available online.[1]

While it is fascinating to browse each DLF member's collections, it is not an efficient way for LSS to help patrons find items. Let us begin our exploration of our national treasures by first learning how we can search DLF members' collections more easily that we can, in turn, share with our patrons.

DIGITAL PUBLIC LIBRARY OF AMERICA

What was lacking in the DLF was a way to link directly to collections of primary sources. The newly created Digital Public Library of America[2] (DPLA) is just the solution—it is a seamless way to search many collections at once! The DPLA resolves the problem of having to search each major digital collection individually, as we did in my example at Purdue. The Digital Public Library does not hold collection *content* of files on its servers. Rather, it is a powerful search interface to locate by keyword and metadata digitized primary sources cataloged and stored on servers of universities, libraries, and other national institutions. DPLA is a **portal** and acts on our search requests to connect us to the appropriate digital library collection of its members.

It is important to know that while Google and others are excellent search engines, they do not get us to the item or metadata level and depth of DPLA. DPLA uses the metadata records of the collection, whereas search engines create their own indexes of web addresses (see table 4.2). It is because DPLA locates with metadata that we can find exact items within large collections. Search engines do not locate with metadata and thus cannot get us to that level of detail.

Now that we know the differences between DPLA and search engines, let's talk just a bit about metadata and why it is different than key word searching.

Table 4.2.   Comparisons between DPLA and Search Engines

Features	DPLA	Search Engines
Basic Structure	DPLA is a portal with direct connections to the digital collections of member sites.	Own servers of indexes of key words and other information gleaned from websites.
Searching	Cataloged descriptions called metadata is created for each item in a collection by the owning institution. Members' collections are searched simultaneously.	Common or important keywords of web pages are compiled in the search engine indexes and matched to people's search queries for results.
Search Limitations	Searches can be done by keywords, timeline, map, virtual bookshelf, format, subject, co-owning partner, or other descriptions.	Advanced search can limit by domain, country, language, or other Boolean features.
Breadth	Searches are limited to members' collections of digitized primary sources.	Search engine web crawlers aim to search every web page on the Internet for information.
Usage	DPLA membership increases usage to member collections.	Search engines enhance their profit margin with increased usage from advertising or other sources.

Metadata

Librarians have long used Machine-Readable Cataloging (MARC) standards to identify, describe, and catalog data of library books, serials, and media. Metadata is the standard for cataloging objects and artifacts. Dublin Core, developed with the Online Computer Library Center (OCLC), is one of the most common metadata systems. Dublin Core metadata elements are used by most digital libraries and museums in English speaking countries to classify and catalog their collections. The elements of Dublin Core are more extensive than MARC standards and offer many more ways to search and find an object. There are fifteen elements or metatags for searching: *contributor, coverage, creator, date, description, format, identifier, language, publisher, relation, rights, source, subject, title,* and *type.*

Metadata elements may be used multiple times for each object. For example, at the Smithsonian hangs The Spirit of St. Louis, the airplane Charles Lindberg flew solo across the Atlantic Ocean to France.[3] In searching the digital object of this plane, the element "materials" is used several times. From the metadata we learn the plane was made of metal, fabric, and glass. Because this metadata is searchable by keyword, The Spirit of St. Louis can be searched using any of these words. It is important for LSS to become familiar with metadata to be able to successfully search by any or all of the elements for objects and artifacts found in DPLA or other large library and museum collections.

Searching the Digital Public Library of America

Now that we know about interfaces, portals, and metadata, let's have some fun searching the primary sources of photographs, images, artwork, music, videos, records, and other resources of DPLA. There are several helpful video tutorials posted at DPLA to help us get started. Even though DPLA is relatively new, it currently links to over one thousand digital collections with more than six million items and growing daily. DPLA is free and can be found by only typing *dp.la* in the URL line (no other letters are needed).

DPLA is a **portal** that moves you from the DPLA search screens to the actual library collection. The portal points to the digital collection that contains the item. DPLA does not have its own collection of items. Once you locate the link to the resource, you click the button or link that says "View" to see the resource at holding collection. At the collection you can access and download the item. DPLA has the goal of being the portal to all digital collections in the United States.

There are currently six ways to search DPLA (see figure 4.1). These six ways are listed across the top of the home page in links called *Home, Exhibitions, Map, Timeline, Bookshelf,* and *Apps. + more*

1. *Home:* To do a basic search, use the search box on the home page of DPLA. Type in your search words. The resources with links to the digital collection where it is located are found on the right side of the screen. Limit the results by media type, time, date, etc. by choosing the refinement on the left. Look closely at these limiters as you will see some of the metadata categories we discussed above. Remember, if you do not find what you want on the first search you may have to use other terms that also describe or relate to the object.

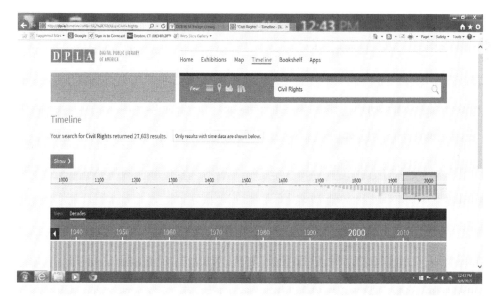

Figure 4.1. Example of a Timeline Search in DPLA. *Digital Public Library of America*

2. *Timeline:* To search by *date* click "Timeline" found on the home page. Type your term in the box that says "Search the Library." A timeline appears that you can view either by decades or years with bars. Where there is a bar, there are digital resources with metadata for this date. Click on the bar to obtain a list of links to the items.

3. *Map:* To search by *location of the digital collection* that has the item, click on "Map" found on the home page. Each dot on the map of the United States represents the location of a digital collection or library that has one or more resources on your search term.

4. *Exhibitions:* This link is great for *browsing* for key themes about US history or culture. Within each theme there are many collections about specific topics. For example, click the current exhibition on *Activism in the United States* for specific exhibitions on civil rights, women's activism, anti-war activism, LGBT activism, etc. These are high-quality exhibits and a great way to become familiar with the resources of DPLA. Exhibitions will change over time and are the results of collaboration among DPLA members.

5. *Bookshelf:* The bookshelf is an easy way to search DPLA's books, serials, and journals. The darker the shade of blue, the more relevant the results. Click on a spine for details and related images. Book thickness indicates the page count, and the horizontal length reflects the book's actual height. Type "Jimmy Carter" in the search box and find books about his presidency located in several university libraries. By clicking "View" on each item, the portal takes us to the university library collection that had scanned the appropriate chapters from each book.

6. *Apps:* This page you must try! All data of DPLA is open source, and **apps** are encouraged for new and creative ways to search and use DPLA. Many apps help you narrow down your interests. Right now there are apps for blogs, metadata, collages, a prototype visual search interface that explores content from the Digital Public Library of America, and many more.

DPLA is exciting and has become a vital portal to the digital collections in our country. Try each type of search to become familiar with key collections. Showing patrons how to use DPLA will expand their use of the Internet and lead them to new collections of national and global primary sources.

100 Internat Members

WORLD DIGITAL LIBRARY *Focus on historic/global*

The World Digital Library[4] (WDL) has some of the same members of the Digital Library Federation and the Digital Public Library of America. This is a bit confusing to have so many key groups leading the way for digitalization. Here is how their missions vary:

1. *DLF* establishes *standards and policies* for creating digital resource collections;
2. *DPLA* is the portal interface to *view and use American* digital resources; and the
3. *WDL* is the portal interface to *view and use international* digital resources.

The Library of Congress is a key member of DLF, DPLA, and WDL. The World Digital Library can be accessed directly from the Library of Congress web page or directly from *wdl.org*. The World Digital Library is also supported by the United Nations Educational, Cultural and Scientific Organization (UNESCO), and libraries, museums, archives, universities, and other international organizations around the world.

While the mission or goal of the DPLA is to share primary resources of our country, the United States, the mission of the World Digital Library is to share significant, multilingual primary sources among all world countries and cultures. The focus of WDL is accessing global resources. Our American digital collections also have many international treasures of interest. The principal objectives of the WDL are to:

1. promote international and intercultural understanding;
2. expand the volume and variety of cultural content on the Internet;
3. provide resources for educators, scholars, and general audiences; and
4. build capacity in partner institutions to narrow the digital divide within and between countries.[5]

The World Digital Library is much smaller than DLP but it is anticipated that it will grow significantly in a short amount of time. At the time of this book, the WDL has over ten thousand objects and about two hundred members. These numbers will change as more institutions digitize and share their primary resources. You can search the metadata of WDL by basic keyword searching, timelines, interactive mapping, and themes. Primary sources are found from many countries in all subject areas. For example, the National Library and Archives of Egypt is one of several institutions that have artifacts related to math and science. The *14th Century Guidebook for Students on the Use of Arithmetic* was a standard introduction to arithmetic (figure 4.2).[6]

Keep your eye on the World Digital Library. Its members are growing and so are the number of primary resources for downloading and viewing. It is exciting to think of the impact the WDL potentially has on international sharing and cooperation of artifacts as we explore each other's history and culture through primary, multilingual digital resources.

THE LIBRARY OF CONGRESS

The Library of Congress is the leader in setting standards for digitization and for creating and sharing its collections of digitized primary sources both nationally and internationally. Established in 1800 by Congress by President John Adams when the seat of government moved from Philadelphia to Washington, DC, the initial act called for "such books as may be necessary for the use of Congress—and for putting up a suitable apartment for containing them therein . . ." The Library of Congress was destroyed in August 1814 when the British set fire to the Capitol. In January 1815, Congress accepted Thomas Jefferson's offer to acquire his personal collection and appropriated $23,950 for his 6,487 books. The foundation was laid for a great national library.[7]

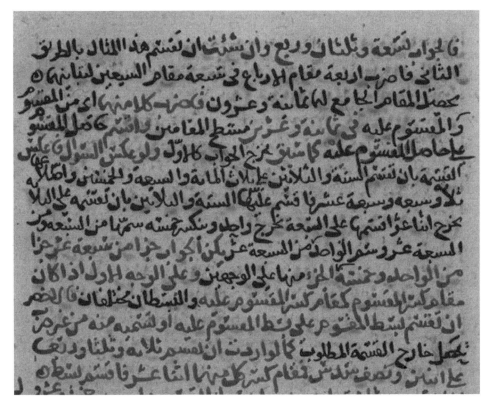

Figure 4.2. Image of the *14th Century Guidebook for Students on the Use of Arithmetic,* National Library and Archives of Egypt, World Digital Library. *World Digital Library*

Today the Library of Congress not only supports Congress in fulfilling its work; it also is the largest library in the world. It oversees copyright law and practices in the United States. MARC cataloging and metadata standards are developed and maintained under its guidance. It leads our country in the preservation of artifacts to archive our culture for future generations. The Library of Congress has the largest amount of digital content to the world and has shown librarians how to use the Internet to collaborate and share resources and collections.

In 1990, the Library of Congress began to explore digitizing as a means of sharing the wealth of their collections. The Internet was very new at that time. With knowledge and research of a five-year pilot, the National Digital Library Program (NDLP) began digitizing selected collections of Library of Congress archival materials that chronicle the nation's rich cultural heritage. NDLP reproduces primary source materials to create the many LC digital collections that support the study of the history and culture of the United States.

We can only dip our toes into the vast oceans of these important digital collections. Look at the broad categories of the eight distinct LC digital collections (see table 4.3). Each collection is subdivided into numerous special collections. To

Figure 4.3. Amelia Earhart, 1898–1937 standing with Mayor James Walker of New York. *Library of Congress, Prints and Photographs Collection*

Table 4.3.   Descriptions of the Main Digital Collections of the Library of Congress*a

American Memory	American Memory provides free and open access for written and spoken words, sound recordings, still and moving images, prints, maps, and sheet music that document the American experience.
Chronicling America	Produced by the National Digital Newspaper Program (NDNP). This is a searchable database of many partial and full US newspapers and historic pages.
Prints and Photographs	Over one million digital images of photographs, fine and popular prints and drawings, posters, and architectural and engineering drawings.
Maps	The largest and most comprehensive cartographic collection in the world with collections of millions of maps, thousands of atlases and reference works, and hundreds of globes and relief models.
Performing Arts Encyclopedia	Hundreds of music, theater, and dance resources searchable by subject, title, or name.
Sound Recordings	Special collections of recorded sound, such as National Jukebox and Songs of America, this collection also has the audio sound recordings of American Memory and Performing Arts and other digital collections.
Film	The Library of Congress began collecting the descriptive material related to motion pictures in 1893. Today it is a collection of the films that numbers in the thousands.
Veterans History	Personal accounts through interviews of American war veterans of World War I to the present day.
Manuscripts	Sixty million manuscript items in eleven thousand separate collections of American history and culture.

* Descriptions adapted from the Library of Congress website.

a. Ibid.

search all library collections (including American Memory) please visit loc.gov/search, or browse collections at loc.gov/collections.

The Library of Congress has many other collections. For example, in its Special Format Collections is the American Folklife Center that, among other projects, fosters Americans telling short, interesting, and meaningful stories that are digitally recorded as part of StoryCorps and often broadcasted on National Public Radio.

The Library of Congress digital collections are cataloged using metadata. Similar to searching DPLA or WDL, we should consider the fifteen elements of metadata when searching to help us target our desired results. You can only become familiar with these eight collections and the wonderment of riches they offer if you *use* them! Collection development is not static. In other words, each day new items are added to DPLA, WDL, and LC. Below are just two requests from patrons where the resources of LC Digital Collections far exceeded their expectations of what was available to help them with their research.

THE NATIONAL ARCHIVES AND RECORDS ADMINISTRATION

The National Archives[8] is a federal agency that we may be least familiar with. What exactly does this agency do? If you have visited a presidential library or if you have

**EXAMPLES OF SEARCHES USING
LIBRARY OF CONGRESS DIGITAL COLLECTIONS**

Question: Where can I find a firsthand account of US slavery in the nineteenth century?

Answer: Enter "slave narratives" into the LC Collections home page search box to find seven hours of recorded interviews of former slaves conducted between 1932 and 1975 in the American Memory collection under the subcategory "Voices from the Days of Slavery: Former Slaves Tell Their Stories."

Question: After learning about the Roaring Twenties, our class assignment is to create a "Speakeasy" day to demonstrate what we know about life and culture of the times. Can you help me find authentic information about speakeasies?

Answer: Enter the term "speakeasy" in the Collections home page search box and further limited it by date range to the 1920s to find web pages, film, manuscripts, prints, and books of authentic interviews, pictures, and articles from several of the main collections of LC.

searched family genealogy using a US Census, you have done so because of the National Archives work. Simply put, the National Archives is the nation's record keeper, yet preserves and archives no more than 3 percent of all records created by the federal government for historic purposes. Because most of the records are text, much of the National Archives is readily available online as digital conversion to text is fairly straightforward. There is so much here of historic significance, such as a wealth of correspondence by and to President Abraham Lincoln (see figure 4.4).

The most common questions patrons have about federal records are related to census data to obtain family history. It is reasonable that LSS can find census data directly using Google and may not always have to go to the National Archives website. Be sure, however, to avoid costly or commercial ancestry sites by setting up your Google search with *site:gov* in the search box! By setting your search for census data to only US government sites, you can link to the digital resources of the National Archives.

US Census

US Census data from the National Archives is particularly robust beginning with the year 1940. This **census** looked deeper into people's lives and occurred at the end of the Great Depression and at the beginning of Europe entering World War II. The online 1940 census records were released by the US National Archives on April 2, 2012. The commercial site, Archives.com, partnered with the National Archives to make this possible. A US 1940s Census search requires knowledge of the **enumeration district** number to view images and documents (see table 4.4).

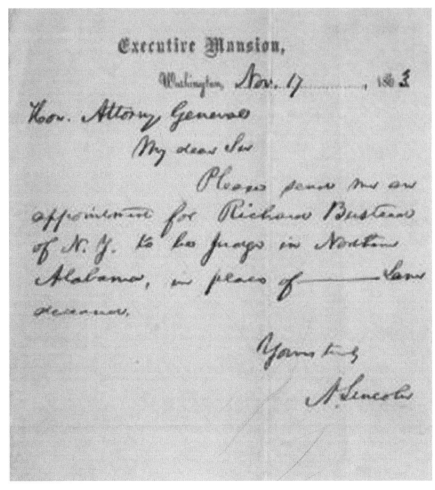

Figure 4.4. Letter from President Abraham Lincoln to Attorney General, November 17, 1863.
The National Archives

Table 4.4. How to Search the Online 1940 Census

Step	Action
1	Access the National Archives US 1940 Census at http://1940census.archives.gov/.
2	Drop menu for state, county, town, and street.
3	Select either "Map," "Descriptions," or "Census Schedules."
4	Map will provide several pages of maps of the town or will be specific to the street area.
5	Descriptions option will provide a scanned image of the actual page from the 1940 US Census book.
6	Census Schedules are located by enumeration number (EN). The EN references the actual page in the census book or schedule.

Data on the census schedules of 1940 is in numerical order by street and includes address, number living in household, family living in household, name, relationship to those in household, home data such as ownership, value, farm or residence, personal data of age, sex, race, married, age of first marriage, whether the person attended college, and if he or she could read and write. Next is the person's place of birth and that of his or her parents. Then they asked the native language (mother tongue) if foreign born. There are questions about citizenship, occupation, and employment and if the person is a veteran of war. The 1940 Census provided more comprehensive data that never had been collected by the federal government before.

Archives.com provides the means to search by person. The site gives a small amount of "free" downloads but then charges for the records. A genealogist needs both sites. Archives.com is a subscription database a large library may license for its patrons. Go ahead and search the 1940 Census for a grandparent or other family member. It will be a rewarding personal experience as well as give you knowledge on how to use this site for genealogy questions by library patrons.

CHAPTER SUMMARY

There is so much to view and experience through the global and national digital libraries and collections introduced in this chapter. Try to become familiar with each resource on a personal level. Look up people or topics you are interested in to make these libraries more meaningful for you. If you do this, you will think about them when patrons ask for help, and you will be a knowledgeable navigator in these digital libraries. A major idea of this chapter is that these national digital collections are cataloged using metadata, and are not typically found with basic Internet keyword searching. Become familiar with using the DPLA for searching these libraries and their collections. LSS can expand their knowledge of Internet resources by becoming familiar with these global and national collections.

DISCUSSION QUESTIONS AND ACTIVITIES

Discussion Questions

1. What is the purpose of the Digital Library Federation (DLF) and how does it work?
2. Which of the six ways to search the Digital Public Library of America (DPLA) do you prefer the most? Why?
3. Discuss the four principal objectives of the World Digital Library. Which principal objective do you think is the most important and why? Which one has the most impact on your local library patrons?
4. How has the Library of Congress demonstrated leadership in technology and digitations of our country's resources?
5. Which of the digital collections of the Library of Congress do you find the most interesting, and why?
6. How does census information support research and learning?

Activity

This chapter introduced us to several of the key national digital libraries LSS can familiarize themselves with in order to help patrons find important resources. These resources are primarily preserved from American history and culture and are now available for us to view, listen, read, and use online.

Let's become familiar with our key national digital libraries or collections and explore some of the important artifacts and information that they offer.

In this activity the LSS is preparing for programs and displays around the themes of civil rights in January as part of the remembrance of Martin Luther King, Jr. The goal is to find information that can be shared with patrons via the library resource web page for January on the topic of MLK Jr.

Use the four links below in table 4.5.

1. *Digital Library Federation*: Members. Select four members from this large list of institutions and browse their collections for online information on MLK Jr. for your library web page. Make your selections based on "hunches" about where MLK Jr. lived, spoke, or traveled. For example, he was killed in Memphis, Tennessee in 1968. One of the digital collections I would search for information may be the University of Tennessee. Search until you find four members of the DLF who have useful material on MLK Jr. or civil rights for your January library web page.
2. *Digital Public Library of America*: Use this portal interface to find additional information for your January library web page on civil rights or MLK Jr.
3. *Library of Congress*: Locate the digital collections *American Memory*, *Chronicling America*, and *Sound Recordings*. In each collection find a digital resource that would be informative to your library patrons about civil rights or MLK Jr. For example, search "Chronicling America" for newspaper articles on the decade of the 1960s or even find articles on April 4, 1968, when MLK Jr. lost his life. Seek out sound recordings of his speeches or those of other civil rights leaders.
4. *The National Archive and Records Administration*: Search the archive for additional information on civil rights leaders, documents, speeches, or other important information you can share with patrons.

For all information located be sure to:

- copy the URL correctly; and
- cite the source on your web page to give proper credit.

Table 4.5.   URLs of National Digital Libraries

Digital Library Federation—Members	http://www.diglib.org/members/
Digital Public Library of America	http://dp.la/info/
Library of Congress—Digital Collections	http://www.loc.gov/collections/
The National Archive and Records Administration	http://www.archives.gov/

NOTES

1. Amy Neubert, "Earhart's Legacy Thrives at Purdue University," Purdue University News, last modified October 19, 2009, accessed November 19, 2014, https://news.uns.purdue.edu/x/2009b/091019CordovaEarhart.html.

2, "DPLA," Digital Public Library of America, last modified 2014, accessed November 20, 2014, http://dp.la/.

3. Ryan NYP "Spirit of St. Louis," Charles A. Lindbergh. (2014). Retrieved December 31, 2014, from Smithsonian National Air and Space Museum website: http://airandspace.si.edu/collections/artifact.cfm?id=A19280021000.

4. "World Digital Library Home," World Digital Library, last modified 2015, accessed February 21, 2015, http://www.wdl.org/en/.

5. Ibid.

6. Mary Alice Anderson, "The World Digital Library," *Internet@Schools* 20, no. 2 (2013), http://search.ebscohost.com/login.aspx?direct=true&db=f5h&AN=85833772&site=eds-live.

7. "The Library of Congress," Library of Congress, last modified 2014, accessed November 20, 2014, http://www.loc.gov.

8. "National Archives," National Archives and Records Administration, last modified 2014, accessed November 20, 2014, http://www.archives.gov/.

REFERENCES, SUGGESTED READINGS, AND WEBSITES

Anderson, Mary Alice. "The World Digital Library." *Internet@Schools* 20, no. 2 (2013). http://search.ebscohost.com/login.aspx?direct=true&db=f5h&AN=85833772&site=eds-live.

Digital Library Federation. "About the Digital Library Federation." Digital Library Federation. Last modified 2014. Accessed November 18, 2014. http://www.diglib.org/about/.

Digital Public Library of America. "DPLA." Digital Public Library of America. Last modified 2014. Accessed November 20, 2014. http://dp.la/.

"Dublin Core Metadata Element Set, Version 1.1." Dublin Core Metadata Elements. Last modified 2014. Accessed November 20, 2014. http://dublincore.org/documents/dces/.

Library of Congress. "Digital Collections & Services." Library of Congress Digital Collections. Last modified 2014. Accessed November 16, 2014. http://www.loc.gov/library/libarch-digital.html.

"The Library of Congress." Library of Congress. Last modified 2014. Accessed November 20, 2014. http://www.loc.gov.

Library of Congress. "World Digital Library Home." World Digital Library. Last modified 2015. Accessed February 21, 2015. http://www.wdl.org/en/.

"Metadata Innovation." DCMI Home: Dublin Core. Last modified 2014. Accessed November 20, 2014. 00-caption list.docx.

"National Archives." National Archives and Records Administration. Last modified 2014. Accessed November 20, 2014. http://www.archives.gov/.

Neubert, Amy. "Earhart's Legacy Thrives at Purdue University." Purdue University News. Last modified October 19, 2009. Accessed November 19, 2014. https://news.uns.purdue.edu/x/2009b/091019CordovaEarhart.html.

"Ryan NYP 'Spirit of St. Louis,' Charles A. Lindbergh." Smithsonian National Air and Space Museum. Last modified 2014. Accessed December 31, 2014. http://airandspace.si.edu/collections/artifact.cfm?id=A19280021000.

CHAPTER 5

State and Local Collections

LSS know the role of technology in creating, identifying, retrieving, and accessing information resources and demonstrate facility with appropriate information discovery tools. (ALA-LSSC Technology Competency #7)

Topics Covered in This Chapter:

- State Digital Libraries
  - Lifelong, Self-Directed Learning
  - Authentication Required
- iCONN.org—Connecticut's Search Engine
  - Special Historic Digital Collections
- Local Digital Collections
- Preservation
  - Archival Supplies
- Grants for Digital Projects
  - Institute of Museums and Library Services
  - National Endowment for the Humanities
  - Regional and Local Grants
  - Bank of America

Key Terms:

Authentication: This is the method of identification needed to access an online digital library or a database that is agreed upon by the library and the data provider. The proof for access could be such things as the patron barcode, unique username and/or password, or using an authorized library computer.

Grants: These are funds provided by others to pay for materials, equipment, labor, or other supports to advance the work of an important project. The library commits to mutually agreed upon goals, conditions, and activities with the funding agency.

In-Kind Contributions: Grants often fund part of a project and require the applicant to contribute the rest. The share or match required by the library for a grant could be things the library already has in place like staff time and skills, existing equipment, or materials. The library may have to do fundraising to acquire their amount of the project. Each grant will stipulate whether there is any matching effort required. Library staff can help with reaching the required match by providing their own expertise or skills for a project or outside activities like training volunteers and fundraising.

Preservation: The action or process of keeping an item from harm or decay so that it is maintained in its original state. There are many ways to maintain library artifacts beginning with climate control, secure handling, and protective covering. Library staff can locate artifacts within the library and research the correct archival supplies that can help maintain original integrity.

Virtual Library: This is another name for multiple online digital collections. Library staff should be familiar with this term as some people or places prefer to use it to describe their digital resources collections.

In the previous chapter we explored some of the digital resources of our national libraries and institutions. Programs and policies of the Digital Library Federation, Digital Public Library of America, and the Library of Congress have helped set the cataloging and metadata standards that are being followed by world institutions to allow searchable Internet access to their digital collections.

In this chapter we will look at a sampling of state and local digital library collections. There are similarities between practices of national libraries and how state and local libraries plan, implement, and share their digital collections. We will learn about the basic preservation of library materials so that they can be digitized and shared. Grants as a source of funding for digitization projects and how staff may obtain them will be explored.

STATE DIGITAL LIBRARIES

There are fifty state libraries that support the work of their academic, public, and school libraries. While most of the state libraries are departments or entities that report directly to the governor or state legislature, a few, like Wisconsin and Colorado, are divisions of the Department of Education. State libraries primarily support the research of the state legislature and preserve or archive important information. Secondary responsibilities of state libraries vary but often include leadership, materials, programming, education, and funding supports for academic, public, and school libraries.

Lifelong, Self-Directed Learning

An expanding role for the majority of state libraries is to provide digital resources for state residents which provide information and promote lifelong, self-directed learning. Libraries strongly support self-directed learning. Patrons take the initiative to use library resources[1] to acquire new knowledge and skills. Every state library has its own unique purpose or mission. For example, the New York State Library in its *Creating the Future: A 2020 Vision Plan for Library Service in New York State* recommends, in part, being a vital part of all New Yorkers' lifelong learning experience. Libraries "function at the front lines of e-resources (including e-books) purchasing, licensing, digital rights management, digital curation, resource-sharing, and preservation."[2]

While all libraries have a critical role in supporting inquiry, the public library is a key resource for patrons when they are no longer enrolled in school or college. State libraries recognize the importance of providing these kinds of digital resources that enhance the public libraries collections and can be accessed by all residents for life-long, self-directed learning:

EXAMPLES OF DIGITAL RESOURCES THAT SUPPORT LIFELONG, SELF-DIRECTED LEARNING

- electronic subscriptions that are licensed for the use of state residents;
- databases of government, educational, health, and other information;
- online digital collections of primary sources such as original artifacts, manuscripts, texts, or other materials that preserve the history of the state and are shared with the public; and
- accessible e-books with free access privileges.

The number of state libraries that offer digital resources to their residents is increasingly growing. Most state libraries offer subscription databases on their home page, but each state varies in the titles, providers, and quantity. For example, in addition to databases, Indiana offers a **virtual library** called *Inspire*[3] that is a very large and comprehensive directory of web links of importance to Indiana residents. New York has a separate interface to its digital collections held in the New York State Archives.[4] Montana Digital Library offers access to EBSCO databases and the Montana Memory Project,[5] as well as an organized approach to a unified catalog, government and educational links. The State Library of North Carolina[6] has a well-organized framework of the subscription databases and reference sources from Gale and EBSCO, journals, newspapers, state and local history resources, and government links. Each state has its own unique presentation of digital resources.

Authentication Required

Residents access subscription databases of their state digital libraries with some kind of **authentication**, such as library patron barcode or user name and password to assure the state that they are legitimate users. Some state digital libraries post free links to important educational and government resources that do not require authentication. Commonly found on state digital library pages is PubMed,[7] a free government database for biomedical literature. There are many other fine government, legal, medical, educational, and nonprofit databases which state digital libraries include in their digital resources for residents.

Research I+CT

ICONN.ORG: CONNECTICUT'S SEARCH ENGINE

One of the first state digital libraries in the country was iCONN, sponsored by the Connecticut State Library (CSL) (see figure 5.1). The goal of iConn is to support the core information needs of all Connecticut residents. iConn.org[8] is a comprehensive offering of an online catalog, databases, e-books, and web links. iCONN[9] began in 1990 as a statewide catalog of Connecticut library holdings and it continues today with regular updated holdings of school, academic, and public libraries. The staff of the CSL creates, negotiates, coordinates, collaborates, and maintains digital library services for Connecticut residents. It provides expansive databases directly to every public library and educational institution in Connecticut through the Connecticut Education Network. Residents can also access iCONN from any Internet accessible location.[10]

At the time of this writing iCONN has licensed agreements for databases from EBSCO and ProQuest. Other databases are obtained individually, such as Ancestry .com, or are created by the Connecticut State Library or other educational or cultural organizations. There are also many links to other subject sites that promote inquiry and learning that are free (see table 5.1). You do not have to be a Connecticut resident to access links to other useful sites. Following are the current categories and databases for the public.

public, Schools, Colleges

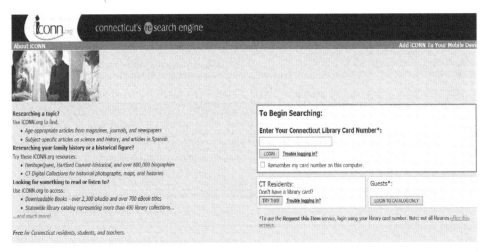

Figure 5.1. Connecticut Digital Library Home Page for Public and K–12 Libraries. *Connecticut Digital Library*

Table 5.1. iCONN Resources for the Public

Category	Databases
Resources for Students	• Kids Search, MAS Ultra—School Edition • Middle Search Plus, Primary Search, Searchasaurus • Student Research Center, TOPICSearch, Main File • 2-1-1 Community Resources, GreenFILE
Health and Science	• Connecticut Physician Profiles, Medline Plus • CT Consumer Health Information, PubMed • Science Reference Center • *Links to Other Science and Health Sites*
Magazines and Journals	• Academic Search Premier, iConn One Search • Advanced Searching EBSCO Host, ERIC • MasterFILE Premier (includes *Consumer Reports*) • Professional Development Collection, Referencia Latina • Teacher Reference Center • E-Journal Finder; Popular Magazines
Law	• Legal Information Reference Center • *Links to Other Law Resources*
Business	• iCONN OneSearch for Public Libraries—Business Profile • *Links to Other Business Resources*
Newspapers and Images	• Christian Science Monitor (ProQuest) (1988–) • Hartford Courant (1992–) • Hartford Courant—Historical (1764–1922) • iCONN Newsstand (ProQuest) • Los Angeles Times (ProQuest) (1985–) • Newspaper Source Plus • New York Times (ProQuest) (1985–) • Wall Street Journal (ProQuest) (1984–) • Washington Post (ProQuest) (1987–) • *Free Streaming Video, Free Images on the Web*
History, Biography, and Genealogy	• Biography Reference Bank, HeritageQuest • Biography Reference Center, History Reference Center • Connecticut Digital Collections (to be replaced in 2015 by the Connecticut Digital Archive)[a] • CT State Library Collections in Ancestry.com • Hartford Courant (1764–1922) • Remembering World War I • American Civil War Resources • *Links to Other History Resources*
E-Reference Books and Reading	• Nonfiction Book Collection—High Schools • Nonfiction Book Collection—Middle Schools • Nonfiction Book Collection—Elementary Schools • Book Recommendations • eAudio and eBooks, Free E-Books

[a] William Sullivan, "Draft from Chapter 8," e-mail message to author, January 9, 2015.

Special Historic Digital Collections

The Connecticut Digital Collections[11] and Connecticut History Online[12] are special historic collections that are free to the public. As one of the original thirteen colonies, Connecticut has extensive primary source materials on Colonial history, the American Revolution, the War of 1812, the Civil War, and other eras and events that shaped the nation. The Connecticut State Library received an award from the National Endowment for the Humanities to digitize from microfilm one hundred thousand pages of historically significant Connecticut newspapers between 1836 and 1922. The digital images will be included in the Library of Congress newspaper site *Chronicling America*[13] and eventually in the Connecticut Digital Collections. These newspapers contain firsthand accounts of historic events of interest to all of America.

In addition to newspaper accounts, the primary sources digitized in Connecticut Digital Collections provide significant research on historic topics and people. As an example, let us research primary sources about Benedict Arnold, a native of Connecticut. Remember, there is no authentication needed to access these resources (see table 5.2).[14, 15]

LSS can explore and use these primary sources for research of early American history and those of their own state library. Take a few minutes and explore. Find the digital library of your state, and explore its offerings. Remember, your federal and state tax dollars support your access to the resources there. Encourage your patrons to use their state library databases to help them find primary sources and

CT Digital Collection ↓ *CT* ↓ *Digital Archive* *

Table 5.2.   Use Connecticut Digital Collections* for Historic Research

Q. What primary source information can be found on Benedict Arnold?

Source	URL	Search Results
Connecticut Digital Collections	http://www.cslib.org/iconnsitemap/staff/digitalcollections.aspx	Access the links to the source sites.
Connecticut History Online**	http://www.cthistoryonline.org/cdm/landingpage/collection/cho	Images of him, his birthplace, homes, maps, the Battle of Fort Griswold.
Connecticut State Library Digital Collections	http://cslib.cdmhost.com/ *Treasures of CT libraries (humanities) CT History.org*	Images, Revolutionary War newspapers, court files, militia archives, pamphlets, excerpts from books, maps, etc.
Newspapers of Connecticut	http://cslib.cdmhost.com/cdm/landingpage/collection/p15019coll9	Scanned copies of newspapers from the eighteenth and nineteenth century.
ProQuest Historical Papers—Hartford Courant 1764–1922	http://search.proquest.com/hnphartfordcourant/index?accountid=47180	Over six hundred results, many of which are from the original newspaper accounts during the Revolutionary War.

*Connecticut Digital Collections will be called Connecticut Digital Archive some time in mid to late 2015.

**Name to change to Connecticut History Illustrated some time in 2015.

Henry Ford Museum
Digital Resource →
Caring for an facts
→ paper

other information. Most state libraries have a goal to preserve and digitize historic artifacts of the state.

Museum of CT Hx

LOCAL DIGITAL COLLECTIONS

LSS have a large role in promoting and creating digital resources at the local level. There are uncountable artifacts, texts, manuscripts, and images of important historic and cultural heritage existing in local libraries, historical societies, and museums.

National and state institutions aim to support the preservation and digitization at the local level. For example, in 2012, the National Archives funded over $2.5 million for the preservation of state and local historical records.[16] The Texas State Library digital library, TexShare,[17] not only provides a full complement of journal, reference, and e-book databases to its residents, it also provides grants for TexTreasures.[18] TexTreasures are locally created library digital collections. Each year libraries that are awarded TexTreasures grants are posted with a project description. Usually within a year of being awarded a grant, some or all of the new digital collection is posted online and available to the Internet public. Examples of award-winning digital collections of interest to all Americans are:

1. Materials documenting the history of the Mexican Revolution (1910–1920) on the US–Mexico border.
2. Documents, records, and artifacts of Lady Bird Johnson's work to transform the way Americans think about the natural environment.
3. Documents relating to the Prairie View Interscholastic League (PVIL) that served as the basis for African-American grade school and high school athletic and academic tournament competitions from 1920–1970. The PVIL occurred during a time of segregation.[19]

Across the country local library collections are the foundation for larger state resources. The Ohio State Library offers funds to local institutions through the Ohio Memory digital library.[20] Ohio Memory funds over three hundred fifty local Ohio libraries' and institutions' efforts to digitize local artifacts for online access. Indiana State Library's Hoosier State Chronicles—Digital Historical Newspapers Program[21] provides free access to hundreds of thousands of state and local digitized and searchable pages. The Online Archive of California[22] provides free public access to primary source collections created and maintained by over two hundred libraries and other institutions. These are just a few examples of how state libraries are collaborating and supporting the local digitization efforts of local libraries. I suggest LSS explore their state library and the state historic preservation websites[23] to find opportunities for financial and other guidance on how to digitize the treasures of local libraries that remain unseen by the public.

Digital projects, however, do not have to be expensive nor do the artifacts always have to be housed in the library. A fine example of this is the Groton History Online[24] project (see figure 5.2). Several years ago librarians at the Groton Public Library in Groton, Connecticut, asked patrons to share with them old postcards they had of historic scenes or past events that occurred in Groton. Over a thousand

Figure 5.2.   Groton History Online. *Groton Public Library, Groton, CT*

postcards were shared. Staff scanned each postcard and entered simple metadata about the creator, location, date, event, and related terms for the database. The postcard was returned to the owner.

Groton is known as the submarine capital of the world. It is the home of a submarine Navy base as well as a major builder of submarines, Electric Boat. By searching the word "submarines," one finds historic postcards of submarine history. The Revolutionary War Battle of Fort Griswold also occurred on the banks of Groton. Searching the battle by name brings up a variety of images. You may want to create a local postcard project around a theme of historic pictures or events that occurred over time in your library's town or city.

Students in my course, "Introduction to Digital Resources," learn about the postcard project as an example of an effective digital collection created by local library staff. For their final project students research and propose a digital collection of historic or important primary sources currently housed in a library where they work or frequent. In a presentation proposal, students describe the purpose of the collection and several items they have digitized and hyperlinked for additional information about the artifacts. They may share their prototype collection with a librarian or supervisor. I have found this final project gives students both the experience and confidence to begin to create digital collections around a theme or topic of hidden library treasures. Students have proposed digital collections on a variety of topics such as US Coast Guard Academy athletic history, members of a local founding family who lived in the late eighteenth and early nineteenth century, Colonel Ledyard who died in battle leading Connecticut soldiers at the Battle of Fort Griswold, and a digital yearbook of famous alumni from a nearby large private high school academy. Each project has potential and merit as it can bring dispersed or hidden artifacts to the public.

PRESERVATION

The first step in digitizing artifacts often is preservation. According to Dr. Walter Havighurst,[25] "The past is not the property of historians; it is a public possession. It belongs to anyone who is aware of it, and it grows by being shared. It sustains the whole society, which always needs the identity that only the past can give" (pp. 1–2). Dr. Havighurst's words in *With Heritage So Rich* support the goals of the National Historic Preservation Act of 1966.[26] The act, amended in 2006, mandates that government agencies consider preservation of historic land and buildings before any renovations or changes. The idea of the past belonging to the public is fundamental to the act and supports the work of libraries to preserve significant artifacts, documents, text, and images. Creating local online digital library collections is an important way to share unique and fragile artifacts with the public.

What are the best ways for library staff to preserve the original items, particularly if they show wear or distress? Look around your library to identify items that are not properly stored. Are there artifacts too close to heating or water sources? Even simple measures can prolong the lifespan of an artifact. What vulnerable materials or fabrics is the item made from? Papers, journals, documents, or texts that are not properly stored can grow mold or otherwise be damaged. Climate control for preservation is not often available in library buildings that are decades or centuries old.

Archival Supplies

Archival supplies can help maintain the life of primary sources. A local resident was about to discard his extensive collection of *Life* magazines. He had every issue from 1937 through 1952, all in excellent condition. These World War II primary sources were an opportunity for students to conduct authentic research. Unfortunately, mold and mildew were an ongoing library problem. With special archival slips or plastic bags, we were able to protect and seal each magazine. Not only did this step maintain the physical integrity of the magazines, it also provided a way to teach patrons about how to care and preserve important primary source materials.

Library companies sell archival supplies (http://nysa32.nysed.gov/a/records/mr _hrecords_cons_arcsupplie.shtml) such as paper, tissue, storage boxes, plastic bags, fasteners, cleaning materials, archival identification tags, and pens (see figure 5.3). Seek training from experts in local museums or historical societies to learn how to handle and best preserve the integrity and original characteristics of an item. Often state libraries will either provide training workshops or have an expert on staff who can provide guidance. A good place to begin your learning about how to preserve artifacts and materials is from the Henry Ford Museum.[27] From its extensive website we can learn how to:

1. handle archival documents and books;
2. avoid factors that cause damage;
3. store, exhibit, and frame items; and
4. repair and clean (especially mold).

The Henry Ford suggests ways to preserve objects made of different materials made of metal, wood, or glass. It also offers advice on the preservation of textiles, paintings, photographs, furniture, and other items.

Figure 5.3.   Library Archival Workspace and Supplies. *Bill Library, Ledyard, CT*

In addition to the Henry Ford, another resource LSS can search is the Directory of Preservation Organizations and Resources.[28] From this site you can reach more than 4,500 historical societies and 7,000 museums, many of which have information about preservation. Library staff can learn much from these institutions that are committed to Dr. Havighurst's goal of preserving our past in order to share it with others. Once an item has been preserved or repaired properly, it can be digitized for online access by the public. We will next look at grant opportunities to fund local library digital projects.

GRANTS FOR DIGITAL PROJECTS

Federal, state, and endowment grants support large digitization projects of important primary resources. Grantors may require applicants to adopt digitization standards established by national libraries so that the project may potentially contribute to a larger effort like the Connecticut historic newspapers and Chronicling America. By using common standards and metadata, states and local institutions can plan and later share their digital collections in a more purposeful and global way.

Institute of Museums and Library Services

The United States Institute of Museums and Library Services (IMLS)[29] is a federal agency that supports over 123,000 libraries and 35,000 museums in the United States. The IMLS "Grants to States" program is a major source of federal funding that distributes over $150 million per year. The grants are distributed to the fifty state libraries and agencies of US territories that develop library services as mandated by the Library Services and Technology Act (LSTA).[30] LSTA grants have many purposes, including the support of digitization of special collections and primary sources as well as access to electronic databases and e-books. They also promote the development of library services that provide all users access to information through local, state, regional, national, and international collaborations and networks.[31] State libraries disburse LSTA grants to local libraries who apply for funds, including digitization of primary sources.

National Endowment for the Humanities

While many of the projects that the National Endowment for the Humanities[32] (NEH) funds are of a large scope, it has a program for the preservation and access to collections of cultural value for smaller institutions. Applicants must be small to mid-size libraries, historical societies, museums, or like institutions who have never before received any type of NEH grant. About one-third of the applicants that apply are successfully awarded grants for their projects. The NEH website has extensive resources and examples on how to apply for their grants.

Regional and Local Grants

in kind contributions → greater grant rewards

In addition to national organizations and your state library, public and school libraries may also consider town and regional funding sources. For example my local newspaper, the *Day*,[33] is a nonprofit entity. Twice a year after operating and capital expenses are met, the *Day* disperses any profit to other nonprofit organizations including libraries. Libraries have the opportunity to apply for Bodenwein Public Benevolent Foundation grants twice a year. The Foundation has and continues to fund local library digitization projects.

CT State Library posts successful grant applications

Bank of America

If you are not familiar with the Bank of America website, I suggest you immediately stop what you are doing and check out its "Philanthropic Solutions" page.[34] There are hundreds—if not thousands—of grants available for libraries.[35]

Not only will you find grant descriptions, but on the web page the online application with instructions is provided as well. Bank of America coordinates and supports grant opportunities for nonprofits across the country from its "Philanthropic Solutions" web page.

SEARCH BANK OF AMERICA FOR LIBRARY GRANTS

Go to https://www.bankofamerica.com/philanthropic/grantmaking.go.
You can search by

1. foundation name;
2. category, i.e., education or arts, culture, and humanities;
3. state; or
4. any combinations of the above three.

How can LSS support grant applications for their libraries? There are many ways we can do so! First, LSS work firsthand with library patrons and materials. LSS often have excellent ideas of what new services the public want and would use. Second, a grant has a much better chance of being funded when there are **"in-kind" con- tributions**. In-kind contributions are what the library already has in place to help the project. In-kind may be funding, staffing, materials, or other expertise. LSS can be contributors to digitization projects and identified on the grant application to help with the selection, scanning, and metadata creation. Their time and expertise has in-kind value. Knowledgeable LSS may also be considered in-kind trainers for volunteers. Third, LSS can make themselves familiar with Bank of America and other funding institutions mentioned above and share the opportunities they find with other library staff and supervisors. There are many ways LSS who are interested in promoting and creating digital collections can help locate grants and become a skilled resource for digitizing local primary sources and artifacts.

CHAPTER SUMMARY

In this chapter we learned state digital libraries offer their residents access to high- quality subscription databases. We also learned that state libraries offer support through collaboration, education, and funding local library digitization of primary resources. These resources may be found in local special collections or tucked away in boxes with no public access. There is much LSS can do to support patrons' use of their state digital library databases when they, themselves, are familiar with its offer- ings. LSS use technology in creating, identifying, retrieving, and accessing informa- tion from state digital libraries as well as demonstrate facility when they know how to create local digital collections using appropriate technology and research tools.

DISCUSSION QUESTIONS AND ACTIVITIES

Discussion Questions

1. In what ways do state and public libraries support patrons' self-directed, life- long learning?
2. What does authentication mean in relation to patron access to library databases?
3. Name the four key steps in preserving an artifact or item according to the Hen- ry Ford Museum.
4. Why would local libraries want to create digital collections?
5. Describe two ways libraries may be able to obtain grants for local digitization projects.

Activities

Activity 1: Explore State Digital Library Collections
Using the URLs of the state library digital collections or archives discussed in this chapter (see endnotes):

1. Explore the free resources of the following state libraries:
   * Texas
   * New York
   * North Carolina
   * Connecticut
   * Montana
   * Your own state or others you have interest in
2. Create lists in the categories of Arts, Health and Medicine, Law, Business, and Education.
3. Add to each list three new websites (to you) for each category. Use these new websites regularly to help patrons or for your own self-directed learning.

Share one "best" site with a friend or family member!

Activity 2: Create a Small, Local Library Digital Collection
This activity is to gain beginning practice of planning for a local digital collection.

1. Look around your local library and discuss with librarians and others what artifacts they may have that could be an important digital collection for patrons to access online. If you cannot find anything at the library, expand your search to a historical society, school, or other institution that is interested in history.
2. Develop a theme or purpose of the collection such as historic postcards, an event people in your town participated in, an important industry, etc.
3. Gather five to ten items. Scan or take digital pictures of them.
4. Insert each image on a PowerPoint or other presentation slide.
5. On the slide describe the image and its importance. You can hyperlink to outside websites for additional information.
6. Present your collection to stakeholders, i.e., library staff and administrators. They will be impressed with your research and may want to continue.

NOTES

1. K. Ramnarayan and Shyamala Hande, "Thoughts on Self-Directed Learning in Medical Schools: Making Students More Responsible," School of Education at Johns Hopkins University, last modified 2012, accessed March 11, 2015, http://education.jhu.edu/PD/newhorizons/lifelonglearning/higher-education/medical-schools/.

2. "Creating the Future: A 2020 Vision Plan for Library Service in New York State," New York State Library, last modified 2014, accessed November 22, 2014, http://www.nysl.nysed.gov/libdev/adviscns/rac/2020final/.

3. "A-Z Resource List," Inspire: Indiana's Virtual Library, last modified 2015, accessed March 11, 2015, http://www.in.gov/library/inspire/faq.html.

4. "New York State Archives," New York State Archives, last modified 2015, accessed March 11, 2015, http://www.archives.nysed.gov/aindex.shtml.

5. "Montana Memory Project," Montana Memory Project, last modified 2015, accessed March 11, 2015, http://mtmemory.org/.

6. "Online and On-Site Research," Government and Heritage Library, last modified 2015, accessed March 11, 2015, http://statelibrary.ncdcr.gov/ghl/resources/index.html#online.

7. "PubMed," PubMed, last modified 2015, accessed March 11, 2015, http://www.ncbi.nlm.nih.gov/pubmed.

8. "IConn.org—Connecticut's ReSearch Engine," Connecticut Digital Library, last modified 2014, accessed November 23, 2014, htp://www.iconn.org.

9. William Sullivan, "Draft from Chapter 8," e-mail message to author, January 9, 2015.

10. "IConn.org—Connecticut's ReSearch Engine," Connecticut Digital Library, last modified 2014, accessed November 23, 2014, htp://www.iconn.org.

11. "Connecticut State Library Digital Collections," Connecticut State Library Digital Collections, last modified 2014, accessed November 25, 2014, http://cslib.cdmhost.com/.

12. "Connecticut History Online," Connecticut History Online, last modified 2014, accessed November 25, 2014, http://www.cthistoryonline.org/cdm/landingpage/collection/cho.

13. "Chronicling America: Historic American Newspapers," Chronicling America: Historic American Newspapers, last modified 2015, accessed March 11, 2015, http://chroniclingamerica.loc.gov/.

14. William Sullivan, "Draft from Chapter 8," e-mail message to author, January 9, 2015.

15. Ibid.

16. "National Archives Awards $2.5 Million in Grants for Historical Records Projects," National Archives, last modified January 5, 2012, accessed November 24, 2014, http://www.archives.gov/press/press-releases/2012/nr12-49.html.

17. "TexShare—Special Collections Funded with TexTreasures Grants," Texas State Library and Archives Commission, last modified 2014, accessed November 22, 2014, https://www.tsl.texas.gov/texshare/texcollectionslist.html.

18. "TexTreasures Grant Program," TexShare-TexTreasures, last modified 2015, accessed March 11, 2015, https://www.tsl.texas.gov/texshare/textreasurespage.html.

19. "TexShare—Special Collections Funded with TexTreasures Grants," Texas State Library and Archives Commission, last modified 2014, accessed November 22, 2014, https://www.tsl.texas.gov/texshare/texcollectionslist.html.

20. "Ohio Memory," Ohio Memory, last modified 2014, accessed November 26, 2014, http://www.ohiomemory.org/#ad-image-0.

21. "Hoosier's State Chronicles: Indiana's Historic Newspaper Program," Hoosier State Chronicles, last modified 2014, accessed November 28, 2014, https://newspapers.library.in.gov/.

22. "Online Archive of California," Online Archive of California, last modified 2014, accessed November 28, 2014, http://www.oac.cdlib.org/.

23. "State Historic Preservation Office (SHPO)," Preservation Directory.com, last modified 2014, accessed November 27, 2014, http://www.preservationdirectory.com/preservationorganizationsresources/OrganizationListings.aspx?catid=4.

24. "Groton History Online," Town of Groton, Connecticut, last modified 2012, accessed November 27, 2014, http://www.groton-ct.gov/history/list.asp.

25. Carl Fiess, *With Heritage So Rich* (New York, NY: Random House, 1966).

26. "The National Historic Preservation Act of 1966, As Amended," The National Historic Preservation Act of 1966, as amended, last modified 2009, accessed March 11, 2015, http://www.achp.gov/nhpa.html.

27. "The Henry Ford Museum." The Henry Ford, last modified 2015, accessed February 21, 2015, http://www.thehenryford.org/museum/index.aspx.

28. "Preservation Organizations & Resources," Preservation Directory.com, last modified 2014, accessed November 27, 2014, http://www.preservationdirectory.com/preservationorganizationsresources/organizationcategories.aspx.

29. "Grants to State Library Administrative Agencies," Institute of Museums and Library Services: State Programs, last modified 2014, accessed November 24, 2014, http://www.imls.gov/programs/default.aspx.

30. Ibid.

31. Ibid.

32. "Preservation Assistance Grants for Smaller Institutions," National Endowment for the Humanities, last modified 2014, accessed November 26, 2014, http://www.neh.gov/grants/preservation/preservation-assistance-grants-smaller-institutions.

33. "The Day," The Day, last modified 2015, accessed March 11, 2015, http://www.theday.com/.

34. "Bank of America—Philanthropic Solutions," Bank of America, last modified 2014, accessed November 23, 2014, https://www.bankofamerica.com/philanthropic/grantmaking.go.

35. Ibid.

REFERENCES, SUGGESTED READINGS, AND WEBSITES

Advisory Council on Historic Preservation. "The National Historic Preservation Act of 1966, As Amended." The National Historic Preservation Act of 1966, As Amended. Last modified 2009. Accessed March 11, 2015. http://www.achp.gov/nhpa.html.

"A World of Resources at Your Desktop: Exploring the Montana State Digital Library." Montana State Library. Last modified 2014. Accessed November 24, 2014. http://msl.mt.gov/state/forms/overview_descrpt.asp.

"Bank of America—Philanthropic Solutions." Bank of America. Last modified 2014. Accessed November 23, 2014. https://www.bankofamerica.com/philanthropic/grantmaking.go.

"Connecticut History Online." Connecticut History Online. Last modified 2014. Accessed November 25, 2014. http://www.cthistoryonline.org/cdm/landingpage/collection/cho.

"Connecticut State Library Digital Collections." Connecticut State Library Digital Collections. Last modified 2014. Accessed November 25, 2014. http://cslib.cdmhost.com/.

"Creating the Future: A 2020 Vision Plan for Library Service in New York State." New York State Library. Last modified 2014. Accessed November 22, 2014. http://www.nysl.nysed.gov/libdev/adviscns/rac/2020final/.

The Day Publishing Company. "The Day." Last modified 2015. Accessed March 11, 2015. http://www.theday.com/.

"Digital Collections by Topic." New York Archives. Last modified 2014. Accessed November 23, 2014. http://www.archives.nysed.gov/d/about/browse.shtml.

Fahey, Mary. "The Care and Preservation of Archival Materials." The Henry Ford. Last modified 2014. Accessed November 26, 2014. http://ophelia.sdsu.edu:8080/henryford_org/06-15-2014/research/caring/materials.aspx.html.

Fiess, Carl. *With Heritage So Rich.* New York: Random House, 1966.

"Grants to State Library Administrative Agencies." Institute of Museums and Library Services: State Programs. Last modified 2014. Accessed November 24, 2014. http://www.imls.gov/programs/default.aspx.

"Groton History Online." Town of Groton, Connecticut. Last modified 2012. Accessed November 27, 2014. http://www.groton-ct.gov/history/list.asp.

"Hartford Courant 1764–1922." ProQuest Historical Papers – Hartford Courant 1764–1922. Last modified 2014. Accessed November 24, 2014. http://search.proquest.com/hnphartfordcourant/index?accountid=47180.

The Henry Ford. "The Henry Ford Museum." The Henry Ford. Last modified 2015. Accessed February 21, 2015. http://www.thehenryford.org/museum/index.aspx.

"Hoosier's State Chronicles: Indiana's Historic Newspaper Program." Hoosier State Chronicles. Last modified 2014. Accessed November 28, 2014. https://newspapers.library.in.gov/.

"IConn.org—Connecticut's ReSearch Engine." Connecticut Digital Library. Last modified 2014. Accessed November 23, 2014. http://www.iconn.org.

Indiana State Library. "A–Z Resource List." Inspire: Indiana's Virtual Library. Last modified 2015. Accessed March 11, 2015. http://www.in.gov/library/inspire/faq.html.

Library of Congress. "Chronicling America: Historic American Newspapers." Chronicling America: Historic American Newspapers. Last modified 2015. Accessed March 11, 2015. http://chroniclingamerica.loc.gov/.

Montana State Library. "Montana Memory Project." Montana Memory Project. Last modified 2015. Accessed March 11, 2015. http://mtmemory.org/.

"National Archives Awards $2.5 Million in Grants for Historical Records Projects." National Archives. Last modified January 5, 2012. Accessed November 24, 2014. http://www.archives.gov/press/press-releases/2012/nr12-49.html.

"Newspapers of Connecticut." Newspapers of Connecticut. Last modified 2014. Accessed November 24, 2014. http://cslib.cdmhost.com/cdm/landingpage/collection/p15019coll9.

New York State Education Department. "New York State Archives." New York State Archives. Last modified 2015. Accessed March 11, 2015. http://www.archives.nysed.gov/aindex.shtml.

"Ohio Memory." Ohio Memory. Last modified 2014. Accessed November 26, 2014. http://www.ohiomemory.org/#ad-image-0.

"Online Archive of California." Online Archive of California. Last modified 2014. Accessed November 28, 2014. http://www.oac.cdlib.org/.

"Preservation Assistance Grants for Smaller Institutions." National Endowment for the Humanities. Last modified 2014. Accessed November 26, 2014. http://www.neh.gov/grants/preservation/preservation-assistance-grants-smaller-institutions.

"Preservation Organizations & Resources." Preservation Directory.com. Last modified 2014. Accessed November 27, 2014. http://www.preservationdirectory.com/preservationorganizationsresources/organizationcategories.aspx.

Ramnarayan, K., and Shyamala Hande. "Thoughts on Self-Directed Learning in Medical Schools: Making Students More Responsible." School of Education at Johns Hopkins University. Last modified 2012. Accessed March 11, 2015. http://education.jhu.edu/PD/newhorizons/lifelonglearning/higher-education/medical-schools/.

"State Historic Preservation Office (SHPO)." Preservation Directory.com. Last modified 2014. Accessed November 27, 2014. http://www.preservationdirectory.com/preservationorganizationsresources/OrganizationListings.aspx?catid=4.

State Library of North Carolina. "Online and On-Site Research." Government and Heritage Library. Last modified 2015. Accessed March 11, 2015. http://statelibrary.ncdcr.gov/ghl/resources/index.html#online.

Sullivan, William. "Draft from Chapter 8." E-mail message to author. January 9, 2015. E-mail includes attachment with information about iConn.org and its databases. Background information and future plans are also mentioned.

Texas State Library and Archives Program. "TexTreasures Grant Program." TexShare-TexTreasures. Last modified 2015. Accessed March 11, 2015. https://www.tsl.texas.gov/texshare/textreasurespage.html.

"TexShare—Special Collections Funded with TexTreasures Grants." Texas State Library and Archives Commission. Last modified 2014. Accessed November 22, 2014. https://www.tsl.texas.gov/texshare/texcollectionslist.html.

US National Library of Medicine, National Institutes of Health. "PubMed." PubMed. Last modified 2015. Accessed March 11, 2015. http://www.ncbi.nlm.nih.gov/pubmed.

"Welcome." Preservation Directory.com. Last modified 2014. Accessed November 24, 2014. http://www.preservationdirectory.com/HistoricalPreservation/Home.aspx.

CHAPTER 6

Subscription Databases

Planning, Evaluation, and Acquisition Processes

LSS know the role and responsibility of libraries for introducing relevant applications of technology, including digital literacy, to the public. (ALA-LSSC Technology Competency #2)

Topics Covered in This Chapter:

- The Planning Process
  - Collection Analysis
  - Needs Assessment
  - Common Core State Standards
- The Evaluation Process
  - Reputation
  - Searching
  - Trials
  - Usage Statistics
  - Database Reviews
- The Acquisitions Process
  - Free Databases
  - Funding and Grants
  - Pricing and Discount Purchasing
  - E-Rate
  - Contracts or License Agreements
  - Access
  - IT Support
- Library Support Staff and Training

Key Terms

Dynamic IP Range: Consecutive numbers randomly assigned to library computers which make database searching faster because devices on the library network are preregistered with the provider to be legitimate users.

E-Rate: Implemented in 1997, the E-Rate Universal Service Fund provides discounted rates for Internet service for schools and libraries. The amount or percentage of the subsidy increases with the town poverty level.

Federated Search: This type of search cross-indexes multiple subscriptions simultaneously. The results are viewed in one screen even though the results come from different databases. Library staff should be familiar with federated searching because it is an efficient way to search many products at once.

Internet Protocol (IP): In order to access the Internet network, a computer must be uniquely identified by its IP address. Libraries share their computers and wireless IP addresses with Internet and database providers for authorized patron use within the library.

License Agreement: This is a contract between the library and the database company provider that specifies how long and under what conditions library patrons may use the subscription database or resource. Sometimes one license agreement is negotiated between a provider and multiple libraries for consortium or discount pricing.

Remote Access: This is the ability for a patron to externally access and use a library subscription database from outside of the library. The patron gains access typically with their barcode or a password.

Simultaneous Use: More than one patron may access a subscription database at the same time. Depending on the license agreement between the library and the database provider, the number of users at the same time may be unlimited or restricted to a specific number such as five or ten.

Subscription Databases: These are collections of searchable and authoritative documents, articles, images, sound, media, websites, or other information formats clustered around a broad theme or subject. With editorial review for inclusion of materials, library staff and patrons can rely on information from databases that is likely more reliable and authoritative than that of the free Internet.

In this chapter we will examine how libraries plan for, evaluate, and acquire **subscription databases**. These databases are collections of searchable documents, articles, images, sounds, media, and websites or other information formats built around a broad theme or subject. Expensive to lease or purchase, library staff must be confident in their selection that the database will fill important gaps in the library collections. We will examine the major steps of the leasing/purchasing process beginning with determining the need at the library for the database, evaluating the wide range of products, and acquiring just the right ones. We will also look at how LSS can learn to use these valuable library resources more effectively with patrons.

THE PLANNING PROCESS

Acquiring any type of library materials, whether it be books, media, or databases, is a process that should begin with a plan. Purchasing rights to subscription databases can be challenging and time consuming. Unlike purchasing a book, a database often holds thousands, if not millions of items. Investments in databases are expensive, and they do not often market themselves to patrons as a jacket cover invites one to look at a new book. A database that is underused is a costly mistake no library can afford. We will look at steps library support staff (LSS) can take in the planning process to ensure a library develops the best collection of database services for its patrons.

Collection Analysis

Collection development is the act of selecting and acquiring materials that patrons will use. Planning is an important part of library collection development. The first step in the planning process is to analyze the current collection. Even though we are looking at databases, we need to know what other materials the library has on the topic. Regardless of the type of items or collection, purchases can be made with data to help predict desirability and usage. An analysis of the collection can help determine what materials patrons find desirable, what materials are not, and where gaps or materials may be needed. In a similar way, the current and potential usage of subscription databases can also be analyzed. Comparisons between the content of the current collection and the content of subscription databases can identify gaps in the collection. For example, the hundreds of thousands of journals in Academic One File far exceed the limited periodical holdings of the library.

LSS can support collection analysis by helping to collect data. LSS can also participate in gathering data to help determine the need for subscription databases. They can use circulation reports to identify the age of the library collection, and the type of materials patrons seek. LSS may also read reviews of new databases from library journals, determine if databases offer more current or thorough information than the library's books on the subject (such as medicine and science), and share their observations of patrons' needs with their supervisors.[1]

Analyze the print and e-books owned by your public or school library by these famous classic authors to determine if patrons and students may need additional materials for research (see table 6.1).

The above data could be very helpful in determining if a library should acquire a database that offers research articles, quotations, literary criticism, and other biographical information. By comparing the popularity of each author by the number of titles, supportive materials, and the circulation data, LSS can extrapolate if there is a need for a larger variety of accessible materials for author research.

1. Make several samplings of subjects. Select topics that you perceive a need for more research articles such as history, health, law, science, education, or business.

Table 6.1. Collection Analysis

Author	Number of Books or E-books by Author Owned by Library	Last Circulation Dates of Author's Books	Number of Print Literary Criticisms, Biographies, Etc. about This Author in Library Collection	Last Circulation Dates of Research Books about the Author
William Shakespeare				
Mark Twain				
Jane Austen				
F. Scott Fitzgerald				
Charles Dickens				

2. Obtain data from the online catalog about the number of books or e-books the library has on the subject and how often they have circulated.
3. Determine the popularity of the subject or the lack of materials or gap in the present collection.
4. Find the number and determine the quality of books or other resources in the collection about the subject and if they circulate.
5. Ask staff if patrons seek information about the subject.

The collection analysis is an important first step to learn how the collection is being used and if a database could improve the quantity and quality of information patrons may need. The next step in the planning process is to understand the patrons' interests, hobbies, and other needs for information on the subject.

Needs Assessment

Library Support Staff (LSS) can play an important role in helping to plan for subscription databases by listening to patrons' requests and sharing what they learn with the acquisitions database librarian (see figure 6.1). Collection development shifts from purchasing "just in case" to a patron-driven plan of "just in time."[2, 3] Collection analysis helps LSS identify what patrons currently *use*. But we may not know what patrons *need*. LSS are in a great position to hear what patrons need because they are the ones who most often interact directly with patrons at checkout or other places. They observe what materials patrons use and often patrons tell them what they seek. The simple question asked at checkout by the LSS, "Did you find everything you needed?" is an important way LSS can gather data to share with librarians the shortcomings of the collection and the needs of the patrons.

For example, in my library LSS observed students were struggling with writing bibliographies despite having print guides. As we used more and more online resources, students had increasing difficulty identifying and placing bibliographic data in the citation. After hours LSS were the ones who were called upon to help and shared with me the need to offer something different. Their observations spurred me to find a bibliography subscription database that turned out to be so instructive and helpful for works cited.

How do LSS participate in a needs assessment? There are several ways. OCLC WebJunction, a free online site for library staff training and professional learning, offers many ideas and tools to help conduct a library needs assessment. LSS can familiarize themselves with WebJunction[4] documents which include surveys, worksheets, and focus group or social media methods to explore patrons' library needs. These documents can be readily adapted to obtain the opinions of patrons about what subject or topical subscription databases they would like their library to provide. Surveys can help library staff learn patrons' preferences, such as the format of information or the location that best suits their needs. Patrons can also share their opinion about the usefulness of the present library collection and offer their input about collection development. LSS can encourage patrons to participate in needs assessments as they often interact directly with the public. LSS can also help in the efforts to compile the data and work with the acquisitions librarians to find appropriate resources to fill patrons' needs. In summary, LSS can support needs assessments as shown in the textbox.

Figure 6.1.   Library Subscribes to Popular Databases. *Bill Library, Ledyard, CT*

Subscription databases can greatly support the needs of patrons, and your observations, suggestions, and data will greatly help the acquisitions staff find the right
resources for the library collection.

Common Core State Standards

There is an ever-growing need for quality nonfiction materials with the shift
to national standards in education. Recently adapted by many of the states, the

LSS PARTICIPATE IN NEEDS ASSESSMENT

- Become familiar with documents and suggestions from WebJunction.
- Share with acquisitions librarians your observations of topics that are popular with patrons yet hard to fulfill.
- Ask patrons if they found what they came for.
- Convey patrons' suggestions to acquisitions librarian.

Common Core State Standards (CCSS) are a set of high-quality academic standards in mathematics and English language arts/literacy. CCSS sets national learning goals and objectives for K–12 across the curriculum. These standards set expectations of what a student should know and be able to do at the end of each grade.[5] CCSS requires students to read and understand sophisticated information that contains complex ideas and relationships.

School and public librarians have found subscription databases help meet the requirements of the CCSS because they offer complex text in the various subjects of science, technology, math, history, and literature. Some database providers are marketing to CCSS with structured organization, demanding vocabulary, and written in tone, style, and intricate use of language—all requirements of CCSS. Librarians in their evaluation process of subscription databases can determine if they meet these criteria over many traditional print or books sources.[6]

THE EVALUATION PROCESS

As with any important purchase, subscription databases should be evaluated both prior to and after purchase. Prior to purchase the library staff and, if possible, patrons should have the opportunity to explore the contents of a database and its ease of use. The goal of obtaining subscription databases is to improve information access for patrons.[7] After purchase LSS can help evaluate the usefulness of the database by sharing feedback they glean from patrons.

Reputation

How do librarians select a subscription database (see table 6.2)? Articles and documents within are from a wide variety of journals and publications. The reputation of the journal and its editorial review process are some of the most important criteria. Journals have standards for accepting authors' work. The reputation of the database providers and publishers is also important to consider for selection. How often is the database updated? Do searches link to full text or do you have to seek the document in its entirety elsewhere?

Table 6.2.   Consider These Factors When Selecting a Subscription Database

Authority	Research reputations of journals, providers, and publishers.
Content	Analyze the subjects or topics presented. Are there topics omitted? Compare to other subscription databases in the same general category. What is the depth and breadth of topics? Does the content address the library needs assessment?
Level	Does the subject and writing level meet patrons' needs?
Date	How often is the database updated? Is the information contained in the database date sensitive?
Visuals	Does the database contain media or visuals that help convey information?
Adaptability	Is the database ADA compliant or adaptable for all populations? For example, is media closed captioned? Is the database offered in multiple languages?
Ease of Use	Is the database easy to use and not confusing? Look for a format that is clean and understandable.
Technical Support	Is technical support robust? Will IT work with your staff to ensure 100 percent reliability?

Searching

Searching aggregated or multiple databases at once is called federated searching. The commercial database provider sets up a search box which interfaces with their multiple databases. A way to evaluate a subscription database with many products is through repeated federated searches.[8]

For instance, are there markedly different results between basic and advanced searches? Using different topics, repeat federated searching several times to determine if there are problems with the interface. Does the federated search yield the same results as when you search each database separately with the same terms? If the provider allows you to attach Machine-Readable Cataloging (MARC) records to the documents in the databases, how reliable are the links between your records and the search results? Only by repeated "trial and error" searches will LSS be able to confidently help patrons to use the federated search interface of a provider's databases.

FEDERATED SEARCHES

The database provider offers one search for multiple databases.

- Enter search terms in the *basic* search box. Expect many results! If needed, narrow the results by:
  - using search limiters such as *full text or media type,*
  - using advanced search and select disciplines such as subjects or field options such as searching by *author, journal source, ISBN,* etc., and
  - sorting the results list by *relevance, most recent or earliest* date.

LSS should also become familiar with digital collections management.[9] EBSCO and Innovative Interfaces, Inc. are just two of many businesses that offer the service that combines records of the library collection with the subscription database collections to show together in the online catalog. Patrons are able to use the integrated library system (ILS) or library catalog to locate resources from all collections at once. These systems are becoming more affordable to medium and small libraries where LSS will take a greater role in helping patrons use them appropriately.

Trials

Most providers encourage some period of trial use. This is an opportunity for library staff to introduce a database to patrons and observe its potential use. Because the provider is interested in obtaining a contract, my experience has been that trials are beneficial to establish positive relationships with both provider marketing and IT staff, as well as to evaluate the product. A trial period is exactly that. For a limited time period of typically thirty days library patrons have full use of the database. During the trial LSS can greatly help by introducing patrons to the database and gathering both observational and real data about its popularity and how patrons are using it.

Usage Statistics

Usage statistics are another important evaluation factor. During the trial statistics can be shared by the provider. Once a subscription is purchased, reports of usage statistics often are available automatically from the provider so that the library staff can monitor its activity. These statistics are invaluable when deciding whether or not to renew the subscription. They also help library staff understand patrons' usage patterns (anonymously) such as which items in the database are most popular.

Database Reviews

Last but not least library staff should look to professional reviewing sources to read or hear how other librarians rate a subscription database. Just like the traditional process of reviewing books, database reviews are now common sources to help influence our decisions.

Reviews in library professional literature are very important to the evaluation process because reviews are written by librarians and users. They are not marketing materials that we see in catalogs or advertisements. While marketing materials may catch our eye and are helpful in understanding a database, it is the review by a librarian user who is ethically obligated to uncover the strengths and weaknesses of a product that should be sought in the evaluation process.

A review is typically a firsthand experience written in an annotation or short paragraph. My experience writing reviews suggests it is very challenging to capture the essence of the material in just a few words in a balanced way that also informs the selection process of hundreds—if not thousands—of librarians.

A typical database review in library literature will describe the contents of the database. The reviewer provides an opinion about its overall quality, effectiveness, coverage, and sources within the database. He will also discuss its ease of use and depth of searching features, and any technology requirements the library must have. There are many reviewing sources for databases such as *Library Journal, Choice, Booklist, School Library Journal,* and *Resources for College Libraries* to name a few. Other places to find reviews are in technical journals and columns, professional organizations, and at conferences and workshops.

THE ACQUISITIONS PROCESS

Acquiring a subscription database requires many supports being in place. These supports can be budget and funding sources, contracts or agreements, patron access privileges, and a relationship between library and provider IT. We will talk about each of these important factors.

Free Databases

Subscription databases can be costly, especially for a small public or school library. Before any database is considered for purchase, library staff should be knowledgeable of the subscription or online databases they may be able to access for free.[10] As seen in previous chapters, federal and state governments provide a wealth of free databases that should be considered. Table 6.3 shows just a few other free and excellent databases that library staff should know about before making purchases.

About two-thirds of state libraries offer a wealth of databases to their residents. LSS can help patrons know about these resources by becoming familiar with them and sharing their knowledge with patrons who seek information. In addition to the online databases provided by state libraries, the many Departments of Education provide subscription databases for free to public schools in their state.[11]

Table 6.3.   Free Databases for Consideration for Library Websites

ChemSpider	ChemSpider is a free chemical structure database providing access to over twenty-six million structures, properties, and associated information via text or structure searching.
AP Images	Instant access to AP's editorial photos of today's breaking news, celebrity portraits, historical images across all genres, creative rights managed and royalty free stock photography.
Medline Plus	Extensive information from the National Institutes of Health and other trusted sources on over 740 topics on conditions, diseases, and wellness.
Directory of Open Access Journals (DOAJ)	Online directory that indexes and provides access to high-quality, open access, peer-reviewed journals.
ibiblio	ibiblio.org offers freely available information, including software, music, literature, art, history, science, politics, and cultural studies.

Funding and Grants

Most libraries have shifted funds from magazine print collections to subscription databases. There may no longer be the need to keep large backlogs of magazines if articles are archived to be easily found and retrieved online.

Funding can come from many alternate sources, such as an endowment or special gift. Since many databases are subject specific, the content of a database may align with the goals of a donor or group such as "Friends." For example, my public library had the cost of Ancestry database donated by its Friends group. The Friends recognized and supported the great appeal and interest patrons have in their personal genealogy.

Grants that fund educational initiatives may also fund databases. Dr. Sheryl Abshire,[12] an expert in educational and technology grant writing, offers many excellent suggestions for both writing grants and funding organizations on her website. Grants are available to expand digital resources and archives; subscription databases complement and enhance library collections. In writing any grant, be aware that points are given if what is sought completes a larger goal or objective. Points are also given for sustainability and continuity. An example of sustainability and continuity could be that by acquiring a genealogical database, the resources of the new local history room can better be used and shared across the state because the database encourages users to delve into the print books upon reading introductory articles found in the database.

Pricing and Discount Purchasing

Most providers do not advertise their prices for subscription databases. They negotiate with individual libraries based on formulas that may involve:

- type of library;
- number of users or patrons;
- population of the town or college; or
- expected use.

Subscription databases may cost in the range of $3,000 to $6,000 per year for a medium size public library. Libraries are expected to pay invoices for subscription databases typically within thirty to sixty days.

There is often power in the numbers. Discounts may be offered to consortium or group purchasing. It behooves a library to ask if group discounts are available and if so, to seek partners in purchasing. Discounts may also be given to new users as a means to attract business or to libraries that can pay in advance. A library may receive last year's price if the subscription is renewed before the terms of the agreement are up.

E-Rate

The universal service Schools and Libraries Program, commonly known as the **E-Rate Program**, helps ensure that schools and libraries obtain telecommunications and Internet access at affordable rates.[13] Public and private libraries may apply for funds that will offset the cost of Internet service. Discounts for support depend on the level of poverty and the urban/rural status of the population served and range from 20 percent to 90 percent of the costs of eligible services.[14] The E-Rate Program has advanced Internet use in libraries and schools for more than a decade. This national infusion of funds has solidified the ability for libraries to offer digital resources as a core collection or service.

Contracts or License Agreements

Most subscription databases are not for indefinite library ownership. Libraries and providers enter into a **license agreement** which explicitly states a specified period of time and under certain conditions the provider allows the library and its patrons to use the database. An exception to this may be the first edition e-books that are being replaced with revised editions. Depending upon the publisher or provider, indefinite usage rights of the first edition of the e-book may be assigned to the library.

Each provider has its own legal licensing agreement. Library staff must be versed and informed about each agreement entered into. LSS can help in this way by reading the agreements and asking questions about the database use to ensure the agreement meets the needs of library patrons. The majority of agreements are made for one year. The reasons vary for these factors:

1. public and school libraries are most often not allowed to enter multi-year contracts as their budgets are based on taxes and set on an annual basis;
2. both parties may want to change the terms of the agreement; and
3. the cost is often determined on population which may be unpredictable year to year.

License agreements also specify copyright and ownership of the content. The library will not own subscription databases and typically is not allowed to archive the content. Printing and copying rights are specified in the agreement. The example of EBSCO license agreement with Nebraska Library Commission[15] is helpful for those who are new to library subscription database contracts.

Access

Patron access can vary according to license agreement or contract. Access will always be available within the library or institution. **Remote access**, or access from anywhere outside the library, is important to patrons' needs (see figure 6.2).

In order to use a database remotely, the account is set up so that some identifying data must be patron supplied, such as their library barcode, a password, or a combination of both. An Internet protocol (IP) address allows a computer to connect to the Internet and identifies a specific computer on a network.[16] At larger libraries, universities, and schools, computers have a **dynamic IP range**. Simply put, when a patron logs on, the library computer is assigned the next open IP address that is already authenticated. This efficient process increases access speed for the user and

Figure 6.2. Remote Access to College Databases. *Three Rivers Community College, Norwich, CT*

communicates to the database provider this computer user is cleared to access the database.

Most subscription databases allow **simultaneous use**. Simultaneous use means multiple people can access the database at the same time. Typically simultaneous usage is set to such a high number that it appears unlimited to the patrons because at no time will all accounts be utilized. However, to rein in costs, some subscription databases, such as ProQuest's eLibrary, allow for limited simultaneous use. My library was able to hold down the cost of what would have been an expensive license agreement by agreeing to a maximum of five users simultaneously. When the sixth person tried to use the database, he or she was told to wait until an opening occurred. Simultaneous use was a great "work around" for the lease of this specialized database.

IT Support

My experience has been that provider IT support is at a high level and very helpful. The providers want customer satisfaction, and they are willing to work with local IT and library staff to ensure the network is accepting its databases. Typically there is 24/7 support and with a phone call issues often are resolved.

LSS are often the first to know when patrons cannot access databases. A protocol should be established early on with library management as to what role the LSS plays to work with provider IT. When management is not available, it is reasonable to expect LSS to contact provider IT to seek resolution. Contact information should be shared with LSS for each provider and its products. I suggest that the smaller the library and its staff, the more likely LSS should have the training and authority to work with provider IT support staff to get issues resolved in a timely manner.

LIBRARY SUPPORT STAFF AND TRAINING

Formal technology training of library staff to be prepared to help patrons is sadly lacking in urban, suburban, and rural public and school libraries. Whether it is helping patrons find jobs online or libraries offering technology classes, most libraries fall short.[17] The reality is that most libraries do not have the resources (time and funding) to train staff to be prepared to effectively help patrons with diverse technology needs. It is an important role that the LSS have as they are often the first or only contact with a patron at the circulation desk or other locations with patrons.

In the absence of formal training, LSS can do much to guide their own learning to effectively use subscription databases on the job with patrons. Providers often offer training webinars of their product. A webinar is a real-time shared learning experience with an instructor and others located at different sites. A webinar is scheduled for a specific time, and participants are asked to pre-register so that access information is provided beforehand. At the designated time the participant may call in to the instructor and open the training website. The real-time instructor will guide learning of the product using resources on the website. Participants are encouraged to ask questions. Webinars may be repeated and are an excellent way to become familiar with subscription databases.

Another method of training is for LSS to use provider created tutorials for self-paced learning. It is common for each database to have tutorials or presentations which cover in great detail the functions of the product and how to effectively use its features. Patrons can be directed to provider tutorials. Providers offer many promotion brochures, posters, and even short media clips that can be shared by library staff and patrons. YouTube is another source that is robust with educational tutorials on how to use popular subscription databases.

LSS learn technology from each other.[18] When library management provides support and encouragement for staff learning, there likely will be a climate which fosters collaboration and peer coaching among LSS. Making connections between how to use subscription databases and web technology, LSS can enhance their knowledge by experimenting and practicing searches and opportunities to use a new subscription database. LSS are encouraged to make searching of subscription databases relevant to their patrons as they find new opportunities to use them to improve library service.

CHAPTER SUMMARY

Subscription databases are a core library collection and information service for patrons. These databases often offer a high caliber of information content which advances the research and learning of patrons. Providers or aggregators of content, such as EBSCO, ProQuest, and Gale broker numerous publishers' content and present it as one unit for easy searching and standardized retrieval.

LSS have an important role in the acquisition and subsequent use of subscription databases by helping to determine the need for a new database. LSS also are on the front line and can do much to promote and teach patrons how to navigate and use the resources. Just as LSS learn the features of traditional print and media collections, they are challenged to learn the content, search features, and functionality of subscription databases. LSS who are proficient in using subscription databases advance their role and the responsibility for information services by introducing relevant applications of technology, including digital literacy, to the public.

DISCUSSION QUESTIONS AND ACTIVITIES

Discussion Questions

1. Why is it important for library staff to plan before they purchase subscription databases?
2. Describe the key steps of collection analysis and how collection analysis helps library staff make decisions about subscription databases.
3. In your own words describe what takes place in a needs assessment and when library staff should conduct them.
4. What is a subscription trial and how does it work?
5. Name four important considerations that vendors and libraries use to negotiate discount purchasing of databases.

Activity

Supporting Others to Use Subscription Databases
This extension of your learning is to give you insight and knowledge of two subscription databases that you currently are unfamiliar with or have used only slightly.

Depending on whether you are a student, library employee, or have the benefit of subscription databases from your state library, select two unfamiliar databases from a library where you have user privileges. For each database do the following:

1. Read the online help and view any tutorial provided by the database provider.
2. Search YouTube for instructional videos on the use of the database.
3. Go to the database provider website and see if they offer instructional materials about the database. Read or view all that is offered. If there is a webinar session available, sign up and take the webinar.
4. Construct three searches for the database. Do each search in the basic search. Then do the search again using the advanced search features. Try different search limiters (i.e., select journals, time periods, etc.).
5. Make a list of features you did not know about this database. Include the strengths or usefulness of the content.
6. With your new knowledge of the database, write a simple, one page brochure about the database and how to use it. Write the brochure in a helpful way for someone who is unfamiliar with it.
7. Find a friend, family member, or patron who is unfamiliar with the database and show them how to use it. Use your brochure as part of your instruction. Have the person conduct meaningful searches that he or she has a need of information.

NOTES

1. Kathleen Lehman, "Collection Development and Management," *Library Resources & Technical Services* 58, no. 3 (2014). http://search.ebscohost.com/login.aspx?direct=true&db =aph&AN=97294511&site=ehost-live&scope=site.

2. Stephen Arougheti, "Just-in-Case versus Just-in-Time: A Paradigm Shift in Collection Development," *Keeping Up With . . . Patron Driven Acquisitions*, 2014, http://www.ala.org/acrl/ publications/keeping_up_with/pda.

3. Matthew Pelish, "Redefining the Academic Library: Managing the Migration to Digital Information Services," last modified August 2011, accessed September 2014, http://www.ful lerton.edu/senate/meetings/retreat/Redefining%20the%20Academic%20Library%20-%20 Matthew%20Pellish%20CSU%20Fullerton%208-16-11,%2051%20pgs.pdf.

4. "Needs Assessment," OCLC Webjunction, http://www.webjunction.org/explore-top ics/needs-assessment.html.

5. "Common Core State Standards," Common Core State Standards, last modified 2014, accessed September 23, 2014, http://www.corestandards.org/about-the-standards.

6. Karla Krueger, "Status of Statewide Subscription Databases," *School Library Research* 15 (2012), http://eric.ed.gov/?q=%22database%22&id=EJ994328.

7. F. William Chickering, "Evaluation and Comparison of Discovery Tools: An Update," *Information Technology & Libraries* 33, no. 2 (2014), http://search.ebscohost.com/login.aspx? direct=true&db=aph&AN=96849756&site=ehost-live&scope=site.

8. Sarah Hartman-Calvery, "Using Qualitative Assessment Protocols to Evaluate a New Library Discovery Service," *Computers in Libraries* 33, no. 8 (2013), http://search.ebscohost .com/login.aspx?direct=true&db=aph&AN=91561527&site=ehost-live&scope=site.

9. Marshall Breeding, "Library Systems Report : 2014," *American Libraries* 45, no. 5 (May 2014), http://search.ebscohost.com/login.aspx?direct=true&db=aph&AN=95830652&site=e host-live&scope=site.

10. "Free Publicly-Accessible Databases," UC Santa Barbara Library, last modified 2010, accessed February 14, 2015, http://www.library.ucsb.edu/search-research/free-databases.

11. Karla Krueger, "Status of Statewide Subscription Databases," *School Library Research* 15 (2012), http://eric.ed.gov/?q=%22database%22&id=EJ994328.

12. Sheryl Abshire, PhD, "Funding Your Technology Dreams," Sheryl Abshire, PhD, ac cessed September 22, 2014, http://www2.cpsb.org/Scripts/abshire/grants.asp.

13. "E-Rate," Universal Service Administrative Company, last modified 2014, accessed September 29, 2014, http://www.usac.org/sl/about/getting-started/default.aspx.

14. Ibid.

15. "EBSCO License Agreement for Database Licensing," Nebraska Library Commission, last modified 2014, accessed September 23, 2014, http://nlc.nebraska.gov/discounts/ebsco agreement.aspx.

16. "Tech Terms," Tech Terms, last modified 2014, accessed September 28, 2013, http:// www.techterms.com/definition/ipaddress.

17. Brian Real, "Rural Public Libraries and Digital Inclusion: Issues and Challenges," *In formation Technology & Libraries* 33, no. 1 (2014), http://search.ebscohost.com/login.aspx?dir ect=true&db=aph&AN=95317922&site=ehost-live&scope=site.

18. Marie Keen Shaw, EdD, "Teachers' Learning of Technology: Key Factors and Processes" (PhD dissertation, University of Connecticut, 2010).

REFERENCES, SUGGESTED READINGS, AND WEBSITES

Abshire, Sheryl, PhD. "Funding Your Technology Dreams." Sheryl Abshire, PhD. Accessed
    September 22, 2014. http://www2.cpsb.org/Scripts/abshire/grants.asp.

Arougheti, Stephen. "Just-in-Case versus Just-in-Time: A Paradigm Shift in Collection Development." *Keeping Up With . . . Patron Driven Acquisitions*, 2014. http://www.ala.org/acrl/publications/keeping_up_with/pda.

Breeding, Marshall. "Library Systems Report: 2014." *American Libraries* 45, no. 5 (May 2014). http://search.ebscohost.com/login.aspx?direct=true&db=aph&AN=95830652&site=ehost-live&scope=site.

Chickering, F. William. "Evaluation and Comparison of Discovery Tools: An Update." *Information Technology & Libraries*. 33, no. 2 (2014). http://search.ebscohost.com/login.aspx?direct=true&db=aph&AN=96849756&site=ehost-live&scope=site.

"Common Core State Standards." Common Core State Standards. Last modified 2014. Accessed September 23, 2014. http://www.corestandards.org/about-the-standards.

"Connecticut Digital Library." Connecticut Digital Library. Last modified 2014. Accessed September 30, 2014. http://www.iconn.org.

"EBSCO License Agreement for Database Licensing." Nebraska Library Commission. Last modified 2014. Accessed September 23, 2014. http://nlc.nebraska.gov/discounts/ebscoagreement.aspx.

"E-Rate." Universal Service Administrative Company. Last modified 2014. Accessed September 29, 2014. http://www.usac.org/sl/about/getting-started/default.aspx.

Fishman, Stephen. "Chapter 12: Databases and Collections." *Public Domain: How to Find & Use Copyright-Free Writings, Music, Art & More*, 2014. http://search.ebscohost.com/login.aspx?direct=true&db=lir&AN=95770199&site=ehost-live&scope=site.

Hartman-Calvery, Sarah. "Using Qualitative Assessment Protocols to Evaluate a New Library Discovery Service." *Computers in Libraries* 33, no. 8 (2013). http://search.ebscohost.com/login.aspx?direct=true&db=aph&AN=91561527&site=ehost-live&scope=site.

Krueger, Karla. "Status of Statewide Subscription Databases." *School Library Research* 15 (2012). http://eric.ed.gov/?q=%22database%22&id=EJ994328.

Lehman, Kathleen. "Collection Development and Management." *Library Resources & Technical Services* 58, no. 3 (2014). http://search.ebscohost.com/login.aspx?direct=true&db=aph&AN=97294511&site=ehost-live&scope=site.

"Needs and Assets Assessment Worksheet." WebJunction. Last modified 2014. Accessed September 26, 2014. http://webjunction.org/explore-topics/needs-assessment/documents.html.

"Needs Assessment." WebJunction. Last modified 2014. Accessed September 28, 2014. http://webjunction.org/events/webjunction/Impact_Survey.html.

OCLC—Online Computer Library Center. "Needs Assessment." OCLC Webjunction. http://www.webjunction.org/explore-topics/needs-assessment.html.

Pelish, Matthew. "Redefining the Academic Library: Managing the Migration to Digital Information Services." Last modified August 2011. Accessed September 2014. http://www.fullerton.edu/senate/meetings/retreat/Redefining%20the%20Academic%20Library%20-%20Matthew%20Pellish%20CSU%20Fullerton%208-16-11,%2051%20pgs.pdf.

Real, Brian. "Rural Public Libraries and Digital Inclusion: Issues and Challenges." *Information Technology & Libraries* 33, no. 1 (2014). http://search.ebscohost.com/login.aspx?direct=true&db=aph&AN=95317922&site=ehost-live&scope=site.

The Regents of the University of California. "Free Publicly-Accessible Databases." UC Santa Barbara Library. Last modified 2010. Accessed February 14, 2015. http://www.library.ucsb.edu/search-research/free-databases.

Shaw, Marie Keen, EdD. "Teachers' Learning of Technology: Key Factors and Processes." PhD dissertation, University of Connecticut, 2010.

"Tech Terms." Tech Terms. Last modified 2014. Accessed September 28, 2013. http://www.techterms.com/definition/ipaddress.

PART II

Technologies

CHAPTER 7

Subscription Databases

Providers and Products

LSS know the role of technology in creating, identifying, retrieving, and accessing information resources and demonstrate facility with appropriate information discovery tools. (ALA-LSSC Technology Competency #7)

Topics Covered in This Chapter:

- Different Than the Internet
- State Libraries Offer Databases to Citizens
- Database Providers
  - Working with Providers
  - Sales
  - Account and Technical Support
- Subscription Databases: The Products
  - Federated Searching
  - New Product Reviews
- Newspapers
  - Archives
- Magazines and Journals
  - Popular Magazines
  - Academic Journals
  - Peer Review
- Subject Resource Databases
- Multimedia

Key Terms:

Database Providers: Companies that market, demonstrate, negotiate, sell, and distribute their own or other publishers' online information. The provider may offer training, marketing, and other support to library staff so that they become familiar users.

Lexile Score: A measure of the reading level or difficulty of a text. Aligned to grade level, the scores indicate the reader's knowledge of vocabulary and ability to comprehend the text. Many items in subscription databases have Lexile scores. Library staff who are knowledgeable about Lexile can help patrons select appropriate reading level materials.

Outsource: Work or products the library contracts to have done by an outside company for cost savings or efficiency.

Peer Review: Before a scholarly article is accepted for publication by a journal, experts in the same subject (peers) read the article for accuracy, originality, depth of knowledge, etc., to validate its content. Library staff can guide patrons to authoritative research with confidence when they select *peer review* or *scholarly* as an advanced search limiter.

Streaming: This is the process of data being transferred over the Internet at a very high speed. The database provider sends sound and media data in a continuous steady flow rather than in bunches or packets that can be "jerky." Patrons prefer streaming video because the flow of movement is smooth and more true to watching a film on television or in the movies. Libraries should seek streaming video whenever possible for patron satisfaction.

We learned in chapter 1 that libraries provide many different types of digital resources to meet their patrons' information needs. Library staff plan, evaluate, and acquire databases, one of the most important sources of content for research and information.

In this chapter we will examine some of the more prevalent categories of content of subscription databases: periodicals, subject content, and multimedia.

DIFFERENT THAN THE INTERNET

Subscription databases offer timely and subject specific content which is highly desirable and accessible. However, unlike most of the Internet, subscription databases have restricted access. Libraries enter into agreements with providers to allow their patrons proprietary or legal use of text and media content for a specified period of time and under certain conditions. Librarians guide patrons to seek information from subscription databases because of these important differences from the free Internet (see table 7.1).[1]

There are many reasons why library staff should promote the use of subscription databases with patrons. Information from databases has been selected for a purpose and often has to pass standards of quality and accuracy. For example, most scholarly articles in *Academic Search Premier* are **peer reviewed** by experts in the field and are

Table 7.1. Comparison between Subscription Databases and the Open Internet

Subscription Databases	Open Internet
• Information is regularly updated. • Information is grouped in collections. • Content of databases has been through a review process for inclusion. • Information is archived. • Items in databases are cataloged or classified with bibliographic records for easy retrieval. • Use of the databases is negotiated and purchased by the library for an agreed amount of time and access for patrons.	• No schedule or expectation for updating information. • Information may be sporadic with no standard of organization. • No review or evaluation process. • Websites may change or be removed without notice. • Information is not classified or cataloged. • Free access by the public.

published in journals of high quality and integrity. LSS should be confident about the quality of peer-reviewed information found in subscription databases because experts have already approved the reliability of its content. Patrons should be cautioned about the quality of the information presented on the open Internet that is not reviewed. LSS should also be confident that past articles will be available in the future as there is a commitment by subscription database providers to maintain and archive information.

STATE LIBRARIES OFFER DATABASES TO CITIZENS

State libraries are departments or agencies of state government which support the work of their legislature. They also may be the repository or archive of important state documents and artifacts. In addition, state libraries may guide and support how public, school, and academic libraries deliver services. The New Mexico State Library mission is like many of the states whereby it "is committed to providing leadership that promotes effective library services and access to information to all citizens of New Mexico."[2] The majority of state librarians report directly to the governor; however, in a few states, like Colorado, the state libraries are divisions of the state departments of education.[3]

Many state libraries have expanded their role from acquiring and archiving print materials to now creating digital libraries for their residents. Subscription databases have become a key resource of state libraries. At this writing approximately two-thirds of the state libraries in the United States offer some type of digital library of databases for their residents. Residents benefit when:

- they can gain access to quality databases no matter what town they live in or the ability of their public library to subscribe to databases;
- they gain access to databases with authoritative educational, health, economic, legal, and other important and relevant information they would not have access to over the free Internet; and
- the cost burden of subscription databases is lifted or reduced from libraries allowing them to put their dollars into other important patron services.

State residents are authenticated for use with a library card or other means that identify their residency or library affiliation. The number and quality of databases vary from state to state.

DATABASE PROVIDERS

A library may work with many different **database providers**. These may be small companies that sell a single database or very large companies that broker hundreds of databases. A small company, like Thinkmap,[4] the vendor of the *Visual Thesaurus*, sells one database, while very large companies like EBSCO[5] have a global market of multiple databases and services created by a large and divergent group of researchers, experts, and publishers.

Academic, school, public, legal, medical, and scientific institutions also offer their users access to many subscription databases.[6] Major database providers such as EBSCO, ProQuest, and Gale Cengage, broker or aggregate hundreds of databases for various publishers and deliver the content to libraries with options such as tailoring search boxes to the customer's specifications. See table 7.2 for a sampling of databases from these providers.

There are so many other fine database providers. The company Newsbank licenses the database *America's Newspapers* to libraries, and gives patrons access to full-text articles from over 550 newspapers throughout the United States. *Scopus*, a database popular in academic libraries, is the largest abstract and citation database of peer-reviewed literature and research. A third database, *Pscyh Info*, is licensed by the American Psychological Association with more than three million articles in the behavioral sciences and mental health. Do look for other databases and providers contracted by your state library, university, or other large library institutions that you may have access to.

Working with Providers

As with most businesses, the market dictates change. Library staff should be aware of four ways in which database providers expand to keep in business.

Table 7.2. Sampling of Databases

EBSCO	Gale Cengage	ProQuest
Medline (Full Text)	LegalTrac	Historic Newspapers
MasterFile Premiere (Journal articles)	(Law reviews, law journals bar association journals, legal newspapers, etc.)	ProQuest Digital Microfilm (recent microfilmed newspapers)
Reference Centers (K–12 Student, Biography, History, etc.)	Gale Virtual Reference Library	Statistical Abstract of the United States
	InfoTrac Databases and Editions (Newsstand, Student, etc.)	

1. They may buy competitive and complementary companies to increase their market share,
2. They may develop services that will **outsource** traditional library services to their company.
3. They may take away accounts from competitors.
4. They may expand the market by creating new products.[7]

Should we be concerned about database providers taking over traditional library services from staff? Outsourcing means that the work is no longer done in the library but rather by an outside company. Some database providers offer to do the work of library staff would normally do. Here are some of the outsourced tasks providers can do for libraries:

- compile statistics and other reports of patron use;
- provide 24/7 reference service;
- archive thousands—if not millions—of back issues of magazines and journals thus minimizing the work of a serials librarian; and
- share readers' advisory and other literary applications across customers for book recommendations and reading suggestions.

LSS can find ways to work with database providers to enhance library services. There is a great need for knowledgeable library staff to understand many database services and to suggest and monitor ways patrons can make better use of them. For example, rather than always relying on my own book suggestions for patrons, looking at the readers' advisory options of our databases together we would discover new titles that interested each of us. The focus also was on instructions for the patron to become a user of the readers' advisory service. The key idea here is that library staff that know the product features of databases can offer better library services to patrons.

As in most businesses, sales forces vary in size. The larger the company, the greater the marketing sales force. Small companies cannot compete with the large sales and marketing forces of the larger subscription database companies. However, they do develop their products around a niche they developed their product around. For example, Noodletools[8] is a database resource for note-taking, outlining, citation, document archiving/annotation, and collaborative research and writing. Its primary customers are schools whose students gain excellent support from its resources when conducting research and writing papers.

Sales

LSS may interact with provider sales representatives to obtain new product information or hear about changes to existing databases. Carving time from a busy librarian's day for sales is difficult, and LSS can be very helpful by handling routine calls. Most sales representatives check in several times a year with product enhancements, new releases, or ideas for stretching the limited library budget for subscription databases.[9] Representatives can be very helpful with suggestions about features or demonstrating ways to use a database efficiently that LSS can share with other librarians so that everyone is knowledgeable about product features.

Account and Technical Support

LSS can also provide essential help with the management of provider accounts to ensure that the library is fully using the databases. It is invaluable to have an organized system of contact information, licenses, title lists, expiration dates and renewal information, statistics, or usage reports. LSS can also become knowledgeable about routine technical issues with databases. They can be given responsibility for contacting the provider's IT to run small tests to ensure the library network is functioning. LSS may keep information about IP ranges or other authentication methods, URLs, and proxies.[10] LSS can be valuable key contacts with vendors and their IT staff when issues arise, especially at times when the library may be understaffed such as early mornings or evenings or when the technical services librarian is not present.

SUBSCRIPTION DATABASES: THE PRODUCTS

Subscription databases have extensive current and archival items from newspapers, periodicals, and subject resources that are not available on the free Internet. There is an enormous amount of published material that is protected under copyright law and not released on the free Internet. A search on the free Internet often does not result in the most reliable or best quality of information. Database providers either own copyright or pay the publisher or owner for the right to resell or lease items for the use of others. In a straightforward way, most information on the free Internet:

- has never been copyrighted;
- has an expired copyright;
- the copyright owner allows its use; or
- it is otherwise protected by the owner or publisher and requires a fee for use.

This leaves a substantial amount of information that is protected under United States or other countries' copyright laws which is not available for free. It is quality copyrighted items that are the products sold in subscription databases.

Federated Searching

The large database providers often offer a seamless interface or single search box to search many of their databases at once. This kind of multiple searching is referred to as an integrated **federated search**.[11] For example, Gale Cengage *Powersearch* and *EBSCOhost Integrated Search* allow users to search multiple resources with one familiar search screen that interfaces with their different products. Users can select the different databases that they want their search to reach or default the search to all databases. Results from the integrated federated search of individual databases are compiled into one view and ranked by relevance or data together. The single result list has links to each resource within the databases that meet the search criteria. LSS should become familiar with the benefits of integrated federated searching as it is a very efficient way to help patrons obtain resources from many sources at once.

New Product Reviews

Each year there are more and more fine products to choose from on numerous topics. Just as it is challenging for library staff to keep current with all of the new print publications, it is also difficult for us to be knowledgeable about all of the information products available in databases.

How do we find out what is new in databases? Just as library staff do with books, they can go to professional library and educational print and online magazines and journals. *Library Journal, Booklist, School Library Journal, Library Media Connection (LMC), VOYA, Education Today, Teacher Librarian*—these are just a few of many excellent journals you can use to find reviews of new database products that are annotated and rated in regular columns. There are also annual or semi-annual reports such as *Library Journal* "Best Databases" or *Booklist* spring and fall "E-Reference Updates." Regular reading of current technology reviews in popular newspapers and magazines is also a way for LSS to help identify new subscription databases. There are also great leads in professional and popular magazines in the areas other than library science related to history, literature, science, geography, and other interesting subjects.

While it is not the author's intention to endorse a particular database provider or product, in the course of our investigation some databases will be named while other excellent ones may not be discussed. The author does not endorse any particular database, but rather encourages the reader to use selection criteria discussed in a previous chapter to investigate many other subscription databases and form his or her own opinions about them.

In the next sections we will explore the features and functions of different types of subscription databases. These databases are in collection types of newspapers, magazines, journals, multimedia, and subject resource databases. E-books, while often available from subscription databases, are discussed in another chapter.

NEWSPAPERS

Newspapers are one of the most common and popular type of subscription databases (figure 7.1). Most newspapers offer a free website with a few of the key articles in the current daily paper. Do not expect to see the entire daily newspaper free and available online, as typically only lead or key articles are posted for the current day.

Many people get their news today through the Internet. One of the largest sources, Google News,[12] does not keep its own archive of all the national and international newspaper stories they link, just like they do not keep all of the world's websites on their servers. Instead, Google creates robust indexes of headlines and other key terms with links to newspaper stories. When you click a link, you are connecting to the newspaper website that carried the story. Yahoo News, America Online, and other search engine companies provide links to news services. Links are offered to

Figure 7.1.   Patrons Read Newspapers, Print and Online. *Bill Library, Ledyard, CT*

every newsworthy story so readers can choose a variety of perspectives from different papers.

Most newspapers are owned by a parent company which supports their online products. The database provider ProQuest offers *ProQuest National Newspapers* and *ProQuest Historical Newspapers*. These two products have archival and current issues of renowned and respected regional, national, and international newspapers such as the *New York Times*, the *Wall Street Journal*, the *Washington Post*, the *Los Angeles Times*, and the *Chicago Tribune*. EBSCO has a product called *Newspaper Source Plus*. EBSCO has important newswires, National Public Radio transcripts, the *Times* (United Kingdom), *USA Today*, and many other newspapers. Both vendors have a large and impressive number of titles, and most libraries purchase subscriptions through these vendors to acquire multiple papers for varying geographic locations, perspectives, and diverse points of view.

There is no one standard for online newspaper access from regional or local newspapers. Depending upon the publisher, a limited number of articles may be archived and available for some period of time, perhaps two weeks or a month. Most newspapers, however, offer anyone the ability to purchase their archived articles directly from them. Some offer subscribers online access when they order the print or paper copy. The need to purchase may occur when the user has used up or expired their free access to the daily paper or if they are looking for an article that goes further back in time than the limited free archive. Patrons expect their library to have back issues of newspaper articles, and it is a challenge to meet all of their needs. LSS can investigate all of the ways the library can offer archived newspapers, finding arrangements with local and regional papers who may want to offer access to their databases.

An interesting and growing project for creating online access to newspapers nationally is through the Library of Congress project "Chronicling America: Historic American Newspapers."[13] A feature of this project is the US Newspaper Directory which can help identify what titles exist for a specific place and time, and how to access them.

Archives

Finding copies of older newspaper articles can be problematic. Only a few large newspapers have scanned and made available every article beginning with the first issue. The *New York Times Historical Papers*,[14] carried by ProQuest, is one such database, a model for others as it offers all articles and images in PDF format beginning at its inception in 1851. Many newspapers that do have digital archives have not yet been able to offer every article. There is a real need to "catch up" to go backward; in other words, the majority of newspapers have yet to scan their paper copies from years ago into a digital resource. Most papers began to scan issues with the inception of personal computers in the mid-1990s. They do not have the resources to scan fifty, one hundred, or even more years of their print copies.

While database providers maintain limited archives of major regional, national, and international newspaper articles, archives of local papers are often not available at all. Graphic design and digitizing companies are capable of scanning local newspapers because they have the proper equipment and experience to tackle the job efficiently and properly. These companies can be found through simple web searches. The larger the project, the more costly it will be. Often a library cannot support such projects from its normal operating budgets. The National Digital Newspaper Program, or Chronicling America, supports academic or library initiatives to digitize newspapers that would have wide appeal and benefit. The National Endowment for the Humanities also has funded projects to digitize local newspapers.

But for the LSS working in a small to medium size library, grants from these institutions are not realistic. Small grants may be available from state libraries, local towns and cities, and other interested parties who will benefit from having access to articles published by local papers. Library staff can also seek small grants from groups such as library Friends, local historical societies, or patrons. Fundraisers can be had for the purpose of digitizing. The LSS who are knowledgeable about scanning and have a passion for sharing primary sources can support or even lead the effort to digitize local newspaper collections and thus enhance library services. LSS can begin the effort to scan library collections of local newspapers that are decomposing and off limits for future online access.

MAGAZINES AND JOURNALS

Similar to newspapers, large database providers broker millions of periodical articles to libraries. There are distinctions between popular magazines and academic journals. Audience, writing style, graphics, content, purpose, authorship, vocabulary, and reading level are a few of the differences generally found between these two types of periodicals.

Popular Magazines

The first type of periodical to discuss is the popular magazine. These magazines are readily available for sale from stores or by home subscription. Patrons have traditionally come to the library to browse or read popular magazines for such reasons as to keep up with current events or news, learn more about their special interests or hobbies, or enjoy sports and entertainment news. Many libraries have been able to reduce their need to purchase as many paper magazine subscriptions because they are already acquiring them through a database. *Popular Magazines* by Gale Cengage and *MasterFile* by EBSCO permit patrons to download articles from general or popular magazines at any time or location with their library card. Online magazine databases have also reduced, if not eliminated, the need for public and school libraries to purchase a periodical index or to archive back issues of popular magazines for extended years.

Some libraries offer patrons access to online magazine services such as *Magzter* and *Zinio for Libraries*. *Zinio for Libraries* provides "popular magazines that can be downloaded as PDFs and seen just as you would in print . . . no wait for an issue to return and the number of people looking at an issue at the same time is unlimited."[15] New issues are released simultaneously with the print edition. Many publishers offer embedded interactive multimedia in the articles which has great appeal to readers who download the issues for unlimited time on their own devices. Libraries that use an online magazine service are free of serial circulation management. LSS can be very supportive by showing patrons how to sign up for such magazine services, establish an account with their library card, and demonstrate how to download popular magazine issues to patron devices.

Academic Journals

The second type of periodical for discussion is the academic journal. *Academic One File* by Gale, *Academic Search Premier* by EBSCO, and *JSTOR* provide access to scholarly, professional, or research journals. Patrons who seek these journals often do so for research, work, or to advance their own learning. Academic journals lean heavily on reporting and analyzing current research studies and new discoveries in all disciplines.

LSS can be very helpful to patrons who are seeking information from studies or are writing a school or college research paper by recommending academic journals. Suggest that the patron use advanced search features of the databases to find specific authors, terms, or even journals. Advanced search features often give the option of limiting the results of a search by specifying journal titles and dates of the journals.

Peer Review

An important tool for researchers is to limit the search by selecting the option "scholarly" or "peer review." What this means is that before the article was published, it had to be read or "vetted" by one or more experts in the field who agreed to the substance of the research or theories proposed by the author. Peer review assures the reader that the author's work has been checked for authenticity and accuracy. Results can also be scoped by relevance or date. Relevance means that the search words occur most frequently. The date can be newest to oldest or the reverse. By selecting these advanced search features—date, peer review, or journal title—the LSS can help the patron limit his or her search to find the best fit for his or her research needs.

SUBJECT RESOURCE DATABASES

Many topic or subject digital packages of resources are available by subscription. These can be topic resources grouped by educational level:

- elementary school;
- middle school;
- high school; and
- higher education.

Databases may also be about specific subjects. More common subject databases are on the disciplines shown in the textbox.

Common to each of these resource packages is the content. Similar to the idea of "one-stop-shopping" found in department stores, subject resources typically offer preselected magazine and journal articles, reference content, chapters from or entire e-books, images, interviews, sound, and media clips.

The goal of the subject resource database is that the patron will find a variety of research on the topic in one place. Subcategories of a broad subject make browsing easier. Abstracts or short summaries help one get the gist of the article. One can search by date, relevance, or **Lexile** reading level. Being able to select items by their reading level has great importance with schools. Teachers are able to select appropriate materials for their students based on their reading comprehension and vocabulary. Today having the Lexile level available is even more important with the great emphasis in schools on students being able to read and analyze nonfiction articles. Often vendors provide text-to-speech for most articles and different file formats such as PDF and HTML to accommodate a variety of computing devices.

COMMON SUBJECT DATABASES

- Biography and genealogy
- Health, wellness, and medicine
- Business and economics
- United States and world history or specific time periods or events
- Sciences, nature, environment
- Literature by genre, country, or time period
- Languages or translations of databases into a specific language such as Spanish
- Other academic or specialty topics

There are many fine subject resource databases that libraries subscribe to. EBSCO and Gale Cengage are two of the largest providers to libraries of subject resource databases. Gale Cengage has available online spec sheets on each of its databases that introduces the database and gives visual examples of its content and how it can be used by patrons. Free trials are offered to sample products, and vendors work with both individual libraries to large consortiums and states to offer competitive pricing. Vendors keep their subject resource databases current with new articles appearing each month. They also may provide federated searching so that patrons can search multiple subject databases at once. LSS can guide patrons to use the subject resource databases available from their library. Become familiar with the subject resource databases so that when questions arise you have a great "one-stop-shopping" response that patrons will undoubtedly find useful.

MULTIMEDIA

Multimedia is digital film, sound recordings, or combinations of both. Most patrons seek multimedia from their libraries for either research or entertainment. Patrons may want to research "how to" do a task or to enhance their learning about a topic. They may also want to view movies to be entertained, relieve stress, relax, follow a favorite performer's work, or even just to fill a time void. There are many reasons why library patrons seek multimedia from their libraries, and LSS are often involved with helping them make selections by sharing favorites and reviews. LSS often recommend multimedia to patrons but, more importantly, with the onset of streaming video services, they may be called upon to help patrons set up accounts or devices.

Libraries have several options for multimedia service. They may purchase their own hard copies of media, or purchase subscriptions or licenses to stream video from services. There are also many purposeful free multimedia sites available on the Internet. DVD collections are standard and are still in use in most libraries. Some large academic or school libraries host their media on a central console and network it to classrooms or users in the building. These central distributing systems can be thought of as a local network for multimedia. The systems are expensive and often require trained staff to manage. LSS who work in school libraries that have this kind of equipment may be trained to manage the system and support users. Benefits of such systems are a control of content by the institution, simultaneous and proprietary rights to the media, and immediate access by the users.

There are many companies that sell multimedia to libraries, schools, and the public, offering different packages and prices (see table 7.3). Netflix is a leader in entertainment and film for the public although many schools also use Netflix to support the curriculum. Discovery[16] offers full curriculum support, K–12, with **streaming video** aligned to learning standards. Local cable companies may also offer streaming video of television programs and movies to libraries. Check with the company in your area to see what they may be able to do on a limited basis.

Information about movies is available through databases. Internet Movie Database[17] offers film information, including credits, plot summaries, character names, movie ratings, year of release, running times, soundtracks, country of production,

Table 7.3. Examples of Streaming Video Services for Library Consideration

Name	Description
Hoopla	Hoopla is a digital platform which offers streaming movies, TV, music, and audiobooks. Think of it like a Netflix for libraries.
Freegal	A library subscription service that offers over eight million songs and fifteen thousand music videos.
YouTube	Free and universally popular self-posted shorts. Good for instructions and "how to."
Netflix	Entertainment and classical films
Discovery	Curriculum based for learning
PBS Videos	Popular educational films
Overdrive	A great collection of streaming movies
IndiFlix	Stream independent shorts, film festival selections, and classics

genres, production companies, distributors, special effects companies, reference literature, filming locations, and movie trivia from 1892 to the present. Having this kind of information online is very helpful to patrons to make decisions about their viewing and replaces reference materials that were difficult to keep current.

Some companies target streaming video services for libraries. For example, Overdrive, a provider of subscription e-books for library patrons, is just one company which also offers libraries the ability to license accounts for multimedia. Patrons use their library card to access Overdrive and download available multimedia. If a film is in use by another patron, one can place a hold on the item to check out for a limited amount of time set by the library circulation policy. LSS help patrons set up accounts and offer support for instructing patrons how to download their first media.

There are many excellent free multimedia websites LSS can guide patrons to. Julie DeCesare[18] created an annotated list of video services which covers a broad spectrum of subjects. From classic film to history to science to the arts, one can find research documentaries hosted by nonprofit or educational institutions. Finally, for those who want to learn "how to" do something in just a few minutes, YouTube, a free hosting service for the public to post video, often does the job. Try out as many of these free or library-provided media databases to become familiar with them. If your library does not subscribe to streaming or media databases, look to see if the provider offers a limited free trial.

There are also music database libraries for special collections. Naxos Music Library offers sound recordings of western music from the Middle Ages to the present. Smithsonian Global Sound[19] is a subscription database of streaming audio world music to over 42,000 tracks from the Smithsonian archives and world music archives in Asia and Africa.

LSS can be knowledgeable and supportive of their patrons when they are familiar with the multimedia services the library provides or subscribes to as well as the free and educational video websites on the Internet.

CHAPTER SUMMARY

In this chapter we learned about how a positive working relationship between database providers and library staff can improve and benefit research and information services for patrons. There are many different products between and within subscription databases. Unlike books, databases do not come with colorful jackets which catch patrons' eyes. It is difficult to "browse" a database as it is not colorful and attractive as websites are. It is important for LSS to become familiar with the content and features of subscription databases. These are large and important investments by libraries and provide a much higher quality of information than the free Internet.

LSS can provide guidance to patrons if they themselves are knowledgeable of their library subscriptions and interact with providers. By knowing how to identify, retrieve, and access information subscription database resources, LSS can help patrons discover appropriate newspapers, magazine, journals, multimedia, and subject resource databases that meet their needs.

DISCUSSION QUESTIONS AND ACTIVITIES

Discussion Questions

1. How does information content differ between subscription databases and the open Internet?
2. Who are two of the major database providers for libraries? Give examples of their products.
3. What are some of the options library staff have to locate historic newspaper stories for patrons?
4. Describe three key differences between popular and academic or scholarly magazines.
5. What is the peer review process and why should library staff be familiar with it?

Activities

Activity 1: Advanced Search Practice

This activity is to gain practice using the Advanced Search features of academic journal subscription databases.

If you cannot gain access to an academic journal EBSCO database or Gale Cengage Powersearch, or through your public or college library, please simulate this activity using one of these database providers' trials found on their website.

1. Create a search on a health or scientific topic such as "e-cigarettes and nicotine," "global warming and climate," or a topic of your own interest.
2. Do a basic search in an academic journal database and note the quantity of your results.
3. Use the advanced search feature of an academic database and search your topic setting limiters of peer review, titles of magazines (that are related to your search topic), and date within the last twelve months.
4. Compare your results to the basic search. Were the articles more on target for what you expected?
5. Continue to experiment with limiters and decide which ones are most useful.
6. Show a patron or a friend how to use advanced search features.

Activity 2: Integrated Federated Searching

This activity is to gain practice using integrated federated searching. If you cannot gain access to EBSCO databases or Gale Cengage Powersearch through your public or college library, please simulate this activity using one of these database providers' trials found on their website.

1. Create a search on a topic of your own interest and search it in an integrated federated search box.
2. Look at the results.
3. Use the advanced search feature of the federated search box and set limiters as above.
4. Continue to experiment with limiters and decide which ones are most useful.
5. Show a patron or a friend how to use federated searching.

NOTES

1. "How Databases and Search Engines Differ," University Library, last modified August 6, 2014, accessed February 11, 2015, http://www.library.illinois.edu/ugl/howdoi/compare1.html.

2. "History and Mission," New Mexico State Library, last modified 2015, accessed February 13, 2015, http://www.nmstatelibrary.org/about-nmstatelibrary/history-and-mission.

3. "Colorado State Library," Colorado State Library, last modified February 12, 2015, http://www.cde.state.co.us/cdelib.

4. "Products," Thinkmap, last modified 2015, accessed February 18, 2015, http://www.thinkmap.com/products.jsp.

5. "Home Page," EBSCO Information Services, last modified 2015, accessed February 18, 2015, https://www.ebsco.com/.

6. Dan Tonkery, "The Future for Library Searching," *Searcher* 20, no. 10 (2012), http://search.ebscohost.com/ login.aspx?direct=true&db=aph&AN=84299221&site=ehost-live&scope=site.

7. Diane H. Smith, "The Reality Is . . . Everyone Is Selling Something," *Reference & User Services Quarterly* 53, no. 4 (2014), http://search.ebscohost.com/login.aspx?direct=true&db=aph&AN=96802873&site=ehost-live&scope=site.

8. "Noodletools: A Powerful, Integrated Platform for Research & Literacy," Noodletools, last modified 2015, accessed February 19, 2015, http://www.noodletools.com/tools/index.php.

9. Diane H. Smith, "The Reality Is . . . Everyone Is Selling Something," *Reference & User Services Quarterly* 53, no. 4 (2014), http://search.ebscohost.com/login.aspx?direct=true&db=aph&AN=96802873&site=ehost-live&scope=site.

10. Heidi J. Webb, "Managing E-Resources: Did You Choose Your Stuff or Did It Choose You?" *Computers in Libraries* 34, no. 8 (2014), http://search.ebscohost.com/login.aspx?direct=true&db=aph&AN=98763344&site=ehost-live&scope=site.

11. "What Is Federated Search?," Extensity, accessed October 22, 2014, http://www.library.extensity.com/page/FedSearch_LIB.html.

12. "About Google News," Google News, accessed October 22, 2014, http://www.google.com/intl/en_us/about_google_news.html.

13. "Chronicling America: Historic American Newspapers," Chronicling America, last modified 2015, accessed February 20, 2015, http://chroniclingamerica.loc.gov/.

14. "New York Times Article Archive," *NewYork Times* Article Archive, last modified 2015, accessed February 19, 2015, http://www.nytimes.com/ref/membercenter/nytarchive.html.

15. Elizabeth Michaelson, "Best Databases 2013," *Library Journal* (2014), http://reviews .libraryjournal.com/2013/11/best-of/best-databases-2013/.

16. "Discovery Education: Solutions for Districts," Discovery Education, last modified 2015, accessed February 20, 2015, http://www.discoveryeducation.com/.

17. "Internet Movie Database" Internet Movie Database, last modified 2015, accessed February 20, 2015, http://www.imdb.com/.

18. Julie DeCesare, "Multimedia and Video Resources," *Library Technology Reports* 50, no. 2 (2014), http://search.ebscohost.com/login.aspx?direct=true&db=aph&AN=95655440&site =ehost-live&scope=site.

19. "Smithsonian Global Sound for Libraries," Smithsonian Global Sound for Librar-ies, last modified 2015, accessed February 20, 2015, http://alexanderstreet.com/products/ smithsonian-global-sound%C2%AE-libraries.

REFERENCES, SUGGESTED READINGS, AND WEBSITES

"About Google News." Google News. Accessed October 22, 2014. http://www.google.com/ intl/en_us/about_google_news.html.

Alexander Street Press. "Smithsonian Global Sound for Libraries." Smithsonian Global Sound for Libraries. Last modified 2015. Accessed February 20, 2015. http://alexander street.com/products/smithsonian-global-sound%C2%AE-libraries.

Colorado Department of Education. "Colorado State Library." Colorado State Library. Last modified February 12, 2015. http://www.cde.state.co.us/cdelib.

DeCesare, Julie. "Multimedia and Video Resources." *Library Technology Reports* 50, no. 2 (2014). http://search.ebscohost.com/login.aspx?direct=true&db=aph&AN=95655440&sit e=ehost-live&scope=site.

Discovery Communications. "Discovery Education: Solutions for Districts." Discovery Edu-cation. Last modified 2015. Accessed February 20, 2015. http://www.discoveryeducation .com/.

EBSCO Industries, Inc. "Home Page." EBSCO Information Services. Last modified 2015. Ac-cessed February 18, 2015. https://www.ebsco.com/.

"Guidelines for Digitizing a Newspaper." State of Michigan. Accessed October 22, 2014. http:// www.michigan.gov/documents/hal/GuidelinesForDigitizingANewspaper_181557_7.pdf.

IMDb.com. "Internet Movie Database." Last modified 2015. Accessed February 20, 2015. http://www.imdb.com/.

Library of Congress. "Chronicling America Historic American Newspapers." Chronicling America. Last modified 2015. Accessed February 20, 2015. http://chroniclingamerica.loc .gov/.

Michaelson, Elizabeth. "Best Databases 2013." *Library Journal* 138 (2013). http://search.eb scohost.com/login.aspx?direct=true&db=aph&AN=91882516&site=ehost-live&scope=site.
———. "Best Databases 2013." *Library Journal* (2014). http://reviews.libraryjournal .com/2013/11/best-of/best-databases-2013/.

New Mexico State Library. "History and Mission." New Mexico State Library. Last modified 2015. Accessed February 13, 2015. http://www.nmstatelibrary.org/about-nmstatelibrary/ history-and-mission.

The New York Times Company. "New York Times Article Archive." *New York Times* Article Archive. Last modified 2015. Accessed February 19, 2015. http://www.nytimes.com/ref/ membercenter/nytarchive.html.

Noodletools, Inc. "Noodletools: A Powerful, Integrated Platform for Research & Literacy." Noodletools. Last modified 2015. Accessed February 19, 2015. http://www.noodletools .com/tools/index.php.

PR Newswire. "Library Journal Awards Best E-book Database to Ebrary's Academic Complete." November 1, 2012. http://eds.a.ebscohost.com/eds/detail/detail?vid=9&sid=ad223364 -cab1-4315-a990-d554d86132bf%40sessionmgr4002&hid=4205&bdata=JnNpdGU9ZWR zLWxpdmU%3d#db=n5h&AN=201211010800PR.NEWS.USPR.DE03806.

Smith, Diane H. "The Reality Is . . . Everyone Is Selling Something." *Reference & User Services Quarterly* 53, no. 4 (2014). http://search.ebscohost.com/login.aspx?direct=true&db=aph& AN=96802873&site=ehost-live&scope=site.

Thinkmap. "Products." Thinkmap. Last modified 2015. Accessed February 18, 2015. http:// www.thinkmap.com/products.jsp.

Tonkery, Dan. "The Future for Library Searching." *Searcher* 20, no. 10 (2012). http://search.eb scohost.com/login.aspx?direct=true&db=aph&AN=84299221&site=ehost-live&scope=site.

University of Illinois at Urbana-Champaign. "How Databases and Search Engines Differ." University Library. Last modified August 6, 2014. Accessed February 11, 2015. http://www .library.illinois.edu/ugl/howdoi/compare1.html.

Verma, Henrietta. "Best Databases 2012." *Library Journal*, 2012. http://reviews.libraryjournal .com/2013/11/best-of-best-databases-2013/.

Vnuk, Rebecca. "Fall E-Reference Update." *Booklist* 107, no. 5 (2013). http://search.ebscohost .com/login.aspx?direct=true&db=aph&AN=91805180&site=ehost-live&scope=site.

———. "Spring E-Reference Update, 2014." *Booklist* 110, no. 16 (2014). http://search.ebsco host.com/login.aspx?direct=true&db=aph&AN=95574020&site=ehost-live&scope=site.

Webb, Heidi J. "Managing E-Resources: Did You Choose Your Stuff or Did It Choose You?" *Computers in Libraries* 34, no. 8 (2014). http://search.ebscohost.com/login.aspx?direct=tru e&db=aph&AN=98763344&site=ehost-live&scope=site.

"What Is Federated Search?" Extensity. Accessed October 22, 2014. http://www.library.exten sity.com/page/FedSearch_LIB.html.

CHAPTER 8

E-books

Library Support Staff (LSS) know the general trends and developments in technology applications for library functions and services. (ALA-LSSC Technology Competency #1)

Topics Covered in This Chapter:

- Background
- E-books
  - Benefits
- E-Readers: Devices and Formats
  - Amazon and the Kindle
  - Apple
- File Extension Formats
- E-book Providers
  - NetLibrary
  - Overdrive
  - Project Gutenberg
  - Subscription Vendors and Publishers
- E-Books: Continuing Issues and the Future
  - Pricing
  - Circulation
  - Future
  - LSS Support E-Books and E-Reading

Key Terms:

Encryption Code: Instructions in the code of the e-book that cripple or make it no longer usable upon expiration of the loan time. Library staff can show patrons how to renew a library e-book to avoid it becoming encrypted before they are finished reading. E-book circulation is controlled by the computer instructions embedded in the e-book code.

File Extension: Appearing at the end of a computer file name, this three- or four-letter code represents the software application of the file. Common e-book file extensions are .doc for Word files, .azw for Kindle, .html for web hypertext, and .pdf for Adobe. Library staff help patrons download e-books to e-readers with knowledge of the how extensions work.

Open Source: This is software that has been developed by programmers that is free and without license or copyright. It is available for anyone to download and use. The software is often a collaborative effort among many contributors who improve the application. Libraries often have substantial technology cost savings when they use open source; however, they may also take a risk because the products often lack formal vendor or other technical support.

Tablet: This is a light and compact computer that has a built-in screen. The keyboard is typically a touch pad from the screen. Many patrons bring their own tablets into the libraries and use the library Wi-Fi to access the Internet. These devices also serve as e-book reader devices for many of the different types of e-book file types, particularly .html and .pdf.

E-books are fiction and nonfiction books created in computer file format of text and images. E-books are meant to be read on a computing device. Some e-books were originally published in print and have been scanned. Other types of e-books are only published electronically. One of the first e-books by a famous author to be published digitally and not in paper was Stephen King's novel, *Bag of Bones.* Since the release of King's book in 2000, many e-books are only published in digital format depending upon such factors as genre, market share, and potential audience.

E-books are read on a variety of devices by people of all ages. Reading text on computers has been around as far back as the mainframe computers of over fifty years ago. It was not until technology advanced in ways that computing devices became small and portable that the idea of e-books for the public was launched.

In this chapter we will examine many aspects of e-books and how LSS can support both their acquisition and use in libraries. We will learn about different e-readers and file extensions. We will also look at e-book collections and how libraries acquire and lend e-books to patrons. We are still in the infancy stages of e-books. How they will influence patrons' reading and digital literacy, as well as library collections and services in the future, is still anyone's guess.

BACKGROUND

Electronic books, otherwise known as e-books or digital books, have been around for a long time, particularly in the early computer industry. Electronic workbooks began to be published as early as 1984[1] when microcomputers were appearing in the workplace and managers needed to be able to use them. By the end of the 1980s, CD-ROMs that held electronic books, such as Microsoft's Encarta, an encyclopedia geared for students, became available for desktop computers. About the same time e-books were written to motivate and support reluctant readers or math students in school. Electronic books geared for "drill and practice" usually had some kind of animation to reward learning progress. School media centers and public libraries developed collections of electronic educational discs that were geared for children or teens to support their learning.

Reading electronic or e-books would not become popular in the next decades without several conditions in place. These conditions had to do with:

- improved devices to read e-books on;
- availability of titles;
- real and perceived economical cost effectiveness; and
- skill, adaptability, and acceptance of people to read in a new format.

We will look at how each of these hurdles has been overcome and the role libraries have had to promote acceptance of e-books.

E-BOOKS

E-books have become a core library service. While e-books are a fairly recent phenomena, they have gained popularity quite quickly. People had already become accustomed to reading newspapers, magazines, and other short pieces on a screen. Amazon was a major player in creating a market for e-books by discounting the cost of e-books in order to sell Kindle readers. People early on acquired Kindles in large numbers and found that once they purchased the device, they could buy e-books at less cost than a hardcover paper book of the same title.

Benefits

Despite some of the digital literacy issues we have already discussed with reading on a screen, people find that particularly for fiction, e-books are great for travel and leisure reading. E-readers can hold hundreds of e-books on one device thus eliminating the need to pack heavy print books when traveling. Battery life is good, and devices are power efficient and can be charged with a regular outlet. E-books seem to be made for the traveler!

Searching text is another benefit of e-books. Keyword searching makes it easy to find a passage. The reader can go back to a sentence or paragraph easily if they highlight or mark it. These features of searching and highlighting particularly can be

BENEFITS OF E-BOOKS

- Libraries lend e-books without much staff overhead.
- E-books are quick and easy to download.
- E-books from vendors can be acquired 24/7.
- E-books available in the library collection can be acquired 24/7.
- In some cases e-books may be less expensive than print books.
- Multiple e-books on one device make it easier for travel.
- Anytime, anywhere access once the e-book is downloaded to a reader.
- E-readers may now be used for other Internet uses.

helpful for nonfiction reading. Digital reading seems to work best when the story is compelling and entertaining, such as a bestselling adventure or mystery.

In this chapter we will examine both the benefits and the concerns around e-books. We will also look at e-readers and file formats, the providers of content, and the impact of e-books on reading.

E-READERS: DEVICES AND FORMATS

With the breakthrough of portable devices at the end of the 1990s, people began to slowly accept e-books as a viable choice for their leisure and informational reading. Librarians were a bit blindsided by the idea of e-books replacing print books because no one could imagine themselves curling up to read at night with a large computer in their bed! We did not anticipate the rapid development of e-readers that came at the end of the twentieth century, and how, with advances in e-reader devices, people's mindset shifted to accept reading with new technology devices.

Let's look at some of the highlights of e-book reader development.[2] Already tried and accepted in Japan in 1991, Sony Discman was the first commercial e-book reader sold in the United States. It played audio and data CDs in a proprietary e-book format. A few years later the e-reader Rocket enabled one to download e-books from a computer using a serial cable. These two handheld devices opened the market for e-readers.

In the year 2000, Microsoft released its own proprietary software called Microsoft Reader which could turn a personal computer (PC) into an e-reader. Laptops were emerging and gaining popularity in the marketplace, and with Microsoft Reader, could become transportable e-reading devices. Microsoft Reader was easy for me and staff to download e-book content onto patrons' laptops.

But something much more innovative and in time proved to be long lasting was just around the corner. In 2001, Adobe, the creator of the **file extension** format PDF, marketed the Adobe Acrobat eBook reader. Pages of the e-book were displayed side by side, and it was very easy for the user to zoom up and down the text. The early Adobe Acrobat eBook was the first e-reader acquired by my high school library, and it introduced us all to this new way of experiencing books.

Amazon and the Kindle

The first Kindle e-reader was introduced in 2007. Amazon, the largest online paper bookstore had its own e-reader developed by E-Ink, a company that developed a screen that people found much more acceptable for reading text. Amazon continues today to lead the market in e-reading. The business model that solidified Amazon in the market began with deep discounts of the e-books that attracted both publishers who wanted to sell books, and readers who wanted to fill their Kindles with high-quality books at a low cost. People were willing to purchase Kindles if they could get their e-books at a reasonable price.

Amazon was also a leader in using wireless technology. The original Kindles could only connect to Amazon's proprietary network that was used for purchasing and transferring e-books by Amazon online network to the user's device. The idea of transferring e-books over Amazon's own wireless network, Whispernet, was revolutionary as Amazon controlled the content and readers transferred their e-book purchases with ease. Owners of Amazon e-books manage the rights of their books using the Kindle application found on the Amazon website. The system set up in 2007 continues today effortlessly and flawlessly.

Apple

In 2008, Steve Jobs put Apple in the huddle of e-readers with the MacBook Air. Apple has struggled to compete with Amazon in the e-book market. With much success, Apple held market share in online music or iTunes. iPods were everywhere, and people were familiar and comfortable purchasing music from the iTunes store. Apple assumed that people would also be as willing to purchase e-books from the iTunes store.

But the problem was that Apple did not offer a comparable e-reader to the Kindle to read iBooks on. **Tablets** had not been invented, and Apple laptops were too expensive and cumbersome to use as e-readers. Reading from a desktop Mac did not provide an adequate e-reading experience. Compounded with the problem of using the iTunes store, Apple did not discount e-books at the same level that Amazon did. iTunes did not have a large inventory of iBooks compared to Amazon; the e-books were expensive and not discounted. Today Apple's tablets are top of the line as reading devices and with file extensions being easier to transfer or convert, people successfully use iPads as e-readers.

Recently the Pew Research Center reported an upward trend of Americans owning devices that can be used to read e-books.[3] Of Americans sixteen years and older, 24 percent owned e-readers compared to 35 percent who owned tablets. A whopping 91 percent of Americans in this study own cell phones, 55 percent of which are smart phones. By the data it is predicted Americans will continue to acquire Internet and communication devices which serve multiple purposes, including e-reading (see figure 8.1).

Today Kindles and iPads are the most popular e-readers. Both come in several versions. Consumers can choose among Amazon line of Kindles from inexpensive grayscale to the full HDX color Fire tablet. Apple customers have an array of iPads to select from with full color, Retina display, and the desirable features of a tablet.

Figure 8.1.   Patrons Reading E-books in Library. *Bill Library, Ledyard, CT*

Undoubtedly devices will continue to become smaller, lighter, and enhance our e-reading experiences. Can other devices take market share? As with all technology, sit back and enjoy the ride as the one thing we can be certain of is that new products will undoubtedly be in our future!

We will now look at a few of the most common or popular file extensions for e-readers.

FILE EXTENSION FORMATS

E-books are created in many file types or extensions. The type of file an e-book is created in is important to the brand of e-reading device we use. As we saw not all devices are the same (i.e., Kindle and Apple), and not all e-books are created in the same file extension. Amazon Kindle has its own proprietary file extension.

It was important for me to understand about common e-book file extensions in order to make better decisions with confidence about downloading e-book content to different devices. There are a few common file extensions for e-books as well as many specialized ones. The file extension is determined by the requirements of the e-reader or device. Many e-readers are compatible with scanned pages. One of the most common file types for e-books is PDF or Adobe portable document format.

PDF is the common file format for scanned pages, and many e-books are available simply because they were scanned in their entirety from print books.

Another common file type is HTML, or hypertext markup language. HTML, and now advanced versions of it, are the most frequently used language of the Internet and web design. HTML e-books have three great advantages.

1. The capability to be read by multiple e-reader devices.
2. The ability to hyperlink to places within the e-book itself.
3. The ability to hyperlink book content to external Internet websites.

A third common e-book file extension is, of course, the Kindle proprietary AZW3. AZW3 can only be read on Kindle e-readers, giving Amazon a great advantage for selling these devices. Table 8.1 lists some of the most common file extensions for e-books and the main e-readers they are compatible with.

Using programs such as the free Calibre E-book Management,[4] some file extensions—but not all—may be converted to anther e-book type so they can be read on different devices. My students write a children's story in Microsoft Word. They then use Calibre to change their DOC file to Kindle's AZW extension. Once done, the student's e-book is uploaded and read on the Kindle. This assignment gives students practice and understanding in manipulating e-book file extensions.

As e-books have evolved, so has the versatility of e-readers. People will not purchase numerous reading devices to keep up with a plethora of different file extensions. We will next look at the many ways to obtain e-book content.

Table 8.1. Common E-Book File Extension Formats[a]

Extension	Description	E-Reader Device
txt	Simple text file	Any PC or Apple device except Kindles
PDF	Adobe Portable Document Format	Any PC or Apple device that accepts scanned images; Kindles read PDFs
Open PDF	**Open source** PDF that is based on several open source software applications.	All readers that accept PDF should also accept open PDF
HTML	Hypertext Markup Language	Any PC or Apple device except Kindles
AZW, AZW2, AZW3, AZW4	Amazon Kindle eBook file extensions	All Kindles
EPUB	Open Publication structure eBook file	iBooks, iPhones, iPads, Barnes & Noble Nook, Sony Reader, etc. Any device EXCEPT the Amazon Kindle.
Open EPUB	Open source EPUB	Same as above
MOBI	Mobipocket E-book Format	iPhones and Android Phones
iBooks	Apple iBooks	Apple
Lit	Microsoft Reader E-book File	Microsoft Reader

[a] File-Extensions.org. "E-book file extension list." E-book file extensions. Last modified 2014. Accessed December 18, 2014. http://www.file-extensions.org/filetype/extension/name/e-book-files.

E-BOOK PROVIDERS

Already mentioned are Amazon and Apple as two commercial e-book providers. There have been many ventures for creating e-book content, some more successful than others for libraries. The Million Book Project and Google Book Search, worldwide efforts to digitize libraries of academic books, were halted due to copyright infringement. Amazon, while discounting its content, was not agreeable to open lending of its e-books, thus not making it a provider for the library community. Apple did not have the array of titles that libraries sought, and their devices were out of range for what libraries could afford.

NetLibrary was one of the first e-book providers for libraries. Recorded Books was also one of the first companies libraries could work with. Today Overdrive is the most successful lender of e-book content to library patrons. EBSCO and other database providers offer subject content. Explore the e-books offered by your state library and other library collections you have access to in addition to those discussed in this chapter.

NetLibrary

Just a little over a decade ago lendable e-book content for libraries was scarce. NetLibrary, a product of OCLC[5] (https://www.oclc.org/en-US/home.html?redirect =true) had close to 12,500 nonfiction books that were cataloged and offered to OCLC libraries. The titles were mostly nonfiction and geared for college level reading. A special web interface was needed on the computer to read and manage (such as printing pages) the e-book. Searching was fairly good, but the limitation was that libraries did not have small, portable devices to read the e-book on. Patrons used NetLibrary e-books for research similar to a journal article at desktop computers.

NetLibrary was sold to EBSCO in 2010. EBSCO dropped the name and today offers its own e-book collection to database subscribers. Some e-books from NetLibrary's collection that were copyright free and scanned are now offered by Project Gutenberg or the World Public Library.

Overdrive

Overdrive (https://www.overdrive.com) is the current leader of providers that lend e-books directly to library patrons. With thousands of fiction and nonfiction books to choose from, Overdrive patrons self-manage their own selection and circulation of e-books. Very little support is needed from library staff other than initial training. Patrons automatically have an Overdrive account that is linked to but separate from their library account that uses their library barcode number. In other words, patrons have two library accounts with the same one barcode: one account for local library borrowing and subscription database use and a second account linked to Overdrive for borrowing its e-books.

Overdrive lends e-books for a wide variety of publishers. Librarians like Overdrive because they select individual titles to build their "own" library collection of e-books. Library staff have control over e-book collection development unlike EBSCO or Gale Cengage which provide mostly core collections.

Overdrive manages the circulation of the materials whether it is media, audio, or e-books. Circulation with Overdrive is very different than with subscription vendors. Only one person can check out the e-book at a time. If you have an e-book title checked out, then another patron cannot also check it out unless the library has purchased an additional copy. Overdrive manages the circulation of checkout and renewal through its unique **encryption code** that disables the e-book once the lending period is over. These actions occur via the Whispernet with the Kindle. Library staff have no extra circulation tasks with Overdrive as patrons place holds and receive notices via e-mail from Overdrive. Parameters for circulation are set up library by library.

Overdrive is the only outside e-book provider Amazon works with to have Kindle e-books lent to library patrons.[6] Library patrons with Kindles can select Overdrive books in Kindle format and have them downloaded to their devices in a similar manner that they do if they were to purchase a Kindle e-book from Amazon. With Overdrive my patrons were fully able to engage in borrowing e-books for all types of e-readers and devices.

Project Gutenberg

Project Gutenberg is a website of over fifty thousand e-book titles. The titles are in numerous languages and file extensions. The e-book files are stored and hosted on servers all over the world. Anyone can use Project Gutenberg without cost or registration. It is free! Project Gutenberg began at the University of Illinois in 1971 when Michael Hart typed the US Declaration of Independence into a mainframe computer.[7] He is credited for creating the first electronic book. By 2003 there were ten thousand e-books available. The collection has only grown and has both fiction and nonfiction books. All books are copyright free either by expiration or by authors' permitting their e-books to be part of this wonderful resource for use or exposure to their writing.

Project Gutenberg is particularly good for obtaining classic fiction titles. Typically as classes were changing a student dashed into my library panicked because he left his text, such as Mark Twain's *The Adventures of Huckleberry Finn*, at home. The student could either print the pages of the novel that he would need for class or take the link to the e-book and access the novel on his own computer device. Some made a habit of using Project Gutenberg for English classes because it was easier to upload the book than carry it in an overstuffed backpack. Project Gutenberg provided the opportunity to educate students about copyright law and the public domain.

The more popular the title, the more file extensions Project Gutenberg offers. Using my example of *The Adventures of Huckleberry Finn*, figure 8.2 shows the different file extensions currently available.

This e-book is available in the file extensions of HTML, EPUB with images, and EPUB with no images, Kindle with images, Kindle with no images, plain text, and more. This information is for just one edition of *The Adventures of Huckleberry Finn*. Other editions are also available on Project Gutenberg in multiple languages.

LSS should become familiar with Project Gutenberg. It is a great resource for historic and classic titles. If using a Kindle version, see table 8.2.

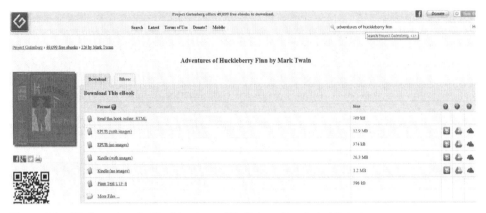

Figure 8.2.   File Extensions for *The Adventures of Huckleberry Finn. Project Gutenberg*

You may keep Project Gutenberg books indefinitely on your e-reader or computer as there are no limitations with digital copyright.

Subscription Vendors and Publishers

In earlier chapters of this book we learned about subscription vendors who sell or lease databases of periodicals and subject content to libraries. Most vendors also now offer e-book databases to libraries which are available to their patrons as part of the annual lease.

Gale Cengage is both a publisher and a provider of quality nonfiction e-books. Gale Cengage has a long history of publishing books acquired by librarians for reference and nonfiction collections. Their print books are of the highest quality and authority covering a broad spectrum of content. E-book format is now available for the majority of print titles. The division, Gale Cengage Learning,[8] offers Gale Virtual Reference Library (GVRL), among other e-book collections. GVRL has a seamless search interface for thousands of e-books that are delivered in HTML or PDF format. HTML format provides audio script for those who would prefer to listen to the content. For some titles there is a short lag between the print publishing data and the release of it in e-book, but that gap appears to be lessening as titles are being simultaneously released in print and e-book formats. Gale Cengage also provides e-book collections of nonfiction for academic, K–12 schools, and public libraries of their own books and other publishers.

Table 8.2.   Using Project Gutenberg with a Kindle

Step	Action
1	Download the e-book AZW file to your desktop computer.
2	Plug the Kindle into a USB drive on the computer similar as you would a thumb or jump drive.
3	Copy and paste the e-book file onto the Kindle like you would do any file from computer to jump drive.

A second large vendor of subscription e-books is EBSCO.[9] EBSCO does not publish its own books, but rather sells other publishers' e-books in either PDF or HTML format. While a PDF is a scan of the original book, HTML format compromises on charts and figures but offers some desirable features to the user. Like Gale Cengage, if the book is offered in HTML then audio format is available for listening. EBSCO also provides Lexile or reading level as selection criteria for its HTML e-books. EBSCO offers a variety of e-book collections such as academic, public, K–12 schools, corporate, medical, and government. Librarians can select a few individual titles or choose collections of several titles around a theme or subject. Collections can be popular in theme such as the bestsellers, or very specific such as the American Association of Pediatrics Core Clinical collection aimed for medical libraries. Most libraries, however, purchase an already preselected collection of e-books aimed for their type of library. For those libraries that subscribe to other EBSCO databases, the e-book collections follow a similar format for searching and downloading. PDF and HTML e-books can be read on all tablets and PDFs can be downloaded to Kindles, Sony readers, etc. With both Gale Cengage and EBSCO, similar to their journal articles, there is no restriction on how many people can use an e-book simultaneously.

Many publishers today offer their print books in e-book format. In some arrangements, such as Salem Press,[10] libraries receive the e-book version when they purchase the print copy. Publishers use a variety of ways to market and sell e-books, including selling their e-books through their own marketing staff, selling e-books through Amazon, and leasing their e-books through vendor arrangements.

LSS can become familiar with how publishers sell e-books to libraries. Read the contract agreements the library director has made with the provider. Often if print books are purchased, there may also be complimentary access to the title in e-book format.

Second, if there is such an agreement, be sure that staff and patrons know how to access the e-books. A unique URL or web address will be provided by the vendor for your patrons' access that may also require a password or other form of authentication. The URL is meant to be posted on the library website. You may need to work with provider support and local IT staff to ensure that the URLs are not blocked by your network.

Third, providers will share statistics and other reports about patrons' use of e-books and other databases. You may offer to be involved with collecting and relating the data from the reports to your library director so that use is being monitored.

LSS who use e-books for their own research and information will be better able to guide patrons to these wonderful digital resources!

We have looked at some specific examples of how library patrons can obtain e-books. Table 8.3 provides additional opportunities for LSS to learn about and become familiar with ways to offer patrons e-books.

A problem librarians and publishers are working hard to resolve is the pricing of e-books. Overdrive passes on the publishers' price to the library, and with wide fluctuation of costs, libraries were stymied to afford e-book collections. We will next turn to pricing and other issues libraries are working through with publishers in order to ensure a solid future for e-books.

Table 8.3. Additional E-book Providers for Consideration

Provider	Description	URL
World Public Library	Copyright free e-books from countries around the world. Nominal membership fee of under $10. All of the e-books are in PDF file format, and all audio e-books are in MP3 file format.	http://www.netlibrary.net
Ipl2—Internet Public Library	Links to free e-book websites, information about e-readers and file extensions.	http://www.ipl.org/div/ ereader/#0.1_libraries
3M Cloud Library	Offers more than one hundred thousand e-book titles, and hopes to capture library market share. Works with most readers including Kindle Fire.	http://www.3m.com/us/library/ eBook/howitworks.html
Baker & Taylor Axis 360	The digital media platform is powered by the Blio e-reading software and currently offers more than one hundred thousand e-book titles, as well as other media.	http://www.btol.com/axis360 .cfm
Recorded Books	OneClickdigital brings exclusive Recorded Books e-audio, as well as content from all major publishers, together with an e-book service. Combines e-books and e-audio in one collection.	http://www.recordedbooks.com/ index.cfm?fuseaction=rb.ocd
DOAB	Directory of Open Access Books. The primary aim of DOAB is to increase discoverability of Open Access books for academia. Free access to approximately three thousand books in PDF format.	http://www.doabooks.org/doab
Google Books	Thousands of scanned books. Books without copyright restriction are offered in entirety. Copyright restricted books are for preview and partially viewable.	https://books.google.com/
Open Culture	Free art e-books from the Metropolitan Museum of Art and the Guggenheim Museum	http://www.openculture .com/2013/08/free-the -metropolitan-museum-of-art -and-the-guggenheim-offer -474-free-art-catalogues -online.html

E-BOOKS: CONTINUING ISSUES AND THE FUTURE

Electronic journals were more widely accepted by people and easier to launch by publishers than e-books have been. This could be for several reasons.

1. Some authors of journal articles are on staff and paid a salary by the journal or publisher for their articles. Staff writers typically sign over copyright to their employer.

2. Other journal authors are paid by the piece and compensated accordingly. They typically are asked to sign over copyrights.
3. Researchers and authors of academic articles desire to share their research with a larger community. Academic articles most likely are copyrighted.
4. Unlike books, journal articles are typically short in length and have a shelf life of typically one week or a month. Also because of the small amount of text, people can read the articles on any online device within a few minutes and get the gist of the article.

Magazine and journal articles were more adaptable and accepted to electronic format early on. Let's look at reasons why this was not the case for e-books.

Pricing

E-books, like print books, often have one or two authors who expect compensation. In addition, publishers commit vast resources for the printing of books that include editorial staff, production, marketing, and sales. Book publishers have formulas that have proven to work adequately and fairly over the years for both the authors and themselves that ensure a revenue stream that covers the expense and has the potential to make a profit on each book.

When Amazon entered into the market with Kindles, it discounted the cost of e-books. Amazon absorbed the cost of the e-books in order to sell the Kindles. This worked for a few years, but as publishers became more eager to sell e-books, they were not willing to compromise on their profits.

Circulation

A fundamental problem e-book publishers have with libraries is the way we circulate books. In the traditional library model we purchase one copy of a book and circulate it many times over until the binding and paper wear out. Library staff are great at repairing books to stretch out the least amount of usage, and it is only at last resort would I repurchase a book. Publishers were reluctant to sell e-books to libraries because they feared they could not make a profit. In 2012, Harper Collins and other publishers decided they would limit the number of circulations of an e-book sold to a library to twenty-six (assuming the book would be "lent" a maximum of twenty-six times for two-week intervals per year).[11] Some publishers, such as Simon & Schuster, refused to sell e-books to libraries at all fearing that libraries, once they had one copy of a digital file, would duplicate it and share it among patrons without compensation. Random House took another tactic where they would sell e-books to libraries but only at a significantly marked up price. Libraries both small and large appealed to publishers, state libraries, and national organizations such as the American Library Association to intervene on these issues that were blocking the ability of libraries to develop collections and circulate e-books to their patrons.

Future

Today libraries and publishers are working toward a more common ground.[12] In 2014, the American Library Association reported that all major publishers will now sell e-books to libraries, but that not all issues are resolved to both parties' satisfaction. While cost and fair distribution of e-books are major issues still to be resolved equitably and fairly, some of the other issues between libraries and publishers found in the ALA report are: privacy protection of the patron, accessibility to patrons with disabilities, digital preservation of collections, conflicting file extensions, and how libraries collect, disseminate, and save information for future generations. E-books initially were seen as a threat to publishers, but today publishers can also sell e-book copies of printed works to readers without the expensive overhead of printing, warehousing, and shipping. Libraries say some of the e-book profit should be passed on to libraries that will promote and grow a new customer base of e-book customers.

The future of e-books is still evolving. For libraries and publishers e-books are here to stay, but both sides have to keep up the hard work and negotiations to understand each other's position. Large libraries and major publishers are leading the way, but it is important that policies and practices they adopt should be universal, not favoring large academic libraries over small school or public libraries. Just as the traditional system of lending books and adhering to copyright laws works for all types and sizes of libraries, so should the new practices created to resolve problems of e-books between publishers and libraries.

LSS Support E-books and E-reading

Nonfiction reading is often deep reading and is harder to do on a screen. Fiction and novels are often more desirable for e-book format. LSS who use e-books can do much to promote and help patrons navigate through the issues. Table 8.4 shows how you can help patrons become comfortable with e-books,

---

ADDITIONAL ISSUES WITH E-BOOKS

1. Nonfiction reading on small devices or screens does not adequately support deep reading.
2. Images and pictures, while good on tablets, are not the same quality as paper.
3. Not all content is available in e-books.
4. Libraries are reluctant to purchase multiple titles and there is no interlibrary loan for e-books thus making it harder to obtain e-books from libraries.

CHAPTER SUMMARY

In concluding this chapter, there are so many more things to say about e-books and e-reading. However, by knowing general trends and developments about e-books,

Table 8.4. LSS Support Use of E-books

Steps	Actions
1	Become an e-book reader yourself if you have not already done so! While it may be difficult at first for "deep reading," select a book that you would enjoy and be motivated to read.
2	As you read think about the process of reading on a screen. What do you like about it? What may be more difficult? Experiment now with downloading books from Amazon, Overdrive, or other vendors and publishers you have access to.
3	Think of your tablet or Kindle as a "jump drive" using the USB features. Turn off and on the wireless of your e-reader to see how that affects the amount of circulation time.
4	Borrow different types of e-readers to compare some of the differences. Do you prefer to read in grayscale or color? Do you like the ability to "flip pages," or do you want more text on your screen? Try changing font styles, size, and color. Think about how people with disabilities may benefit from these changes.
5	Try other features of readers such as audio text, highlighting, and searching. Organize the e-books you borrow into folders on the device. The more you are comfortable with the technology, the better able you will be to help others.
6	Similarly, download different types of file extensions. Compare reading a book in PDF to HTML or to AZW. Be able to talk to patrons about the differences of file extensions, particularly if they want to view images, charts, and figures.
7	Finally, team up with an expert on staff and offer a workshop on e-books. People will come! I did this several times for seniors in my community, and with high school students and library staff supporting me, we had much fun helping each individual participant with their unique challenges. Gain confidence so that you can potentially lead other informal or formal sessions in how to use e-books effectively.

you will be able to support the functions and services that patrons seek with their own e-reading. By challenging yourself and practicing some of the ideas discussed in this chapter, LSS will be able to ensure patrons have equitable access to the fairly new technology of e-books. In this chapter we did not discuss e-textbooks, but they are closely related and share many of the same issues as fiction and nonfiction e-books.

DISCUSSION QUESTIONS AND ACTIVITIES

Discussion Questions

1. What advantages do you personally see with e-books over paper books? What are the disadvantages?
2. Download an e-book from either a vendor or a free service onto your cell phone and read it. What was the experience like? Were you able to sustain your reading with the cell phone as an e-reader?
3. Look up a classic title in Project Gutenberg and compare the formats and file extensions. What file extension do you prefer and why?
4. What do you predict the future of e-books will be for libraries? Will they affect how libraries traditionally offer services? If so, how?

Activity

My students create their own e-book. They learn from this assignment how to plan, create, and manage an e-book that they are vested in. Below are brief instructions for this assignment.

Self-Publishing an E-book

Your goal is to write a short e-book that will be published through Amazon KDP (Kindle Direct Publishing) (use table 8.5). This could be a children's story, or an instructional or informational e-book. We are doing this to create e-book ready files as well as to evaluate the process of self-publishing digitally.

Below are parameters for you to follow. Some of these guidelines are suggested by Amazon to be compatible for file conversion.

Clear instructions are important. Be an expert on your short topic and focus on the age of interest of your target audience.

Table 8.5.   Activity Table

Step	Task Description
Initial Story Line	Develop a story line that has an introduction, main body or message, and an ending. These are your notes to refer back to during the process.
Concept Map	Using your notes, create a concept map of your story. The concept map should be in the form of a hierarchy, flow chart, or process. Be sure to capture the action steps of your story in the concept map.
First Draft—Peer Conference	In Word, create your first draft of the text of your e-book. Lay out your information so that it fits within the eight-page guideline.
	Have a peer read it and provide feedback to you. Do the same for another person.
Images—Jpegs	Find images that are copyright free and in the public domain or take your own images.
	All images should contribute to the visual literacy of your work. All images should be saved in jpeg format.
Table, Chart, or Diagram	All e-books must have one of these formats which will provide condensed information to your audience.
Hyperlinks	Aim to have three hyperlinks in your story to websites that contribute to the information or story of your book.
Grammar and Spelling	Read carefully for proper grammar and spelling. Do an "audience check" meaning that your words are appropriate and understandable for your intended audience.
Formatting	Format text for a consistent look.
Second Draft—Conference	In Word create a second draft of your e-book for instructor review.
Bibliography	Bibliography of all sources
Publish your E-book	Open the link to Kindle Direct Publishing (KDP)
	https://kdp.amazon.com/
	View Video
	Click Learn More: (to set up an account)
	Warning: Amazon requires your Social Security number. If you prefer not to go forward, save your e-book as both PDF and HTML files and load them onto a tablet using a USB connection.
	https://kdp.amazon.com/help?topicId=A37Z49E2DDQPP3&ref_=gs
	Read the Kindle Direct Publishing Simplified Guide and follow instructions:
	https://kdp.amazon.com/help?topicId=A17W8UM0MMSQX6
E-book Files	Transfer your e-book to an e-book reader! Celebrate your success!

Your goal is to create an **eight-page** e-book which can be published using Amazon's Kindle Direct Publishing.

NOTES

1. John Van Zwietzen, "Managers and Microcomputers: Getting the Right Mix." *Training and Development Journal* 38, no. 4 (July 1984): 30–36, accessed December 18, 2014, https://search.ebscohost.com/login.aspx?direct=true&db=aph&AN=9076021&site=ehost -live&scope=site.

2. Nancy Herther, "The Ebook Reader Is Not the Future of Ebooks." *Searcher* 16, no. 8 (September 2008): 26–40, accessed December 18, 2014, https://search.ebscohost.com/login .aspx?direct=true&db=aph&AN=34172354&site=ehost-live&scope=site.

3. Lee Rainie and Aaron Smith. "Tablet and E-reader Ownership Update." Pew Research Internet Project, last modified October 18, 2013, accessed December 18, 2014, http://www .pewinternet.org/2013/10/18/tablet-and-e-reader-ownership-update/.

4. Calibre, "About Calibre." Calibre Ebook Management, last modified 2014, accessed December 18, 2014, http://calibre-ebook.com/.

5. Barbara Quint, "NetLibrary Offers 1,500 E-Book Titles to 100 Large Public Libraries in Trial Program." *Information Today* 17, no. 3 (March 2000): 18–19, accessed December 18, 2014, http://search.ebscohost.com/login.aspx?direct=true&db=aph&AN=2882976&site=eh ost-live&scope=site.

6. Andrew Richard Albanese, "Life with E-books." *Publisher's Weekly* 259, no. 35 (August 27, 2012): 34–41, accessed December 21, 2014, http://search.ebscohost.com/login.aspx?dir ect=true&db=aph&AN=79447100&site=ehost-live&scope=site.

7. Paula Hane, "Project Gutenberg Progresses." *Information Today* 21, no. 5 (May 2004): 28–52, accessed December 18, 2014, http://search.ebscohost.com/login.aspx?direct =true&db=aph&AN=13134255&site=ehost-live&scope=site.

8. Gale Cengage Learning, "Gale Virtual Reference Library (GVRL)," Cengage Learning— Gale, last modified 2014, accessed December 19, 2014, http://www.cengage.com/search/ showresults.do?N=197+4294904997.

9. EBSCO, "EBSCO eBooks and Audiobooks," EBSCO eBooks and Audiobooks, last modified 2014, accessed December 20, 2014, http://www.ebscohost.com/ebooks.

10. "Salem Press Special Offers," Salem Press, last modified 2014, accessed December 20, 2014, http://www.salempress.com/special_offers.html.

11. Shannon Acedo and Cathy Levercus, "Updates on Ebooks: Challenges & Changes," *Knowledge Quest* 43, no. 1 (September/October 2014), accessed December 20, 2014, http://search.ebscohost.com/login.aspx?direct=true&db=aph&AN=97937362&site=ehost -live&scope=site.

12. "Libraries Annual Report: Relations between Libraries and Publishers Over Ebooks Improving," Digital Book World, last modified April 14, 2014, accessed December 20, 2014, http://www.digitalbookworld.com/2014/libraries-annual-report-relations-between-libraries -and-publishers-over-ebooks-improving/.

REFERENCES, SUGGESTED READINGS, AND WEBSITES

Acedo, Shannon, and Cathy Levercus. "Updates on Ebooks: Challenges & Changes." *Knowledge Quest* 43, no. 1 (September/October 2014): 44–52. Accessed December 20, 2014. http://search.ebscohost.com/login.aspx?direct=true&db=aph&AN=97937362&site=eh ost-live&scope=site.

Albanese, Andrew Richard. "Life with E-books." *Publisher's Weekly* 259, no. 35 (August 27, 2012): 34–41. Accessed December 21, 2014. http://search.ebscohost.com/login.aspx?direct=true&db=aph&AN=79447100&site=ehost-live&scope=site.

Calibre. "About Calibre." Calibre Ebook Management. Last modified 2014. Accessed December 18, 2014. http://calibre-ebook.com/.

DBW. "Libraries Annual Report: Relations between Libraries and Publishers Over Ebooks Improving." Digital Book World. Last modified April 14, 2014. Accessed December 20, 2014. http://www.digitalbookworld.com/2014/libraries-annual-report-relations-between-libraries-and-publishers-over-ebooks-improving/.

Dobler, Elizabeth. "Looking beyond the Screen: Evaluating the Quality of Digital Books." *Reading Today* 30, no. 5 (April/May 2013): 20–21. Accessed December 18, 2014. https://search.ebscohost.com/login.aspx?direct=true&db=aph&AN=87064637&site=ehost-live&scope=site.

EBSCO. "EBSCO eBooks and Audiobooks." EBSCO eBooks and Audiobooks. Last modified 2014. Accessed December 20, 2014. http://www.ebscohost.com/ebooks.

File-Extensions.org. "E-book file extension list." E-book file extensions. Last modified 2014. Accessed December 18, 2014. http://www.file-extensions.org/filetype/extension/name/e-book-files.

Gale Cengage Learning. "Gale Virtual Reference Library (GVRL)." Last modified 2014. Accessed December 19, 2014. http://www.cengage.com/search/showresults.do?N=197+4294904997.

Hane, Paula. "Project Gutenberg Progresses." *Information Today* 21, no. 5 (May 2004): 28–52. Accessed December 18, 2014. http://search.ebscohost.com/login.aspx?direct=true&db=aph&AN=13134255&site=ehost-live&scope=site.

Herther, Nancy. "The Ebook Reader Is Not the Future of Ebooks." *Searcher* 16, no. 8 (September 2008): 26–40. Accessed December 18, 2014. https://search.ebscohost.com/login.aspx?direct=true&db=aph&AN=34172354&site=ehost-live&scope=site.

Project Gutenberg. "Free ebooks—Project Gutenberg." Project Gutenberg. Last modified 2014. Accessed December 19, 2014. https://www.gutenberg.org/.

Quint, Barbara. "NetLibrary Offers 1,500 E-Book Titles to 100 Large Public Libraries in Trial Program." *Information Today* 17, no. 3 (March 2000): 18–19. Accessed December 18, 2014. http://search.ebscohost.com/login.aspx?direct=true&db=aph&AN=2882976&site=ehost-live&scope=site.

Rainie, Lee, and Aaron Smith. "Tablet and E-reader Ownership Update." Pew Research Internet Project. Last modified October 18, 2013. Accessed December 18, 2014. http://www.pewinternet.org/2013/10/18/tablet-and-e-reader-ownership-update/.

Salem Press. "Salem Press Special Offers." Salem Press. Last modified 2014. Accessed December 20, 2014. http://www.salempress.com/special_offers.html.

Van Zwietzen, John. "Managers and Microcomputers: Getting the Right Mix." *Training and Development Journal* 38, no. 4 (July 1984): 30–36. Accessed December 18, 2014. https://search.ebscohost.com/login.aspx?direct=true&db=aph&AN=9076021&site=ehost-live&scope=site.

CHAPTER 9

The Internet

Directories and Search Engines

LSS know role of technology in creating, identifying, retrieving, and accessing information resources and demonstrate facility with appropriate information discovery tools. (ALA-LSSC Technology Competency #7)

Topics Covered in This Chapter:

- Directories
  - Selection
  - The Internet Public Library, Second Edition (IPL2)
  - Academic LibGuides
  - Directories by Professional Organizations
  - Local Directories
  - Yahoo! Directories
- Search Engines
  - Basic Steps of the Search Engine
- Advanced Shortcuts
  - Boolean Operators
  - Quotations
  - Google's Use of the Word *Site*
- Analytical and Critical Thinking Websites
- Intenational Search Engines
  - Country Codes

Key Terms:

Algorithms: These are formulas created by search engine companies that determine how certain web pages show up in the results list. Results may be based on such things as the number and quality of other websites that are linked to a page, how many times key words appear on the page, or the quality of the sites that appear within the page. Library staff can recommend search engines to patrons with confidence when they know how result lists are determined.

Boolean Operators: Words added to the search that limit or expand the results. The words AND, OR, and NOT are common. For example, "AND" actually limits the search results because at least two words—this AND that—must be present in the web page. Library staff perform or assist with more effective searches when they use operators.

Directory: A list of websites organized around a subject or theme for the purpose of guiding searchers to recommended sites. Library staff use authoritative national and state directories to help patrons find information. Library staff may also create their own directories of valid websites for research, local history, reading selection, or other topics that are important to patrons.

Search Query: These are the actual words typed into the blank box of a search engine to locate information on the Internet. How the query is constructed determines the results. Library staff can suggest ways to improve a patron's search by using different combinations of shortcuts, words, and operator options to find desirable results.

Spider: Not the arachnid, this type of spider, also called a web crawler, is a program created by search engine companies to scan through all Internet web pages. Searching for key words, images, and other information, these programs search uncountable Internet sites to identify pages searchers would like to find. The selected websites are then referenced in the search engine index for quick retrieval.

URL: This is the abbreviation for the term Uniform Resource Locator, the global address of documents and other resources found in servers on the World Wide Web. Because it would be impossible to remember all of the different numbered addresses of servers, the numbers have been converted into names such as www.mylibrary.com that are uniform for locating a web page. Librarians use URLs in their work as they recommend websites to patrons or retrieve information from reliable sources.

Many people rely on library staff to help them find information. In fact, some people credit librarians with knowing the answers to everything! Our secret is we have developed and practiced research and information skills. Where once library staff dealt primarily with paper, today our research skills extend into many digital resources, including the Internet.

The goal of this chapter is to help improve our proficiency as Internet searchers. Search engines are made to be simple and easy to use by everyone. For basic or factual information most people find the information they seek on the Internet.

However, it is much more difficult for people to find higher level information. This is where library staff that have developed their search skills can make a real difference for patrons.

Some web designers adhere to a three-click rule. Our tolerance for Internet searching is limited to three clicks of the mouse.[1] The theory states if we do not find what we want on the Internet in three clicks, we give up and change our search to move on to something else. We will learn in this chapter how library staff can search the Internet for patrons so that they can quickly locate the most optimum results available.

Directories and search engines are used to navigate the Internet. **Directories** are preselected lists of websites on a theme or subject which provide quick access to reliable Internet web pages. We will look at some of the best directories for library staff to be aware of to use or share with patrons. Most searching on the Internet takes place using search engines. We will also learn how library staff can effectively use search engines to quickly obtain high-quality information for patrons (figure 9.1).

Figure 9.1.   Patrons Use Library Computers to Search the Internet. *Frances Hart Ewers Library Media Center, East Lyme High School, East Lyme, CT*

DIRECTORIES

One way to distinguish directories from search engines is how each compiles results. Search engine results are generated by a set of computer instructions. Directories are specific lists of websites created by people. Each website on the selected list has been evaluated and recommended for inclusion. While numerous other websites may exist on the topic, directory sites are typically chosen for their quality and authority.

Directories have important value for library staff. Our patrons today are comfortable Internet users, and their skills are quite good. When patrons require help with searching, they have often already done basic searches and need "something else." Patrons who are shown directories are often pleased with the results and may ask why they had not known about them. Directories provide library staff with a quick way to produce excellent results to guide patrons in their Internet searching.

Directories are usually arranged by subject or time period. Within each category, often in alphabetical order, will be the name of the website, a hyperlink to its web address, and a brief description or annotation that introduces the website, its purpose, or special features. By browsing web page titles and reading accompanying annotations, users make selections by clicking on likely websites from the list under the topic of interest. Updates occur either on a planned schedule which could be as often as daily, but more likely directories are updated as needed, or, if the directory is abandoned, not at all.

Selection

LSS should determine who the sponsor of the directory is by checking the credentials of the publisher. Select and guide patrons to academic or school directories that have been created by university or school librarians. See the textbox for the many reasons to select academic and school directories.

REASONS TO SELECT ACADEMIC AND SCHOOL DIRECTORIES

1. These directories are authoritative because they have been created by library specialists for educational purposes.
2. These directories may have been created as part of an instructional lesson or library guide and offer high-quality websites.
3. Subject classifications found in these directories align with school curriculum or categories of information librarians are familiar with.
4. These directories are updated regularly because they are key digital resources of the academic library and are in demand by students.
5. These directories are educational tools that support students in their learning. They will work well for all patrons who seek information on a variety of topics and subjects.

There are also many directories that are of high quality posted by state and national government, professional, and nonprofit organizations. We will now look at the more important directories for library staff to know about so that they, in turn, can use them to provide information and guidance to patrons.

The Internet Public Library, Second Edition (IPL2)

Directories associated with research and academia can be counted upon to have reliable websites with focused results. Internet Public Library and IPL2 have a long and distinguished history. The first Internet Public Library originated at the University of Michigan Graduate School of Information in 1995, in a seminar class taught by assistant professor Joe Janes. Professor Janes created an organized list of websites to teach library students about a relatively new resource called the Internet.[2] Search engines were in their infancy and did not work too well, so the University of Michigan openly shared their directory service with the public to help them navigate for the best results through the Internet. At about the same time the State Library of California developed the Librarian's Internet Index (LII). LII was a reputable directory of excellent lists of websites with annotations categorized by subject for its state residents.

The Library of Congress decided not to create its own national directory and instead supported IPL. In 2010, the Internet Public Library and Librarian's Internet Index merged to become Internet Public Library 2 (IPL2).[3] Lost were the annotations of LII, but gained was the concerted effort to maintain a national directory of websites to support research and inquiry for citizens of the United States. Today graduate library and information programs of Drexel, Rutgers, Syracuse, Florida State, the Universities of Michigan, Washington, North Carolina, and Texas and others, and the Library of Congress, continue the development of IPL2. IPL2 is an excellent place to find websites preselected around numerous subjects and themes. When creating web resource pages for patrons, IPL2 is one of the important sites to begin with for its current and authoritative sites.

Academic LibGuides

As an excellent source of academic directories, LSS should become familiar with LibGuides (http://springshare.com/libguides). LibGuides[4] is a product by Springshare for creating library websites. LibGuides are a concise and easy way to organize, present, and edit library research information and services. One of the reasons most academic libraries and some schools use LibGuides is to make directories of websites for research, coursework, or overall knowledge.

The example of a LibGuide in figure 9.2 was created by the reference librarian at Three Rivers Community College. Each category in the Database and Internet Resources guide is clearly identified: Library Databases, Newspaper Databases, Online Newspapers, and Websites. There is also a guide for Books and one for More Information that supports American government research. Students have a solid place to begin their research and librarians have an organized way to present information resources.

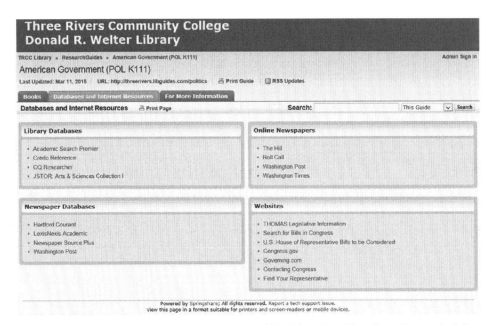

Figure 9.2. LibGuide on American Government. *Donald R. Welter Library, Three Rivers Community College, Norwich, CT and Springshare, Inc.*

LibGuides allowed me to create directories or lists of excellent web resources for students around topics, assignments, courses, or even special events. Students and teachers found the guides helpful and often asked for them for their research assignments. There is a wealth of great directories LSS can tap into by searching "university + LibGuides" or "school + LibGuides." Universities and schools use LibGuides to promote the best Internet websites for their students, many of which are free to the public. Table 9.1 shows just a few examples from universities for your perusal.

Let's examine an academic LibGuide in detail in the textbox and see how it could be an important resource to us.

Directories by Professional Organizations

We can find many fine examples of subject directories by researching professional organizations. The American Association of School Librarians[5] (AASL) provides important information and support for those who work in school libraries including annual directories of "Best Websites for Teaching and Learning."

Table 9.1. Sampling of University Subject LibGuides

Purdue University Libraries	http://guides.lib.purdue.edu/
University of Illinois Libraries	http://uiuc.libguides.com/
University of California-San Diego Library	http://ucsd.libguides.com/
Northwestern University Library	http://libguides.northwestern.edu/
Indian River State College Library	http://irsc.libguides.com/home

LIBGUIDE PRACTICE

Go to Purdue University Libraries,[a] one of many academic libraries with excellent LibGuides directories.

1. Scan the broad core academic topics of arts and humanities, medicine and health, social sciences and education, and so forth.
2. Click on a broad topic that interests you to find the next page of subtopics created by a librarian specialist who is responsible for the directories for this topic.
3. Upon selecting the subtopic, such as anthropology and archeology, there will be a guide or directory of excellent web resources for each topic.

Repeat the process many times and make your own directory of guides from the Purdue University librarians that could be helpful in your studies or library work.

a. "LibGuides—Browse By Subject," Purdue University Libraries, last modified 2015, accessed February 27, 2015, http://guides.lib.purdue.edu/cat.php?cid=24817.

Another example of directories created by professionals within an organization is the American Psychological Association's "Research in Action."[6] Here in one location are lists of websites and studies around current topics that affect our lives.

There are directories of websites from so many professions. Look to career organizations in the areas of science, literature, health and medicine, the arts, technology, business, history, and social sciences to find highly authoritative and recommended web resources.

Local Directories

Directories can also be local and small. LSS may create directories of home web resources or links that support special library programs or call attention to reading initiatives. These directories may have a permanent place on the library website, or they may be created to focus patrons' interest for a special or particular event or program.

For example, around an author's visit there may be a web page or directory made of websites related to the author's work and subject of his or her writings. The directory will be replaced over time with new lists of websites which support future programs. By using the resources from exemplar directories like IPL2 and knowing how to find excellent websites through advanced searching techniques, LSS are capable of creating purposeful directories that support their libraries' programs and collections services.

Yahoo! Directories

To segue into the next section of this chapter on search engines, we will conclude directories with Yahoo! Yahoo! is both a directory and a search engine. Yahoo!

directories link websites in categories such as business, arts and humanities, entertainment, health, science, and recreation or sports. Within each category are subcategories of websites. Yahoo is a commercial venture and LSS should be aware that there will not be the quality of oversight here that is found with IPL2 or professional organizations.

As we end this section on directories, there is a word of caution: while it is fun to browse, using directories may make searching more time consuming and the directory ultimately may not link to sites that patrons' seek. A directory does not provide keyword searching; rather we have to open each site and examine its contents. I recommend LSS become familiar with IPL2 and a few university and professional directories that align to the needs of their patrons. We will now look at search engines, the programs we use to find websites using keywords and other search terms.

SEARCH ENGINES

Unlike directories that are man-made lists, search engines are software programs that use computer instructions to find best matches to keywords. These programs are also called **algorithms**. Algorithms are formulas created by search engine companies which determine how certain web pages show up in the results list. All search engines programs are not the same. Depending upon the search engine you choose, you will obtain different results because what makes search engines unique are the algorithms they use to find and prioritize websites.

There are hundreds of billions of searches every month. The five major search engines today are Google/Google Chrome, Bing, Yahoo!, Ask.com, and America Online (AOL). For much of the world, the most popular and heavily used search engine is Google, followed by every other search engine. Many of the other search engines have consolidated or no longer exist.[7] Table 9.2 gives a summary of the top five search engines and their features.

Table 9.2. "Big 5" Search Engines and Features[a]

Search Engine	URL	Description
Google	www.google.com	Google is the leading search provider in the world. It refines its algorithm regularly to improve search results.
Bing	www.bing.com	Launched in 2009, Bing is an upgrade from Microsoft's previous search engine, MSN Search.
Yahoo	www.yahoo.com	Yahoo continues to strive to achieve market share and attract new users by offering both the search engine and a comprehensive set of directories.
Ask.com	www.ask.com	Originally known as Ask Jeeves, users are encouraged to ask their questions in natural language as an approach to searching that may be more comfortable to them.
AOL	www.aol.com	Founded in 1985, AOL has a loyal customer base for its many services that include its search engine and e-mail.

[a] "Major Search Engines and Directories," Search Engine Watch, last modified 2013, accessed February 28, 2015, http://searchenginewatch.com/sew/how-to/2048976/major-search-engines-directories.

A **search query** is the actual words typed into the blank box of a search engine to locate information on the Internet. How the query is constructed determines the results. Keywords are words the user thinks best describe the information he or she seeks. A basic search uses keywords.

But sometimes the results show there is little to no information on the topic based on our keywords. When this occurs there may be a problem with either the choice of words or even the spelling. LSS can suggest synonyms and other vocabulary to improve a patron's search or use different combinations of words and limiters to narrow results to those that are only highly desirable. We will examine strategies in the next pages on how to help patrons configure their searches to yield best results.

Basic Steps of the Search Engine

LSS who understand the workings behind search engines are more confident in their use. Regardless of the company, search engines are built around some simple principles. We have heard the term web crawlers or **spiders**. These terms refer to the ongoing process of the search engine company to methodically and continually search for quality websites across the Internet. Depending on the search engine formula or algorithm, websites are compiled with addresses. The spider "crawls" through millions of servers of the World Wide Web to gather up all websites as directed by the search engine algorithm.

Similar to creating an index for a book, the search engine now indexes the keywords and websites into a filing system so they can be readily retrieved by Internet searchers. When we search, we actually search the indexes, not the entire Internet. The best matches to our search query are immediately bounced back to us in the form of a result list from the search engine. In addition to the indexes, each search engine has other criteria for what makes the result list. The amount of hyperlinks within a site, the popularity or past usage of the site, and other requirements often unknown to the user frame the result list. Basic steps of the search engine process are as follows.

1. Spider or web crawler computer programs examine keywords on millions and millions of web pages located on servers over the globe.
2. Information about selected web pages is added to the search engine's comprehensive indexes.
3. User's keywords are matched to web page information found in the indexes.
4. These web pages are part of the results list returned for the user to look at by the search engine.

ADVANCED SHORTCUTS

All search engines offer advanced searching, but it is one more click to get to the screen. The LSS who learns and uses advanced shortcuts will find that they can both save time and obtain great results. Each search engine has its own advanced search features and shortcuts. Here we will examine the advanced shortcuts for the search engine Google. However, if LSS use a search engine other than Google, he or she may want to learn the advanced shortcuts by reading help screens offered by the search engine.

Boolean Operators

Boolean operators are universal search terms which enhance searches regardless of the search engine used. Boolean operators allow the searcher to expand or restrict the results of a search based upon the use of conjunctions, punctuation, or modifiers. Three of the most useful and common Boolean operators are the words "AND," "OR," and "NOT" (see table 9.3). The operator AND narrows the search by instructing the search engine to search for all the records containing the first keyword, then for all the records containing the second keyword, and show *only* those records that contain *both*. The operator OR broadens the search to include records containing either keyword, or both. Combining search terms with the NOT operator narrows the search by excluding unwanted terms.[8]

Table 9.3. Basic Boolean Operators Searching Fish and Whales

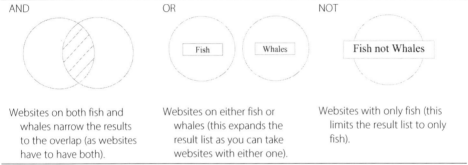

AND	OR	NOT
Websites on both fish and whales narrow the results to the overlap (as websites have to have both).	Websites on either fish or whales (this expands the result list as you can take websites with either one).	Websites with only fish (this limits the result list to only fish).

Quotations

Quotations marks are also a very helpful shortcut for advanced searching. Regardless of the search engine you use, if you place your search terms within a set of quotation marks, the search engine will only return results that contain the exact words or phrase in quotation. Quotation marks restrict the amount of returns you will receive, but at the same time ensure the websites contain the words in the order that you wish them to appear.

Google's Use of the Word *Site*

In addition to Boolean operators, Google has some of its own search operators that are very effective. One that I would like to share with you is the operator word *site*. A domain is an important part of the web address or **URL** that identifies the type or category of sponsorship, such as government, higher education, nonprofit, museum, military, etc. Narrow your search results by domain (e.g., .edu, .gov, .org, etc.) by beginning your search query with *site*. For example, to find the higher education websites that offer web page results on biodiversity, the Google search query would be configured this way:

site:edu biodiversity

Important:

- Do not add any spaces between the operator, colon, or domain (site:edu).
- Do leave one space before the search term (biodiversity).
- Your result list will have only higher education sites that contain this word.

Searching by the site domain is very powerful. Simply by substituting "edu" with "gov" one can flip the search immediately to search only United States government sites with the search term. Or by substituting "gov" with "org," one can now look at results for nonprofit organizations. Top level domains are established by the Internet Corporation for Assigned Names.[9] LSS can enhance their proficiency in searching by becoming familiar with *"site."* This one advanced shortcut is the key way to refine search queries to obtain the best results. Students and patrons have often thanked me for showing them this shortcut.

Analytical and Critical Thinking Websites

Another immensely successful strategy is to include a word that describes the level of thinking you want results to have. Do you wish to find websites that contain mostly facts like almanacs, or do you want websites that provide opinions or evaluations of ideas? The work of two educational theorists, Benjamin Bloom's Taxonomy[10] and Karin Hess's Depth of Knowledge,[11] are particularly helpful to find higher level thinking websites.

Both of these theorists break down levels of thinking from basic facts or knowledge to the highest level of evaluation and creativity. For our discussion, we will look at Benjamin Bloom's work. In the shape of a triangle, Bloom models how people think (see figure 9.3). He said the base of knowledge is factual thinking, and we can progressively move up to the top or peak when we are creative or evaluative. In Bloom's model, facts are at the base of thinking or knowledge. This makes sense because without facts, we cannot expand our ideas. Once we have facts, we can then apply our knowledge to a new situation and analyze or compare it to others. We use facts to form our own opinion so that we can predict, judge, create, or evaluate at the highest level of our thinking.

Bloom's Taxonomy is an excellent model to obtain different levels of information from the Internet. At the knowledge level, LSS answer basic questions such as "how many?" or "name the. . . ." To create an Internet search query for causes of global warming, one may type in the search box *"name the causes global warming."* Resulting sites will name the causes of global warming.

Questions such as *"how is this similar to . . ?"* or *"compare and contrast this event to . . ."* require sites where the topic has been analyzed. If we want to analyze the effects of global warming, the search query could look like this *"analyze effects global warming."* At the top of Bloom's Taxonomy are critical thinking questions such as

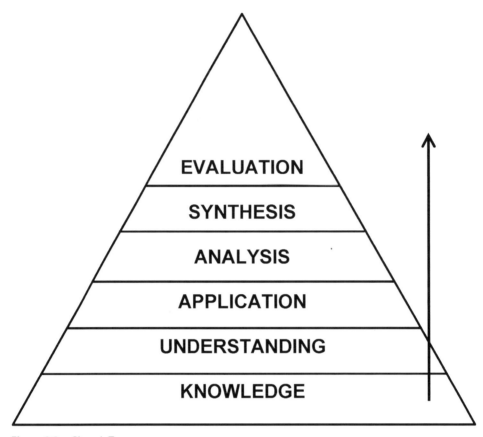

Figure 9.3.   Bloom's Taxonomy

"evaluate these . . ." or *"can you predict the. . . ."* To obtain sites that predict the future of global warming, type in the search box *"predict future global warming,"* adding the word "predict" from the last or highest level of critical thinking. These questions are placed on the triangle so that we can see how facts are at the base and prediction is the highest level of critical thinking (see figure 9.4).

LSS who use the levels of words of Bloom's Taxonomy as a guide for construct-ing search queries will be able to obtain excellent results from the Internet for themselves and for patrons they serve. Combine Bloom's words with Google search operators, and your searching ability has soared (see table 9.4). Try it!

International Search Engines

The Internet is worldwide, and LSS should be aware that searching in the United States does not have an international perspective. The web is global, and there are hundreds of search engines used around the world that are different from what we use in the United States. There are two directories that list international search en-

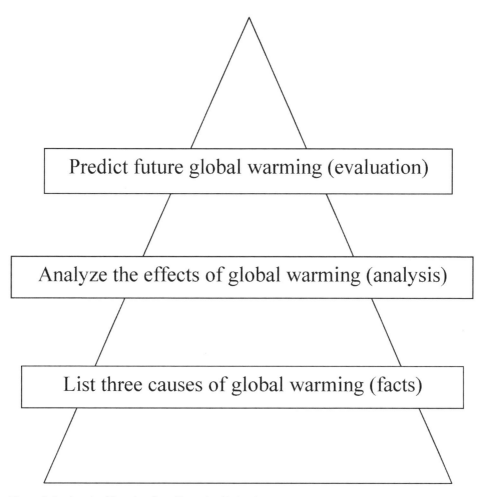

Figure 9.4. Levels of Searches from Factual to Evaluation

Table 9.4. Words for Levels of Searches (Bloom, 1956)[a]

Knowledge	Understanding	Application	Analysis	Synthesis	Evaluation
list	classify	apply	compare	compose	evaluate
identify	summarize	show	contrast	develop	predict
name	describe	change	analyze	assemble	judge
define	explain	discover	differentiate	design	defend
facts	review	illustrate	experiment	revise	value

[a] Benjamin Bloom, "Bloom's Taxonomy Action Verbs," Clemson University, accessed October 27, 2014, http://www.clemson.edu/ assessment/assessmentpractices/referencematerials/documents/Blooms%20Taxonomy%20Action%20Verbs.pdf

gines: Search Engine Colossus[12] and ArnoldIT.[13] Colossus is an alphabetical list of countries. Click each country for search engines either in the language of the country or in English. ArnoldIT also is an alphabetical list of countries but the links to each country's search engine are visibly listed below each country making for easy access. Colossus provides the country flag as well as some factual information about the country. Both Colossus and ArnoldIT are invaluable to find websites with the perspective and culture of the host country.

Country Codes

Another way to gain an international perspective is to add Google international country codes to the Google URL. For example, to search websites hosted in France, modify the Google URL from http://www.google.com to https://www.google.fr. Likewise, the Google search engine in China can be accessed by adding .cn to the URL. LSS can help patrons gain different global perspectives on controversial topics by adding country codes to the Google URL. Lists of all the Google international country codes can be found simply by Googling "*list Google international country codes.*"

CHAPTER SUMMARY

This chapter provides LSS with practical ways to enhance their Internet searching skills by using academic and other credible directories, as well as advanced features of search engines. Search engines can produce better results when we use Boolean logic, shortcuts, or combinations of both. A skilled LSS searcher can offer support to library patrons who still, while being experienced searchers, grapple with ways to find web resources on the Internet. By adding critical thinking words into the search query, LSS define the level of inquiry for the website results. LSS who use academic and professional directories or advanced features when configuring search queries with search engines expand the usefulness of the Internet for identifying, retrieving, and accessing information resources.

DISCUSSION QUESTIONS AND ACTIVITIES

Discussion Questions

1. What are the main differences between directories and search engines that LSS should know about?
2. What is the IPL2 and what important features does it provide patrons and staff? Who oversees and contributes to the quality of IPL2?
3. How would you set up a Google search to only obtain results for universities or higher education websites?
4. List four words that you would use in your search if you were asked to help a patron with an evaluation-type question.

5. Give an example of why you would choose to use an international search engine instead of one based in the United States.

Activities

There are many ideas presented in this chapter to practice or to gain familiarity and proficiency with directories and Internet searching. Below are two activities to enhance your skills. The first activity will give you experience searching academic LibGuides for useful academic directories (table 9.5).

Activity 1: Find Academic LibGuides to Recommend to Others

Table 9.5. Activity Table

Step	Action
1	Using Google enter a search query "university LibGuides." The results will lead you to many pages of university LibGuides.
2	Look for a list of subjects which lead you to guides. Explore the results until you have found five university libraries that offer guides with web resources for topics.
3	You have found academic directories. Look at several of the websites on a topic or subject of your choice. Evaluate the results.
4	Create a list of the sites you would recommend and use with others.

This second activity will give you practice using the words of Bloom's Taxonomy (table 9.6).

Activity 2
Compare how the different levels of vocabulary of Bloom influence search results.

Table 9.6. Activity Table

Step	Action
1	Select a word from each of the six columns of Bloom's Taxonomy, found in table 9.4.
2	For each word construct a search query with Google on genetically modified foods, a controversial topic today.
3	Conduct six searches beginning with your basic, or knowledge word, and ending with a word in the last column, evaluation.
4	Compare the results for each of the six search queries. Do you see the information contained in the websites progressively becoming more analytical and evaluative?

NOTES

1. "Three-click rule," Webopedia, last modified 2015, accessed February 26, 2015, http://www.webopedia.com/TERM/T/three_click_rule.html.

2. Nettie Lagace, "Managing an Internet-based Distributed Reference Service," *Computers in Libraries* 18, no. 2 (1998), http://search.ebscohost.com/login.aspx?direct=true&db=aph&AN=210124&site=ehost-live&scope=site.

3. Barbara Bibel, "IPL2," *Booklist* 107, no. 11 (2011), http://search.ebscohost.com/login
.aspx?direct=true&db=aph&AN=58639138&site=ehost-live&scope=site.

4. "The Most Popular Web Publishing Platform for Libraries," LibGuides by Springshare,
last modified 2015, accessed February 27, 2015, http://springshare.com/libguides/.

5. "Best Websites for Teaching & Learning," American Association of School Librarians,
last modified 2015, accessed February 28, 2015, http://www.ala.org/aasl/standards-guide-
lines/best-websites/2014.

6. "Research in Action," American Psychological Association, last modified 2015, accessed February 28, 2015, http://www.apa.org/research/action/index.aspx.

7. Dave Davies, "Major Search Engines and Directories," Search Engine Watch, last
modified September 26, 2013, accessed October 26, 2014, http://searchenginewatch.com/
article/2048976/Major-Search-Engines-and-Directories.

8. "Boolean Operators," Columbia University, accessed September 24, 2014, http://
www.columbia.edu/cu/lweb/help/clio/boolean_operators.html.

9. "Resources: ICANN: List of Top-Level Domains," Internet Corporation for Assigned
Names, accessed October 26, 2014, https://www.icann.org/resources/pages/tlds-2012-02
-25-en.

10. Benjamin Bloom, "Bloom's Taxonomy Action Verbs," Clemson University, accessed
October 27, 2014, http://www.clemson.edu/assessment/assessmentpractices/referencemate
rials/documents/Blooms%20Taxonomy%20Action%20Verbs.pdf.

11. Karin Hess, "Hess' Cognitive Rigor Matrix & Curricular Examples," Hess' Cognitive
Rigor Matrix & Curricular Examples, last modified 2009, accessed October 27, 2014, http://
static.pdesas.org/content/documents/M2-Activity_2_Handout.pdf.

12. "International Directory of Search Engines," Search Engine Colossus, last modified
2015, accessed February 21, 2015, http://searchenginecolossus.com/.

13. "International Search Engines," ArnoldIT, last modified 2015, accessed February 21,
2015, http://www.arnoldit.com/lists/intlsearch.asp.

REFERENCES, SUGGESTED READINGS, AND WEBSITES

AcademicInfo. "Online Subject Guides." AcademicInfo. Last modified 2013. Accessed Febru-
     ary 27, 2015. http://www.academicinfo.net/subject-guides.
American Library Association. "Best Websites for Teaching & Learning." American Associa-
     tion of School Librarians. Last modified 2015. Accessed February 28, 2015. http://www
     .ala.org/aasl/standards-guidelines/best-websites/2014.
American Psychological Association. "Research in Action." American Psychological Asso-
     ciation. Last modified 2015. Accessed February 28, 2015. http://www.apa.org/research/
     action/index.aspx.
ArnoldIT. "International Search Engines." ArnoldIT. Last modified 2015. Accessed February
     21, 2015. http://www.arnoldit.com/lists/intlsearch.asp.
Bibel, Barbara. "IPL2." *Booklist* 107, no. 11 (2011). http://search.ebscohost.com/login.aspx?
     direct=true&db=aph&AN=58639138&site=ehost-live&scope=site.
Bloom, Benjamin. "Bloom's Taxonomy Action Verbs." Clemson University. Accessed October
     27, 2014. http://www.clemson.edu/assessment/assessmentpractices/referencematerials/
     documents/Blooms%20Taxonomy%20Action%20Verbs.pdf.
"Boolean Operators." Columbia University. Accessed September 24, 2014. http://www.co
     lumbia.edu/cu/lweb/help/clio/boolean_operators.html.
Brian Strome. "International Directory of Search Engines." Search Engine Colossus. Last
     modified 2015. Accessed February 21, 2015. http://searchenginecolossus.com/.

Davies, Dave. "Major Search Engines and Directories." Search Engine Watch. Last modified September 26, 2013. Accessed October 26, 2014. http://searchenginewatch.com/article/2048976/Major-Search-Engines-and-Directories.

Hess, Karin. "Hess' Cognitive Rigor Matrix & Curricular Examples." Hess' Cognitive Rigor Matrix & Curricular Examples. Last modified 2009. Accessed October 27, 2014. http://static.pdesas.org/content/documents/M2-Activity_2_Handout.pdf.

"How Internet Search Engines Work." How Stuff Works. Accessed October 26, 2014. http://computer.howstuffworks.com/internet/basics/search-engine1.htm.

Incisive Interactive Marketing LLC. "Major Search Engines and Directories." Search Engine Watch. Last modified 2013. Accessed February 28, 2015. http://searchenginewatch.com/sew/how-to/2048976/major-search-engines-directories.

Lagace, Nettie. "Managing an Internet-based Distributed Reference Service." *Computers in Libraries* 18, no. 2 (1998). http://search.ebscohost.com/login.aspx?direct=true&db=aph&AN=210124&site=ehost-live&scope=site.

"Punctuation, Symbols & Operators in Search." Google. Accessed October 24, 2014. https://support.google.com/websearch/answer/2466433.

Purdue University. "LibGuides—Browse By Subject." Purdue University Libraries. Last modified 2015. Accessed February 27, 2015. http://guides.lib.purdue.edu/cat.php?cid=24817.

Quinstreet Enterprise. "Three-click rule." Webopedia. Last modified 2015. Accessed February 26, 2015. http://www.webopedia.com/TERM/T/three_click_rule.html.

"Resources: ICANN: List of Top-Level Domains." Internet Corporation for Assigned Names. Accessed October 26, 2014. https://www.icann.org/resources/pages/tlds-2012-02-25-en.

Springshare. "The Most Popular Web Publishing Platform for Libraries." LibGuides by Springshare. Last modified 2015. Accessed February 27, 2015. http://springshare.com/libguides/.

"Webopedia." Webopedia. Accessed October 27, 2014. http://www.webopedia.com.

"Welcome to Infomine: Scholarly Internet Research Collections." Infomine. Accessed September 26, 2014. http://infomine.ucr.edu/.

"Yahoo! Directory." Yahoo! Accessed October 26, 2014. http://dir.yahoo.com.

CHAPTER 10

Appropriate Use

Policies, Confidentiality, Security of Data, and Digital Copyright

LSS know the basic principles and best practices to ensure the integrity of data and the confidentiality of user activities. (ALA-LSSC Technology Competency #3)

LSS know the concepts and issues concerning the appropriate use of technology by different user groups. (ALA-LSSC Technology Competency #4)

Topics Covered in This Chapter:

- Terminology
- Acceptable Internet Use
  - Filters
  - Acceptable Use Policies
  - Regulations, Rules, Procedures, and Guidelines
- Confidentiality
- Integrity and Security of Data
- Copyright Law
  - Brief History of US Copyright
  - Purpose of US Copyright
- Digital Millennium Copyright Act
  - Million Book Project
  - Fair Use
  - Copying and Archiving by Libraries
  - The First Sale Doctrine

Key Terms:

Digital Copyright Protection: Federal law that gives control to the creator of a digital content the right to limit the number of copies and the sales of the work. In order for a work to be copyrighted, it must meet three criteria: it must be tangible or fixed (not an unwritten idea), original, and minimally creative. Library staff should learn the law and report any abuse they see of it to their supervisor.

Fair Use: Educators and students may use copyrighted material for their teaching and learning without seeking permission from the author for a one-time, spontaneous occasion. A small portion of a copyrighted work may be used without permission but never for commercial gain. Libraries receive special consideration because they promote and advance learning, a goal of the US Copyright Act. Library staff should know the basics of fair use. If they are uncertain as to the law, they should seek guidance from their supervisors before making digital copies.

Filters: These are software applications and/or hardware solutions that block inappropriate or damaging Internet content from being viewed or downloaded on users' computers. Library staff are required by federal law to protect patrons under age eighteen from inappropriate Internet sites by equipping library computers and Wi-Fi with such solutions.

Public Domain: In relation to copyright law, this term refers to ***everyone***. Works that are not copyrighted have unrestricted use by all with no obligation to seek permission or compensate to use the work commercially or otherwise. After a set period of time all copyrights expire and the works become available for anyone to use freely. Library staff learn the basics of the law to know how to evaluate if a library material is in the public domain. Libraries are obligated to uphold copyright laws and allow only permissible uses of materials, including digital resources.

In library work LSS are confronted with a wide variety of patron behaviors. When these behaviors are around technology or Internet issues, it is important that the library has clear guidelines, expectations, and policies so there is no misunderstanding of appropriate use and that all patrons are treated evenly and fairly.

This chapter is written to help LSS understand the accepted policies and guidelines around Internet use, the expectations of confidentiality for patrons using library computers, and the role we have to ensure integrity of library data. We will also discuss the Digital Millennium Copyright Act, the federal law that governs the use of software and other digital resources.

TERMINOLOGY

With an unregulated Internet and the expense of technology, there is the need for libraries to establish acceptable rules of use and behavior with technology. LSS can better support patrons' technology use when they themselves know and abide by the rules and understand why they are in place. In this chapter many words describe

Table 10.1. Terminology

Term	Description	Library Examples
Act	National laws passed by the US Congress that are federal legislation.	The Patriot Act requires libraries to share circulation records with law authorities. The Children's Internet Protection Act requires filters.
Law	A legal document that establishes rules and behaviors around specific actions.	US Copyright law affects how libraries circulate and reproduce materials and software.
Statute	State laws that apply throughout the state.	Wisconsin statute 43.07[a] requires the state superintendent to seek advice from the State Council on Library Service and Network development when establishing library networks.
Policy	A contract or plan of action that is strictly adhered to. Policy may include or reference laws or rules.	Libraries are encouraged to have local acceptable use policies that establish the rules for Internet use and behavior.
Regulation	A regulation describes specific ways policies are to be enforced.	Boards of Education have regulations that describe steps or actions for librarians to carry out library policies.
Rule	A guide for action or behavior.	A library may have a rule that food is not allowed next to a computer.
Guideline	A plan or explanation to carrying out a rule that may provide some leeway.	The library has guidelines for how long a patron may use a computer.
Procedure	A logical plan or set of steps detailing how to get something done in a consistent and fair manner.	The library has procedures on how to reserve and set up projection technology for community meetings.

a. State of Wisconsin, "Chapter 43: Wisconsin Legislative Documents." Last modified September 3, 2014. Accessed December 11, 2014. http://docs.legis.wisconsin.gov/statutes/statutes/43.pdf.

how technology use is governed. There is a hierarchy of terms that is helpful for LSS to understand when interpreting library technology policies. We will look at the terms in their hierarchy from national law down to individual procedures libraries may have in place to deal with patrons (see table 10.1).

We will use these terms as we examine some of the acts, laws, policies, regulations, and guidelines of libraries that ensure legal, equitable, accessible, and acceptable uses of technology.

ACCEPTABLE INTERNET USE

Acts, laws, policies, regulations, rules, guidelines, and procedures all govern library patrons' Internet use. LSS need to be familiar with how they govern acceptable use because they are often the staff on the front line who interact and observe how patrons use the library computing services. If staff are not knowledgeable of acceptable use, they may over- or underreact to what they see, thus potentially placing both patrons and the library in jeopardy.

We will begin with a technology act and work our way to procedures that govern acceptable use. Refer back to table 10.1 as we work through these next paragraphs. At the top of the hierarchy guiding how libraries provide Internet to minors is the Children's Internet Protection Act (CIPA). This is federal legislation that was enacted in the year 2000, requiring all schools and public libraries that receive federal funds to **filter** Internet content for children under age eighteen. CIPA was created with the intent of protecting minors from pornography or obscene material considered harmful.[1]

Filters

The act requires every library computer to be filtered, but it does not legislate to what degree the filter must be set. Filters can be set to allow certain content that is age appropriate. Filters may be devices or software, depending on the network and infrastructure of the library. Software filters are often imbedded in Internet services such as America Online (AOL) or reside as an application or program on the computer hard drive. Filters work by blocking specific websites, phrases, or words. Filters can also block larger amounts of data or content such as pornography or obscenity. Most library administrators rely on the filter product's preselected blocked content and may exempt an occasional site. Filters help to protect a computer from incoming viruses or hackers. Library WiFi networks must also have a filter so that children who use their own devices on the library network are protected. There should be no way for library patrons to turn off the filter for the library Internet network or the library WiFi (the network administrator would have this function). Children's room computers often have a fuller or more robust degree of filtering than adult computers.

Acceptable Use Policies

In addition to complying with CIPA law by installing filters for each computing device in the library, libraries are often required by state law or required by their governing boards to have an Internet Acceptable Use Policy (AUP). AUP is a contract or plan of action for how patrons accept their responsibility to use library computers that is strictly enforced by library staff. AUPs may include or reference laws or rules.

My experience with AUP began with chairing my school district technology committee. As we built our school network and made Internet more available to staff and students, it was clear that the school and libraries needed acceptable policy to follow. A district technology committee developed a list of behaviors that were acceptable and also a list of actions that were not. We researched our state guides for board policy and other libraries and school districts to see how policies were written. Once the committee had reached consensus on a draft AUP, it was brought to administration, faculty, and finally the local Board of Education for approval. Each year students are required to read and sign the district AUP that governs their use of school computers and Wi-Fi.

AUP is the basis for determining what is acceptable and what is not, and all users know upfront that to break AUP could cause loss of Internet access (see table 10.2).

Table 10.2. Examples of Acceptable vs. Unacceptable Patron Use of Library Computers

Acceptable Use	Unacceptable Use
Appropriate communications from e-mail, blogs, etc., when using library computers.	Bullying, obscene language, threats, or other unkind or illegal communications.
Educational or informational use of library computers.	Use computers for gambling, ponzi schemes, or participating in other illicit or illegal use.
Accept and use filtering software.	Use virtual private networks (VPN) or other means to by-pass library content filters.
Adhere to copyright laws and library licensed agreements.	Violate copyright law and/or library software or database license agreements.
Respect for other patrons' privacy and work.	Disrespect for other patrons' privacy using technology or trespassing or taking another's files or folders.
Abiding by rules of password security.	Acquiring or using others' passwords.
Careful use of library technology equipment.	Breakage or other damage to technology equipment.

When the AUP is well written and patrons sign or by default accept the policy, staff can feel fairly confident purposeful use of the Internet will take place on library computers. If not, staff has policy in place to impose restrictions or consequences.

The American Library Association (ALA) provides thorough information and guidance for library staff on how to develop acceptable use policies on its Internet Toolkit website.[2] ALA suggests Internet Use Policies include a disclaimer that the library is not responsible for Internet content and to explain the reasons for having an AUP.

The example in table 10.2 of acceptable and unacceptable use of library computers holds true for all three types of libraries. These are common patron expectations for technology use no matter what type of library. Regardless of the library, all patrons are expected to adhere to federal copyright laws. All patrons are expected to respect others' privacy. No patron may conduct illegal or illicit behaviors on library computers. But there are differences in AUPs among public, school, and academic libraries for LSS to be aware of.

> *Public libraries*: Public libraries serve all people. What is acceptable use for an adult may not be acceptable use for a child. While computers in children and teen areas must maintain their filters, adults have the right to ask library staff to turn off or disable the filter during their use. Libraries strive to guarantee adults' First Amendment rights of confidentiality and freedom of speech. This does not mean obscenity or pornographic materials are tolerated in the library, but adults should be provided an element of privacy while they are using the Internet.

> *Schools*: Because the majority of children in K–12 schools are underage, parents are required to co-sign the child's AUP. State Boards of Education either require or strongly encourage schools to adopt acceptable use policies and have them signed each year as an annual contract among the child, parent, and school.

AUP is used as a way to educate children and their families about the Internet and expected behaviors. While teachers and school librarians encourage children to practice the First Amendment, they also are obligated to protect children while they are in school from harm.

Academic Libraries: College and university students are not underage and therefore the Children's Internet Protection Act does not apply and computers do not legally have to be filtered to block content. Academic libraries strive to offer free and unfiltered Internet to enhance learning, research, and teaching. Students and faculty should have access to controversial information and all rights protected by the First Amendment. AUPs should guarantee their freedom of information when using academic computers or Wi-Fi.

In table 10.3 there are examples of AUPs by library type to help further understand how policies guide library Internet and technology services.

Regulations, Rules, Procedures, and Guidelines

Regulations, rules, procedures, and guidelines tell library staff how to respond to patrons' use of technology. The library staff handbook should include such important "how to" information. Procedures and guidelines are often written for staff who may have to make decisions or take actions about patron Internet use without the presence of a supervisor. These documents are written not only for staff information but also to ensure that patrons are treated fairly and equally. Legally it is important for libraries to have these documents approved by either the director or the board—and often both—to ensure that there is no misunderstanding about how patrons are treated. In meetings and other ways library staff are encouraged to learn the nuances of procedures and guidelines so that they can act appropriately and quickly in difficult situations. The state Library of Michigan[3] has procedures on what patrons must do to use the Internet embedded in its Internet Acceptable Use Policy. Notice the level of detail in the textbox.

My own experience is that guidelines and procedures are very helpful to communicate information and expectations to hundreds of computer users each day. The more they were written specifically and to the point, the better the procedures and guidelines were adhered to by staff and students. Remove any ambiguity when writing. Before posting any guidelines ask several people to read them "blind" so that, with their feedback, you can clarify anything that could be misunderstood.

Table 10.3. Examples of Acceptable Use Policies by Library Type

Public	Buffalo and Erie County	http://www.buffalolib.org/content/policies/internet-safety-and-acceptable-use-policy
School	Virginia Department of Education	http://www.doe.virginia.gov/support/safety_crisis_management/internet_safety/acceptable_use_policy.shtml
Academic	Brown University	http://www.brown.edu/information-technology/computing-policies/acceptable-use-policy

EXAMPLE FROM THE LIBRARY OF MICHIGAN INTERNET USE PROCEDURES

1. All Internet users at the Library of Michigan must sign up for a work station.
2. The Library of Michigan is a public building. Library users are expected to maintain a professional, business-like atmosphere conducive to research and study.
3. Before their first session on the library's Internet work station, users must read both the Internet Use Guidelines and Internet Use Procedures statements of the Library of Michigan.
4. Patrons must present a picture ID with birth date and/or library card before they can use the Internet.
5. Patrons under eighteen years of age will be assigned to a filtered Internet workstation.
6. The Library of Michigan's Internet workstations are available to users in sixty-minute time blocks on a sign-up basis. Patrons may sign up for a maximum of two sixty-minute sessions per day. If a patron has used a computer for 120 minutes or more in one day, that patron will not be permitted additional sign-ups.

CONFIDENTIALITY

Patrons expect their library dealings to be private and their First Amendment Freedom of Speech rights to be upheld. Patrons have both legal and personal expectations that what they read and view will not be shared with others. The ALA Library Bill of Rights,[4] in part, states, "Libraries should cooperate with all persons and groups concerned with resisting abridgment of free expression and free access to ideas." Further, the ALA Code of Ethics [5] states confidentiality extends to "information sought or received and resources consulted, borrowed, acquired or transmitted." These library resources could be a patron's database search records, circulation records, and interlibrary loan records, information about materials downloaded, or computer and Internet use. Created in response to potential terrorism, The Patriot Act requires library staff, if asked, to turn over to government officials patrons' records. Librarians across the country have made decisions not to archive circulation or other types of patron search records in order to maintain individuals' rights to privacy about what they read and view.

Databases and computer files are backed up and archived as a matter of standard IT practice. Integrated library systems can be programmed to store circulation data indefinitely. The ALA Code of Ethics[6] advises librarians to uphold the principles of intellectual freedom. In order to do this most libraries purposefully dismantle the archive features of library systems to keep confidential what one checks out of a library.

There are other practical things LSS can do to help educate and support patrons' confidentiality using technology at the library. Public computers can be arranged in a way that patrons have some measure of privacy from main floor traffic. Signage can be posted to remind people to be discrete with their personal passwords. Do

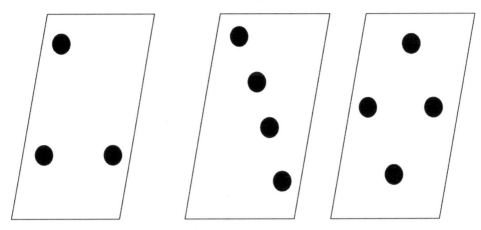

Figure 10.1. Password Patterns to Avoid

not share them with others and be careful to enter them when they are not being watched.

A word about passwords: LSS may want to share with patrons not to use personal passwords to secure phones and tablets that are in a sequence as 1, 2, 3, 4 or in a pattern such as 1, 3, 7, 9 (see figure 10.1). Patterns that form shapes such as a straight or diagonal line, a square, or a cross are easy for someone to recognize and recall.

LSS should scan for library computers not in use to be sure that the last person did not leave an account open. A person who worked with me repeatedly kept her personal Amazon account logged in on a staff computer. With her account open, anyone could place an order as her credit card is on file with Amazon. She was too trusting to protect her account. The LSS who watches for open accounts like this does a great favor for patrons who may be leaving themselves vulnerable.

INTEGRITY AND SECURITY OF DATA

The American Library Association urges librarians to protect patrons' privacy. One way to do this is for libraries to keep limited data on patrons on file and discard information that is unnecessary or outdated. Because LSS most likely collect patrons' data at the circulation desk, work in accounting or billing, or help patrons with Internet searches, they have a responsibility to keep patrons' personal information private, confidential, and secure. Table 10.4 shows the important data topics ALA[7] recommends libraries protect, and my suggestions on how LSS can responsibly and professionally safeguard patron data when using library technology.

Data integrity and security occurs when all library staff are trained and committed to upholding patrons' privacy and confidentiality. LSS collect personal patron data for multiple purposes. When there is no need to retain personal data, it should be purged. Never should patron data be made accessible to outside sources or used in any other way than for the library business it was intended for when it was collected.

Table 10.4. How LSS Safeguard Data

Topic	ALA Recommendation*	LSS Safeguard Data
Data Integrity	Librarians should protect personally identifiable information (PII) and destroy via shredder confidential or privacy protected records from authorized access.	LSS are highly professional in their handling of patrons' data and uphold confidentiality of all library records, including patrons' circulation.
Shared Data	Consortia or multi-branch libraries need to work together to ensure patron records remain accurate and confidential.	LSS avoid choosing passwords or PINs when making patron records that reveal a user's identity, including social security numbers.
Security	Take both managerial and technical measures to protect against loss and the unauthorized access, destruction, use, or disclosure of data. This should include the guarantee of a secure wireless network for patrons to use.	LSS report any suspicious patron or staff activity or corruption of files on any of the library computer systems or servers. If you are involved with backing up data systems, do so responsibly and consistently. Backup your own library work.
Administrative Measures	Implement internal organizational measures that limit access to data while ensuring that individuals with access do not utilize the data for unauthorized purposes.	Never seek to use another's password or authorization to access data outside of your own set of permissions. If you know this is occurring among staff, report it immediately to supervisor.
Electronic Tracking	Neither local nor external electronic systems used by the library should collect PII through logging or tracking e-mail, chat room use, web browsing, cookies, middleware, or other technology usage.	LSS protect patrons' privacy by checking to see that library computers do not store web search history, cookies, or cached files. Set computer hard drives to delete this information.
Data Retention	It is the responsibility of library staff to destroy information in confidential or privacy-protected records in order to safeguard data from unauthorized disclosure.	LSS, with the oversight of the supervisor, purge obsolete patron circulation and use records on a regular basis. If operating surveillance cameras, be sure there is a library policy for protecting confidentiality and treat the tapes with integrity like other library records.

* Used with permission from the American Library Association, 2015.

Maintaining the integrity and security of data is both a legal and ethical responsibility of LSS.

COPYRIGHT LAW

In this last section of the chapter we begin with an overview of copyright law and its basic protections. We will discuss digital copyright and how patrons and staff may legally use digital resources in libraries.

Brief History of US Copyright

The Constitution gives Congress the power to establish a system of copyright protection for authors and their works in the United States. Congress enacted the first federal copyright law in May 1790, and the first work was registered within two weeks. The Copyright Act of 1790 granted American authors the right to print, reprint, or publish their work for a period of fourteen years and to renew for another fourteen. In 1870, copyright functions were centralized in the Library of Congress where they remain today. A major revision of the US Copyright Act was completed in 1909, which broadened the scope of protected categories to include all works of authorship, and it extended the term of protection to twenty-eight years with a possible renewal for another twenty-eight.

A second major revision of the law occurred in 1976, because technology now allowed for new ways works might be copied. US copyright law also needed to be aligned with international copyright law, practices, and policies. The 1976 act preempted all previous copyright law. For the first time the fair use for educational purposes was allowed. Important to library staff, Section 108 was established which allows library photocopying without permission for purposes of scholarship, preservation, and interlibrary loan.[8] Again in 1998, the law was revisited because of rapid advances in technology resulting in the passing of the Digital Millennium Copyright Act.

Purpose of US Copyright[9]

Copyright is law that gives the creator of a work the right to control how the work is used. The intent of copyright is to give an author an economic incentive to create and share his or her ideas with others. Copyright was seen by our forebears as a way to advance the knowledge of citizens and thus give the United States the potential to be a world leader. Only items that are

- tangible or fixed,
- original, and
- minimally creative can be copyrighted.

For example, paper, a computer disk, an audio or a videotape are all legitimate forms of fixation. Original means it precedes all others in time and that it is not derived from something else, such as an original computer program or even e-mail. Creativity need only be slight for the work to be eligible for protection. As a general rule, for works created after January 1, 1978, copyright protection lasts for the life of the author plus an additional seventy years. Once copyright has expired, copying is allowed for generations that follow.

Copyright protects:

- The right to limit copies of the work.
- The right to sell or otherwise distribute copies of the work for profit or gain.
- The right to control who performs the protected work (such as a stage play or painting) in public.

COPYRIGHT SECTIONS OF SPECIAL INTEREST TO LIBRARIES

- US Copyright Law, Sec. 107: Fair Use. Copyrighted material may be used for "criticism, comment, news reporting, teaching, scholarship, or research" without the user paying the producer or asking for permission.
- US Copyright Law, Sec. 108: Copying by Libraries and Archives. Libraries and archives may reproduce and distribute one copy of a work under certain circumstances such as journal articles, book chapters, etc. This section also allows libraries to make copies for preservation purposes.[a]
- Section 109: The First Sale Doctrine. The purchaser of a copyrighted work (library) has the right to resell, rent, lease, or lend the work without paying or asking permission of the copyright holder.

a. *"Section 108: Photocopying by Libraries and Archives," American Library Association: DMCA, last modified 2015, accessed March 12, 2015, http://www.ala.org/advocacy/copyright/dmca/section108.*

It is up to the person who holds the copyright to make sure no one is infringing on their legal right. In some instances the author chooses to give up or sell his or her copyright, such as the case of the Beatles who sold many of the copyrights to their music to Michael Jackson.

Libraries are unique in their practice of lending items to the public. Because the US Copyright Act provides special sections for our services, it is permissible for libraries to lend copyrighted items unlimited times without giving compensation to authors. Libraries are also centers for research. Patrons use resources to enhance their learning. The textbox shows three important sections of US Copyright law that govern how libraries lend materials and promote learning.

The items that are not under US Copyright are considered to be in the public domain. The public domain is *everyone*. A work is in the public domain if it is no longer under copyright protection or if it fails to meet the requirements of copyright.

Examples of what fails to meet the requirements of copyright:

- works, facts, and ideas in the public domain;
- words, names, slogans, or other short phrases. However, slogans, for example, can be protected by trademark law;
- blank forms; and
- government works, which include judicial opinions, public ordinances, administrative rulings, and works created by federal government employees as part of their official responsibility.

DIGITAL MILLENNIUM COPYRIGHT ACT

In 1998, the Digital Millennium Copyright Act (DMCA) was passed by Congress and was incorporated into Title 17 of the US Copyright Act to provide **digital**

copyright protection. Its purpose was to update copyright law to address new situations presented by new technologies and to conform to the policies of the World Intellectual Property Organization.[10] Under the DMCA one cannot copy or sell copyrighted digital content such as computer apps, software, music, e-books, or digital media without the author's permission.

The Digital Millennium Copyright Act, in part

- prevents the circumvention of technological protection measures;
- sets limitations on copyright infringement liability for online service providers;
- expands an existing exemption for making copies of computer programs; and
- provides a significant updating of the rules and procedures regarding archival preservation.[11]

Million Book Project

In January 2007, my family visited HangZhou University in China on a Saturday afternoon during the semester break, making the campus unusually empty. In the library there was a sign announcing the Million Book Project. In a very large open room on the seventh floor were hundreds of people, each at a computer and scanner, as far as the eye could see. They were scanning page-by-page stacks of hard cover books. It was an incredible activity to observe!

Begun as a partnership by academic libraries in the United States, India, and China, the goal was to digitize over one million books that would be the basis of a global online academic library. Carnegie Mellon Libraries was one of the participants.[12] While the goal was admirable, the Million Book Project was halted in the United States due to issues surrounding digital copyright. The scanned pages still exist and may be in use in countries that do not adhere to US copyright laws.

Copyright law differs from country to country. There is no global law. The Million Book Project is an example of the need for global cooperation to adhere to and enforce copyright with world partners. The ease of digitization has created the potential for breaching copyright law in ways that were never possible twenty or thirty years ago.

Fair Use

Why should LSS know about the DMCA? Much of the work that we do in libraries today is dependent upon using digital resources and computers. It is important for us to know when and how Sections 107, 108, and 109 support copying and use of digital materials by library staff and patrons.

US Copyright Law, Sec. 107: Fair use is about using a copyright work for nonprofit or educational purposes. Libraries may fall into this definition depending upon the purpose of use. If the copyrighted work is out of print, it is more likely to be considered fair use. If the work is highly artistic, it may not be fair to use it without the author's permission. Considerations for fair use are brevity and spontaneity. The more you use of the work, the less likely it is considered fair. A good rule of thumb is not to exceed 10 percent of the work without gaining the author's permission. That would be 10 percent of an e-book, computer file, or document. Another guideline is not to use more than thirty seconds of a song or film without authorization.

Spontaneity has to do with the "teaching moment." The instructor may decide the work is important for class and does not have time to contact the author. The instructor may use it in its entirety once, but he or she cannot continue to use the work without copyright permission for future classes. The same copyright protections exist for the author of a work regardless of whether the work is in a database or on the Internet. The Internet is not the public domain. If you make a copy from an online source for your personal use, it is likely to be seen as fair use. However, do not post someone else's work on your website without permission.

Copying and Archiving by Libraries

US Copyright Law, Sec. 108: Library professionals may make a single copy of a journal article or book chapter at the request of a patron or by another library. Libraries may make up to three copies in digital format for preservation and archival purposes not to be used outside of the library. When a replacement cannot be had for a reasonable cost, libraries can make up to three digital copies to replace damaged or deteriorating media. At no times is the library to circulate multiple copies when they only purchased one. Section 108 ensures libraries can both circulate and maintain collections of digital resources. This section also encourages libraries to create archives of primary source and other materials in digital format for future research and use.

The First Sale Doctrine

US Copyright Law, Section 109: The purchaser of a copyrighted work (library) has the right to resell, rent, lease, or lend the work without paying or asking permission of the copyright holder. Second 109 is a "hot topic" with regard to publishers and e-books. Publishers have legitimate concern that libraries purchase an e-book once and circulate it indefinitely, thus limiting their potential profit of the book. Some publishers have priced e-books for libraries at a much higher rate than for individuals. Others have limited the amount of circulations by encrypting e-book code so that the e-book can only be shared for a limited number of times. Libraries cannot afford to pay extraordinary high prices to publishers and authors for e-book titles. Libraries and publishers are working together towards respectful understandings and solutions to this problem of first sale of digital e-books.

Table 10.5 shows potential copyright situations that may occur in libraries and the appropriate response LSS should take.

CHAPTER SUMMARY

As we saw in this chapter, there is much for LSS to know and be able to do to ensure the integrity of data and the confidentiality of user activities. LSS should also know concepts and issues concerning the appropriate use of technology, including copyright law for digital resources and technology. LSS can support the laws and policies that govern staff and patron use of technology when they are trained to use guidelines, procedures, rules, and regulations that specify how library staff should

Table 10.5.   Potential Digital Copyright Situation with Appropriate LSS Response

Potential Digital Copyright Situation	Appropriate LSS Response
The patron is using library equipment to scan and copy an entire popular print book to PDF so he can read it online and not check it out.	LSS should intercede and tell the patron this is not allowed under US copyright, Sec. 109, because the library can only circulate the paper copy it has purchased. Report activity to supervisor.
The library purchases only one copy of a popular children's software program and installs it on multiple computers in the children's room.	LSS should intercede and advise children's librarian that under Sec. 108 libraries can only make one copy for theft or archival purposes. They cannot make multiple copies to get around multiple purchases.
Staff copy and post poetry of a local author on the library website for poetry month without permission of author.	LSS should intercede and advise webmaster or supervisor that poetry is fixed, original, and creative work. Author needs to give permission to have work posted online.
Staff scan all of the annual town reports as a digital collection.	LSS can help with this! Town reports are made by government employees as part of their work and are not subject to US Copyright law. If there are graphics or artwork in the reports, be sure it is copyright free.

act when confronted with situations. LSS can be supportive by suggesting procedures be updated and that training and education be available to all staff so that they are prepared to deal with situations fairly and consistently within the accepted library policies and copyright law.

DISCUSSION QUESTIONS AND ACTIVITIES

Discussion Questions

1. Why is it important for libraries to have acceptable use policies? Whom do the policies protect?
2. Discuss three ways LSS can support the integrity of data in their workplace.
3. Why was it necessary for the Digital Millennium Copyright Act to be written when there were already copyright laws in place?
4. The LSS observes a patron burning a copy of a DVD from the library's new acquisitions on his personal device. What should the LSS do?
5. Staff plan to show a current and popular movie on a Friday night to draw teens to the library. What must occur to be within copyright law?

Activity

Compare Acceptable Use Policies
This activity is to make us aware that AUPs vary from library to library. Some policies are very specific and detailed, others are not.

Your task is to acquire three AUPs from the same type of library and analyze them for similarities and differences. Select the one that you think is the most thorough yet patron-friendly.

1. Select one type of library—public, school, or academic.
2. Acquire online or in person the AUP from three libraries of the type you selected, that is, from three schools, three public libraries, or three academic libraries.
3. Compare each policy. Highlight in yellow similarities. Circle in red differences.
4. Decide which policy you think is the best based on its thoroughness, patron-friendliness, readability, presentation, or other factors.

If you work in a library, compare your library AUP to the policy you selected as the best. You may be in a position to recommend changes to your workplace AUP.

NOTES

1. OCLC, "Children's Internet Protection Act—Summary." WebJunction: The Learning Place for Libraries, last modified 2014, accessed December 11, 2014, https://webjunction. org/documents/webjunction/Children_039_s_Internet_Protection_Act_045_Summary.html.

2. American Library Association, "Internet Use Policies," Libraries and the Internet Toolkit, last modified 2014, accessed December 11, 2014, http://www.ala.org/advocacy/intfree dom/iftoolkits/litoolkit/internetusepolicies.

3. Library of Michigan, "Internet Use Guidelines & Procedures," Library of Michigan Guidelines, last modified 2014, accessed December 12, 2013, http://www.michigan.gov/ libraryofmichigan/0,2351,7-160-19270_28981-52160--,00.html.

4. "Library Bill of Rights" [Intellectual Freedom], American Library Association, last modified 2014, accessed December 11, 2014, http://www.ala.org/advocacy/intfreedom/ librarybill.

5. American Library Association, "Code of Ethics of the American Library Association," Code of Ethics of the American Library Association, last modified 2014, accessed December 11, 2014, http://www.ala.org/advocacy/proethics/codeofethics/codeethics.

6. "Code of Ethics of the American Library Association," Code of Ethics of the American Library Association, last modified 2014, accessed December 11, 2014, http://www.ala.org/ advocacy/proethics/codeofethics/codeethics.

7. American Library Association, "Integrity of Data and Security." Privacy Toolkit, last modified 2014, accessed December 12, 2014, http://www.ala.org/advocacy/privacyconfide ntiality/toolkitsprivacy/Developing-or-Revising-a-Library-PrivacyPolicy#dataintegritysecurity.

8. Association of Research Libraries, "Copyright Timeline: A History of Copyright in the United States," Copyright and IP, last modified 2014, accessed December 13, 2014, http:// www.arl.org/focus-areas/copyright-ip/ 2486-copyright-timeline#.VI2gFcmGtkh.

9. Library of Congress, "United States Copyright Office," US Copyright Office, last modified 2014, accessed December 14, 2014, http://www.copyright.gov/.

10. American Library Association, "DMCA: The Digital Millennium Copyright Act." Copyright, last modified 2014, accessed December 13, 2014, http://0-www.ala.org.librarycatalogs .nnu.edu/advocacy/copyright/dmca.

11. Ibid.

12. Carnegie Mellon Libraries, "Frequently Asked Questions about the Million Book Project." Frequently Asked Questions about the Million Book Project, last modified 2007,

accessed December 14, 2014, https://libwebspace.library.cmu.edu/libraries-and-collections/MBP_FAQ.html#participants.

REFERENCES, SUGGESTED READINGS, AND WEBSITES

American Library Association. "Code of Ethics of the American Library Association." Code of Ethics of the American Library Association. Last modified 2014. Accessed December 11, 2014. http://www.ala.org/advocacy/proethics/codeofethics/codeethics.
———. "DMCA: The Digital Millennium Copyright Act." Copyright. Last modified 2014. Accessed December 13, 2014. http://0-www.ala.org.librarycatalogs.nnu.edu/advocacy/copyright/dmca.
———. "Integrity of Data and Security." Privacy Toolkit. Last modified 2014. Accessed December 12, 2014. http://www.ala.org/advocacy/privacyconfidentiality/toolkitsprivacy/Developing-or-Revising-a-Library-Privacy-Policy#dataintegritysecurity.
———. "Section 108 Photocopying by Libraries and Archives." American Library Association: DMCA. Last modified 2015. Accessed March 12, 2015. http://www.ala.org/advocacy/copyright/dmca/section108.
———. "Internet Use Policies." Libraries and the Internet Toolkit. Last modified 2014. Accessed December 11, 2014. http://www.ala.org/advocacy/intfreedom/iftoolkits/litoolkit/internetusepolicies.
Association of Research Libraries. "Copyright Timeline: A History of Copyright in the United States." Copyright and IP. Last modified 2014. Accessed December 13, 2014. http://www.arl.org/focus-areas/copyright-ip/2486-copyright-timeline#.VI2gFcmGtkh.
Carnegie Mellon Libraries. "Frequently Asked Questions about the Million Book Project." Frequently Asked Questions about the Million Book Project. Last modified 2007. Accessed December 14, 2014. https://libwebspace.library.cmu.edu/libraries-and-collections/MBP_FAQ.html#participants.
"Digital Millennium Copyright Act - Exploring Fair Use Rights." Video file. YouTube. https://www.youtube.com/watch?v=bMugDVv99K0.
"Library Bill of Rights" [Intellectual Freedom]. American Library Association. Last modified 2014. Accessed December 11, 2014. http://www.ala.org/advocacy/intfreedom/librarybill.
Library of Congress. "United States Copyright Office." US Copyright Office. Last modified 2014. Accessed December 14, 2014. http://www.copyright.gov/.
Library of Michigan. "Internet Use Guidelines & Procedures." Library of Michigan Guidelines. Last modified 2014. Accessed December 12, 2013. http://www.michigan.gov/libraryofmichigan/0,2351,7-160-19270_28981-52160--,00.html.
OCLC. "Children's Internet Protection Act—Summary." WebJunction: the Learning Place for Libraries. Last modified 2014. Accessed December 11, 2014. https://webjunction.org/documents/webjunction/Children_039_s_Internet_Protection_Act_045_Summary.html.
State of Wisconsin. "Chapter 43: Wisconsin Legislative Documents." Last modified September 3, 2014. Accessed December 11, 2014. http://docs.legis.wisconsin.gov/statutes/statutes/43.pdf.

CHAPTER 11

Hardware, Software, and Network Infrastructure

LSS are able to assist and train users to operate public equipment, connect to the Internet, use library software applications, and access library services from remote locations. (ALA-LSSC Technology Competency #6)

LSS perform basic troubleshooting of technical problems and resolve or refer those problems as appropriate. (ALA-LSSC Technology Competency #8)

LSS access and use basic assistive technologies, where appropriate, to ensure that all users have equitable access to technology. (ALA-LSSC Technology Competency #9)

Topics Covered in This Chapter:

- Hardware
  - Lease vs. Purchase
  - Evaluation
  - Troubleshooting
- Applications Software
  - Purchase and Installation
  - Operating Systems
  - Internet Browsers
  - Releases and Updates of Software
  - The Cloud: Back-up and Storage
  - Assistive or Adaptive Technologies
- Network Infrastructure
  - Internet Service Provider (ISP)
  - Firewall and Filters

- Broadband Connectivity
  - Wireless
- Technology Professional Learning

Key Terms:

Application Software: Programs installed on computers that are designed for staff and patrons to perform specific tasks or functions.

Information and Communications Technology (ICT): ICT is an acronym used to identify the many technologies for accessing information and communicating with others. ICT used in libraries are the online catalog, subscription databases, special collections, digital media, sound recordings, and digital images. Library staff use ICT to communicate information about programs, materials, and events to patrons and each other via e-mail, the library website, and social media.

Network Infrastructure: The equipment, wiring, software, and other resources needed to move data to and from outside providers of services like the Internet or subscription databases to the patron user. Networks and equipment vary in size according to the location, size, and needs of the library. Library staff who are familiar with key component equipment can communicate with and support ICT staff for quick resolution of problems.

Refurbished Computers: These are used computers that have key component parts such as hard drives wiped clean or replaced. Faster memory and processors may be substituted, and new and updated operating systems or software added. Libraries can acquire these computers for normally half the cost for their online catalog stations or other functions that do not require high end computing.

Troubleshooting: This term describes being able to quickly diagnose and solve a technology problem. Many problems arise with library technology because of the heavy use many patrons give the equipment each day.

This chapter offers practical information for library support staff (LSS) about computer hardware, software applications, and network infrastructure used in libraries. Technology is infused in all aspects of library work, and LSS need to be competent in its use. Responsibility for technology may vary depending upon the size, type, and location of the library. The smaller the library, the more hands-on the staff are. Many public, school, and private libraries do not have municipal **ICT** support. The library staff may have full responsibility for planning, implementing, and managing technology. In most medium size libraries staff share responsibility with others but are often on the front line of setting up systems, troubleshooting problems, and administering day-to-day functions. Large academic and public libraries will likely have ICT staff or outsourced contracts for full support.

No matter the size or type of library, it is important for staff to be able to plan and implement ways technology can improve patron services. The more competent

LSS are with technology, the more confident and successful they will be in helping patrons.

HARDWARE

According to another Pew Research Center study, *Library Services in the Digital Age,*[1] 77 percent of Americans ages sixteen and older say free access to computers and the Internet is a "very important" service of libraries and another 18 percent say it is "somewhat important." It also reported that one in four people who visit libraries either use a library computer or connect to its Wi-Fi. In addition, 35 percent of those asked said they would "very likely" use a library service that gave them access to technology "petting zoos" (http://galibtech.org/?page_id=317) to try out new devices. Survey data such as this indicates how important it is for libraries to provide robust computer services.

LSS work to solve problems for a variety of equipment or devices. These could be any model or age of laptops, tablets, e-readers, mobile devices, cameras, audio, and media equipment that have Internet connectivity. Most libraries have many types and models of public access computers acquired over time through donations, grants, group purchasing, or reallocations from other departments or agencies. A mix of computers makes maintenance challenging because of the differences that can be in computer processors, memory, operating systems, and overall layout. Additionally, LSS are asked to help solve issues with using library applications with patron-owned devices.

Lease vs. Purchase

A way for libraries to have reliable, up-to-date computers is to enter into an arrangement to lease computers for a specific period of time, typically between three and five years. In a standard lease one-fifth of computers will be replaced every year. The library will not have any computers older than five years, and over time leases cost less than to purchase all of the computers new.[2]

There are several advantages to leasing vs. purchasing computers. When a library leases computers, responsibility is shifted away from the library. Benefits of leasing are

- a single point of contact for installation and support;
- annual or monthly payments for technology, rather than large or emergency expenditures;
- little or no maintenance costs;
- a reliable computer replacement plan; and
- removal and disposal of old equipment.[3]

Smaller libraries may consider leasing through a consortium whereby a group of libraries act as a single agent for the discount. Look for consortium discounts from your state and/or regional library and school organizations.

While there are advantages to leasing, many libraries decide to purchase computers. TechSoup for Libraries[4] provides practical guidance for library staff to help with their decision to purchase or lease computers. How will the computers be used? If for video editing, the library will need to allocate funds for high end, more expensive machines. If the plan is for the computer to be primarily an online catalog station, the library may consider purchasing a less expensive or even **refurbished computer**. Refurbished computers typically cost half the amount of a new computer[5] and come with a warranty.

Evaluation

Is the library providing the right technology? The purchase of technology is a large investment which may require special bonding or funding outside of the regular budget. Consider before acquiring technology the users and the equipment.

The users are the patrons and library staff. What are the needs of each group? How will they be using the technology? Determine the needs of the users by observation and surveys. Discuss your observations of how patrons and staff use computers with supervisors. Is the quantity of computers and other devices sufficient in numbers, or do patrons get discouraged because they have to wait? Do staff share computers

Table 11.1. Library Technology Evaluation Checklist

Equipment	Measure	Quantity*	Condition**	Meets Needs
Wi-Fi Network	Available 24/7 from any library space. Plans in place to improve speed as required with new uses.			
Desktop Computers	Look at ALA Factsheet #26 for current guidelines.[a] The national average is 4.5 public access computers for every five thousand people in library legal service areas.			
Laptops or Tablets	These devices provide for flexibility. Have procedures in place that ensure last users' privacy of information and searching.			
Software	Productivity, research, and information applications.			
E-readers	Create a lending library of devices so that patrons have access to the collection of e-books.			
Printers	High end and reliable printers managed with minimal expense to patrons. Scanning ability for PDF files. Consider 3-D printing for makerspaces.			
Scanners, editing, multimedia, equipment	Provide a variety of equipment that patrons can use for their own production, research, and creativity.			

* 1 = insufficient, 5 = meets goal

**1 = poor, 5 = excellent

a. "ALA Library Fact Sheet 26," Internet Access and Digital Holdings in Libraries, last modified 2015, accessed April 28, 2015, http://www.ala.org/tools/libfactsheets/alalibraryfactsheet26.

in ways that make their work less efficient? Are patrons using their own mobile devices and need better Wi-Fi connectivity? There has been a shift that will continue to grow toward patrons using mobile devices.[6] Do library computers have software programs patrons seek? Consider a checklist similar to the one in table 11.1 to evaluate your library's technology.

Troubleshooting

LSS find solutions to technical problems when they approach a problem with common sense and take logical steps.

TROUBLESHOOTING COMMON COMPUTER PROBLEMS

1. *Keep your cool.* The patron has often tried multiple solutions and is upset. Let the patron know that you are there to help and that if it cannot be solved quickly, you will call in additional supports. Do not get flustered!
2. *Check the power supply.* Yes, as simple as it sounds, so often the problem is at the plug end. Make sure all connections are snug and that power sources are on.
3. *Is the Internet site available on other computers?* If the Internet is working but a patron cannot upload a particular site, see if the site is available on other library computers. If so, the settings on the particular library computer or the patron's device may be filtering out the website.
4. *Reboot!* This is the simple act of powering down the computer or other pieces of equipment that is connected to it such as the printer or router. Follow the "ten second rule": hold your finder on the power switch for ten seconds to turn it off, then count to ten, and then turn the power switch back on. This gives the computer enough time to clear in its memory conflicting data that may be causing the computer to hang up.
5. *Is there an incompatibility problem?* Look for incompatibility issues with platforms and software. If the patron's device is old it may not accept your current update of Office. Older Apple products may not work with PC software.
6. *Use RTF and PDF.* Encourage patrons to save work in rich text format (RTF) or PDF. These two formats are universal among computer platforms and allow users to open files no matter what the device as the software application (Word, etc.) is not embedded in a document that is saved in RTF or PDF.
7. *Check printer driver.* If printing is a problem, the patron's device may not have the appropriate printer driver for the library printer. A printer driver is software that is downloaded from the printer manufacturer site that lets your computer communicate (send documents) to the printer.
8. *Carry a flash drive.* A quick solution to give immediate help to a patron is to copy his file to your "work" flash drive and print the document for him. Send the file in an e-mail to the patron. Later focus on the hardware issue.

While these ideas do not solve all problems, they certainly offer support for many of them and give the LSS an approach or framework to helping a patron with a technology issue.

APPLICATIONS SOFTWARE

LSS are knowledgeable and work with many kinds of software programs. Examples of common applications software that are installed or bookmarked on library computers are shown in table 11.2.

Purchase and Installation

It is not unusual for the desktop of a library computer to have applications software acquired from multiple places. This means library or ICT staff have to install, monitor, and/or manage many applications software. There are many ways libraries acquire software. Some applications, such as the browser and word processing programs, may be included with the purchase or lease of computers. Software can also be purchased and licensed directly from individual companies. Other applications may be free or "open sourced" with no cost. Libraries can contract to have outside companies install and manage their software. Providers host applications on their servers that library patrons access through the web. Libraries have proprietary ports or connections with the provider who manages updates, new releases, usage, and other aspects of software. A free and very successful application service is Google apps which provide any person with a Gmail account access to Google docs, a spreadsheet, and presentation software. Microsoft Windows Live provides holders of Microsoft Office licenses remote access to a version of their software.[7] Most common is for libraries to purchase software licenses that allow simultaneous or unlimited use of programs on library devices.

Licensed software may be installed on one computer at a time on individual library computers. This process can be very time consuming. One way to quickly install new programs is to network the software from a server to individual computers via the local area network. A second way to expedite installation is to clone or image all computers to be identical copies of a master computer that has all updated software. There are many products to perform the task of copying the exact software applications or "image" of one drive onto another for a duplicate copy of the original drive.[8]

Table 11.2.   Examples of Library Applications Software

The Internet	ILS—online catalog, patron	Library website
Reader's Advisory programs	circulation account	Microsoft Office
Digital editing sound and media applications	E-book selection and downloading software	Educational and other programs geared for children and teens
	Scanning and printing applications	

Operating Systems

The operating system (OS) initiates the opening screens of the computer in an organized and sequential way so that programs either run as scheduled or can be opened by the operator. OSs are platform specific depending upon the manufacturer or type of computer. The majority of PCs use versions of Microsoft Windows as their OS. The Apple OS is called OSX and works only on Apple computers and devices. The OS comes with the computer when you purchase or lease it. If you purchase a refurbished computer, you may also have to purchase an OS for it. Windows and Apple regularly update operating systems to perform advanced functions. OSs are also updated to provide greater ease of use of the computer.

Libraries with multiple platforms and types of computers have multiple operating systems. For example, a library that has not updated its computers' OS may be using two or more versions of Windows. Patrons' laptops and other devices may have different versions of OSs. Needless to say, it is a challenge, but a necessary one, for LSS to be knowledgeable and able to use many different types of operating systems.

Internet Browsers

A browser is the application software that allows us to access the Internet. We have some choice about our browsers. If you purchase or lease a computer with Windows OS, you most likely will have the Microsoft browser, Internet Explorer (IE), also installed on your computer. Apple computers come with their own browser called Safari. IE and Safari are updated somewhat regularly and new versions can be downloaded quickly by the user.

There are many other browsers that we can select from including the popular Mozilla Firefox, Google Chrome, and Opera. Browsers are really a matter of personal choice or preference, but most libraries use Internet Explorer or Firefox for their PCs and, of course, Safari, for their Apple computers.

Releases and Updates of Software

Normal operations of the library can be affected by updates and releases of software, particularly when they occur to the integrated library system (ILS). An update may be several small changes or refinements to existing software and are installed fairly quickly or overnight. They may also be installed automatically without impacting the library staff or patrons.

A release is a significant revision of existing software and typically occurs every few years. Sometimes the installation of a software release takes hours and cannot be accomplished while users are on the system. Releases often result in training for staff especially when they involve changes in circulation or cataloging software.

The Cloud: Back-up and Storage

Clouds store data, from computers to large servers, which is transferred over the Internet. As users we trust that our data is secure and private. The image of a cloud represents the Internet and simplifies the complexity of all of the hardware, networking, and management that takes place. Any user with an Internet connection and appropriate permissions can negotiate access to the cloud and the services it provides.[9] Clouds today are a routine way of storing and backing up data.

Once a foreign or even an uncomfortable idea, today having an outside company store our communications and data on remote servers around the world is a routine way of doing business. We have become familiar and comfortable with the solution of cloud computing for our mobile phones, e-readers, and computers because the large data we use far exceeds the storage capacity of our handheld and other digital devices. We also do not want to be limited to accessing our data on one computer. We are a mobile society that wants to have our data wherever we may be.

The cloud can be a real asset for storing digital resources. The capacity for storage and retrieval of hundreds—if not thousands—of images, sound, and video would be quickly maximized by library servers. Cloud computing allows libraries and their patrons storage and retrieval to large digital collections. The cloud offers a safety net for backing up library data from fire, theft, and other disasters that would cripple library operations if the library relied only on servers to store their data in only one location or building.

LIBRARIES USE CLOUDS FOR ACCESS AND STORAGE

Here are examples of how libraries are using cloud computing:[a]

1. BiblioCommons: Public libraries upload contents of their online catalogs and special collections. Libraries who are also in BiblioCommons exchange their literary expertise and opinions on the books, music, and movies.
2. The Amazon Kindle Cloud Reader is a web app that allows you to read Kindle Books on any compatible web browser (Mozilla Firefox, Google Chrome, and Safari) from the Amazon cloud.
3. OCLC's World Share Management Services offers member libraries the ability to share data and work from its cloud in ways that save money and time, and streamline labor.
4. EBSCO Discovery Services (EDS) and OCLC have an agreement to have patrons of libraries who subscribe to both systems find and download resources from their shared cloud by a simple search interface.
5. ExLibri's Primo Central Index offers patrons a single search box for searching all of a library's collections and, at the same time, global resources from their index.

[a.] Edward Corrado and Heather Moulaison, "*The Library Cloud*," *Library Journal* 137, no. 4 (March 1, 2012), accessed February 17, 2015, http://search.ebscohost.com/login.aspx?direct=true&db=aph&AN=71940731&site=ehost-live&scope=site.

While there are growing benefits to using cloud computing, there are also concerns for libraries about using cloud computing around privacy and ownership of data. Our profession upholds patrons' rights to privacy, not only for their reading preferences but their personal data. When libraries use cloud computing for circulation data, we must be very careful that the patrons' privacy is protected. We also need to be sure that the companies we deal with will not sell or forward our data to others. Before libraries use cloud computing for circulation, they need to know more about where the servers are located, if there is encryption, and who manages and protects their data.

If a library is not using a cloud, LSS may have a role in backing up and storing library data. Small public or school libraries that run their own automation systems are responsible for making copies of their data, such as library circulation, each day and storing the CD or DVD in a safe and fireproof depository. Back-up and storage of multiple copies of data is routine but critical. Without this process the entire data of a library could be lost in an unfortunate theft or fire.

Assistive or Adaptive Technologies

The Technology Related Assistance Act of 1988 (P.L. 101-407) and the Assistive Technology Act of 1998 (P.L. 105-394) define assistive technology as "any item, piece of equipment, or product, whether acquired commercially, modified, or customized, that is used to increase, maintain, or improve the functional capabilities of individuals with disabilities."[10] ASCLA,[11] a division of the American Library Association, provides suggestions for software and systems which enable people with disabilities to be more independent in their reading and communications with others. LSS can support and help challenged patrons with using both PC and Apple computers with built in accessibility features, such as zoom text or sticky keys that simplify computer commands to one keystroke. For example, the textbox shows quick ways to change text size.

Apple iPads and iPhones facilitate text to speech as part of their operating systems. Simply tap "Settings" and select "General." Go to "Accessibility" and tap "Speak Selection." Slide it on and adjust speaking rate to an appropriate setting. Now you can select any text and have it spoken to you. Text to speech features are

QUICK WAYS TO CHANGE TEXT SIZE

1. While holding the Control Key, press + or − key.
2. In Word, PowerPoint, and other applications increase font size by highlighting text and selecting a number in the font box such as 14, 16, or higher.
3. In Internet Explore open the "Tools" option on the menu bar and choose "Zoom."
4. In Firefox open "View" on menu bar and select "Highlight Text Size" to increase or decrease text.
5. In "Zoom" view you can also increase the percentage of text size (100 percent is normal) to permanently adjust to a larger or smaller text.

found in many programs. Recent versions of Windows offer text to speech. Some websites have already encoded speech capability for html files. Both the vendors Gale Cengage and EBSCO offer text to speech for magazine and journal articles that are in html format.

ASCLA recommends these text to speech programs for patrons with vision loss: *JAWS Screen Reader, Open Book Text Reader, Duxbury Braille Translating Software, Braille* embosser, and *Talking Typer* software. For those with hearing loss, ASCLA suggests using text messaging and *Sound Sentry*, a Windows based program that also works for Apple computers that converts the warning chimes of Windows into flashes the user would see on the screen. For those with learning disabilities or need support with reading, ASCLA recommends *Kurzweil 3000* and *WYNN Wizard* that highlight text to support reading as well as *Read and Write Gold* that supports both reading and writing. LSS who work with disabled patrons can seek trials with these programs and recommend them to supervisors for purchase. They may also contact their state and the National Library for the Blind for recommendations for new advances in assistive technologies. The Hearing Loss Association of America is just one of many national support organizations that can also be contacted for advice and support for working with library patrons.

NETWORK INFRASTRUCTURE

The Internet is a key and vital library service. LSS who have knowledge about how network infrastructure works can be most helpful for Internet services. In small public or school libraries, LSS will have varying degrees of responsibility for maintaining and managing all or part of the library network. We will look at some of the key network infrastructure.

Internet Service Provider (ISP)

Most libraries get their Internet from an Internet service provider (ISP), often the same company that sells the library telephone or cable service. In many communities the utility company, if it is an ISP, provides free Internet to the library or school in the town. The federal government pays most or all of the cost of Internet service to schools and libraries through the E-rate program. In some states, such as Connecticut, the ISP connects all libraries to its fiber optic network. If the Internet is "down," it is usually at the provider end. The LSS may work with the ISP to ensure that the trouble is not inside the library by checking to see that the modem in the library is working properly or that routers and switches are connected.

Figure 11.1 shows a simplistic overview of how the Internet moves through the modem to a router to computing devices. The larger the library, the more routers, switches, and hubs may be in place. A switch or hub is a device that further distributes the Internet to a lab or cluster of computers. Routers, switches, and hubs distribute Internet service to computers in the building and regulate performance and speed. Table 11.3 shows some of the common network devices that LSS may be asked to identify or know the function of.

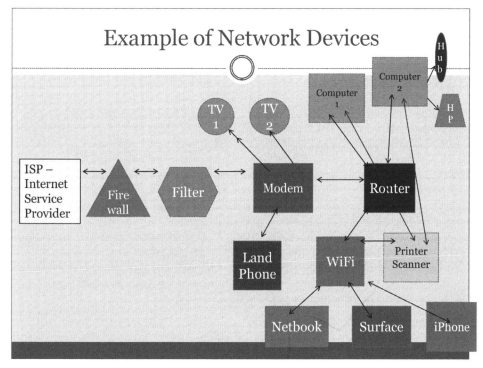

Figure 11.1. Example of Network Devices

Firewall and Filters

While every piece of equipment on a network is essential, an understanding of firewalls and filters is helpful for library staff who may be asked to explain to patrons why they cannot access certain websites. Every network should have a firewall to stop unauthorized data or websites that could potentially harm library

Table 11.3. Common Network Infrastructure Devices

Filter	A program that blocks certain data and websites from computer access by the user.
Firewall	Hardware or software solutions to protect a networked server or client machine from damage by unauthorized users.
Hub	Common connection points for devices in a network with multiple ports.
ISP	Internet Service Provider is the company paid a fee by user to access the Internet.
Modem	MOdulator/DEModulator: A simple analog data communications device for transmitting data over a phone or DSL line.
Peripheral Devices	Equipment used or connected to a computer such as a printer, scanner, digital camera, or flash drive.
Router	A device that forwards data packets along networks.
UPS	Uninterrupted power supply: This is the battery power that keeps a network functioning for enough time (20 to 30 minutes) for safe shutdown.

computers. Firewalls stop corrupted data that may have viruses from entering the local network. A firewall also protects the network from hackers. A firewall policy determines what packets of data that come from the outside should be accepted, denied, or dropped based on its policy.[12] Firewalls have a default setting generally to deny all traffic but rules made by the network administrator will open the firewall to permit appropriate traffic into the network.

As with the need for a firewall, there is also the need for every computer to be filtered. Filters protect the user from obscene or inappropriate content. Filters can be set to allow certain content that is age appropriate. Like firewalls, filters may be devices or software, depending upon the size of the library. Software filters are often imbedded in Internet services such as America Online (AOL) where parents can control the content their child has access to. Filters work by blocking specific websites, phrases, or words. Filters can also block larger amounts of data or content such as pornography or obscenity. Most library administrators rely on the filter product's preselected blocked content and may exempt an occasional site. Filters also work with firewalls to protect a computer from incoming viruses or hackers. Since the year 2000, when the United States legislated the Children's Internet Protection Act (CIPA), all schools and libraries that receive federal assistance for Internet service (see chapter 7) have used filtered computers for minors.[13]

BROADBAND CONNECTIVITY

LSS should be familiar with how the library connects to the Internet so that they can be helpful in communicating with ISP providers or be the first step in solving basic problems. There are different types of connectivity used for the Internet, and depending upon the location of the library, your library will use at least one, if not two of these types (see table 11.4).[14]

Wireless

The demand for libraries to provide reliable wireless or Wi-Fi computing has exploded in the past few years as patrons have acquired more mobile phones, tablets, and laptops. Today in many libraries patrons can check out the materials, place holds, and search the Internet using their mobile phones. Having a robust Wi-Fi has been a priority of libraries so that patrons can access the Internet and other services when they visit the library from their own devices. Public Wi-Fi using any of the above broadband connectivity encourages patrons to use their own equipment in ways such as:

- patrons download library apps to their own devices and use them for library services such as e-books, online catalog, and databases both in and out of the library;
- the library does not need to budget and purchase as many computers when patrons use their own equipment; and
- the library does not need to have every model and make of computing devices to satisfy patrons who have a preference in computer platforms.

Table 11.4. Types of Internet Connectivity

Digital Subscriber Line (DSL)	DSL transmits data faster over multiple traditional copper telephone lines already installed to libraries, homes, and businesses. Distance between the library and the telephone company will often affect the speed of transmission. Video conferencing is compromised if users do not have high speed symmetrical (SDSL) lines. We often see DSL in rural areas where cable service is prohibited or not available. The LSS may interact with technicians from the telephone company when there is a problem with Internet connections.
Cable	If your ISP is your local cable company, it uses the same lines for Internet service, television programming, and, in some places, telephone service. At the point of entry into the building the cable services split from the modem into routers that send Internet to the computers. Speed is usually better than DSL. At any one of these connections the LSS may be asked to work with the cable technician to test to see that the modem or router is functioning before a service appointment is made. Most homes use either DSL or cable broadband.
Fiber	Fiber optic technology converts electrical signals carrying data to light and sends the light through transparent glass fibers about the diameter of a human hair. Fiber transmits data at speeds far exceeding current DSL or cable modem speeds. The same fiber providing your broadband can also simultaneously deliver voice (VoIP) and video services, including video-on-demand.[a] Fiber networks are rapidly replacing DSL. Educational and municipal buildings often first hook up to fiber. Public libraries benefit when a fiber connection can be run from one of these close-by buildings. Fiber networks provide excellent and reliable video and Internet services at the highest speeds. Fiber networks are managed usually by large companies or state institutions. The LSS may support occasional technicians who inspect and improve local fiber connections.
Satellite	Similar to satellite television, Internet service may be the best option for libraries in very remote areas. Downstream and upstream speeds for satellite broadband depend on several factors, including the provider and service package purchased, the consumer's line of sight to the orbiting satellite, and the weather. Speeds may be slower than DSL and cable modem.[b]

a. Ibid.
b. Ibid.

Wireless broadband connects a home or business to the Internet using a radio link between the customer's location and the service provider's facility. Wireless broadband can be mobile or fixed (see figure 11.2).[15] In remote locations wireless transmissions are boosted with an extended antenna and may have intermittent interruptions. Wireless broadband often requires a direct line-of-sight between the wireless transmitter and receiver, thus limiting its range and reliability.

In the library building, a wireless router antenna (Wi-Fi or wireless fidelity) may be connected to the router to transmit Internet service at a limited range to devices that are adapted to receive Wi-Fi connectivity. Hotspots or mobile wireless broadband subscription services are becoming increasingly more common for mobile users who need Internet "on the go." These services can be purchased on a monthly basis. An antenna plugs into a user's laptop computer to pick up the wireless signal.

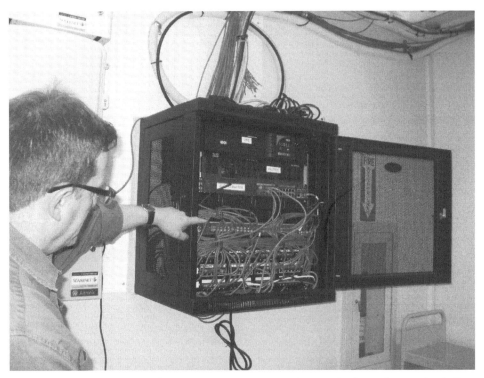

Figure 11.2.   Typical Network Infrastructure of a Medium Size Library. *Rutland Free Library, Rutland, VT*

Library services are dependent upon many types of hardware, applications software, and network infrastructure. However, most library staff do not have formal training in ICT. In the next section we will look at ways LSS enhance their learning of technology through their individual motivation, experiences, and support from others.

TECHNOLOGY PROFESSIONAL LEARNING

In order for a library to offer patrons reliable and functional information and communications technology services, they must have (1) devices to access the resources of a robust network; (2) infrastructure that supports a high level of connectivity to the Internet and other resources; (3) applications software licensed for patron users; and (4) ICT support resources.

The LSS have a key role in each of these areas. LSS can provide critical support for functional and reliable library ICT. According to a report by Pew Research Center on "How Americans Value Public Libraries in Their Communities,"[16] 56 percent of Internet users without home access say public libraries' basic technological resources (such as computers, Internet, and printers) are "very important" to them and their family, compared with 33 percent of all respondents. Likewise in academic and school libraries, reliable ICT is essential for student learning.

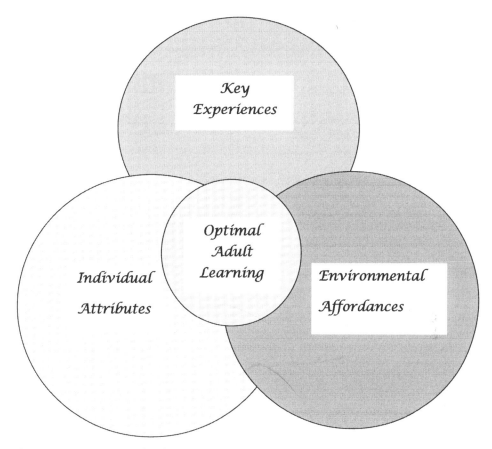

Figure 11.3.   TRIO Model of Professional Learning. *Barry G. Sheckley, PhD*

There is no one place to obtain all of the technical learning LSS need. Technology is ever changing, and LSS need to think of technology training as lifelong learning. There are many ways adults learn. The TRIO Model of Professional Learning (http://adult.education.uconn.edu/wp-content/uploads/sites/656/2014/09/Sheckley_et_al.pdf) (see figure 11.3)[17] suggests that adults learn

1. when we compare new ideas to our own past or key experiences;
2. when we work in an environment (i.e., with other library staff, patrons, etc.) that provides challenge, feedback, and support; and
3. when we are self-motivated to keep learning.

Optimal lifelong learning occurs when all three factors intersect and support each other.

LSS can enhance their learning to work with and support others' use of new technology. We draw upon our past experiences with technology and compare them to what is new. We expand upon what we already know by seeking help from others either in the library or the ICT vendors and specialists who work with library staff.

We are motivated to keep learning about technology because we want to be able to help others use library resources with our equipment or patron-owned devices.

CHAPTER SUMMARY

This chapter is packed with technical information about computers, networks, and infrastructure. It is important that the LSS be active learners and practitioners of technology so that they can in practice support the ever-growing demand for computing services. When the LSS are competent with technology, they are able to assist and train users to operate public equipment, connect to the Internet, use library software applications, and access library services from remote locations. Libraries are hubs of technology, and LSS perform basic troubleshooting of technical problems and resolve or refer those problems as appropriate.

DISCUSSION QUESTIONS AND ACTIVITIES

Discussion Questions

1. Name four key hardware equipment for a library network and tell what each piece does.
2. What are some of the advantages and disadvantages of libraries leasing computers rather than purchasing them?
3. Discuss two reasons why cloud computing is important to libraries and their services.
4. What are the main types of broadband capability and what are key strengths and differences among them?
5. Why should professional learning be ongoing for staff when it comes to technology?

Activities

Activity 1: Creating a Concept Map of Your Home Network
I have found my students learn a lot when they explore the workings of their home network.

Using PowerPoint or Word, draw a concept map of the technologies in your home. Use shapes to represent hardware and lines to represent flow of data or connectivity.

- Include on the map all phone, TV, and computer systems. These may be separate or integrated.
- Include all peripheral devices (i.e., printers, scanners, projectors, gaming systems, etc.).
- Label the location of connectivity to the outside provider(s).
- Include all wired and wireless devices. Use solid lines to show direct wiring, dotted lines for wireless.

Table 11.5. Activity Table

Item	Description	Model No./Vendor	Date Acquired	Location in Library	Estimated Replacement Cost

- The concept map should be one slide or one page.
- Label all shapes.

Activity 2: Inventory Library Hardware and Software

If you work in a library, ask to create an inventory of either the library hardware or applications software. Most likely a full inventory has not been done, especially if you work in a small library that is always short of staff hours.

Your supervisor will thank you for doing this, and you will become much more knowledgeable about the hardware and applications software used in your library.

The inventory form can look something like table 11.5.

NOTES

1. Kathryn Zickuhr, Lee Rainie, and Kristen Purcell, "Library Services in the Digital Age," Pew Research Center, last modified January 22, 2013, accessed October 11, 2014, http:// libraries.pewinternet.org/2013/01/22/library-services/.

2. Deborah Straszheim, "Groton Schools' New Business Manager Wasting No Time Saving District Money," *The Day* (New London, CT), February 16, 2015, sec. A, http://www .theday.com/local/20150216/groton-schools-new-business-manager-wasting-no-time.

3. "Computer Leasing," University of Chicago IT Services, last modified 2015, accessed February 16, 2015, https://itservices.uchicago.edu/services/computer-leasing.

4. "Buying and Deploying Technology," TechSoup for Libraries, last modified 2015, accessed February 17, 2015, https://www.techsoupforlibraries.org/cookbook-3/buying-and -deploying-technology/buying-refurbished-computers.

5. Ibid.

6. Susan Thompson, "Student Use of Library Computers: Are Desktop Computers Still Relevant in Today's Libraries," *Information Technology and Libraries* 31, no. 4 (December 2012), accessed April 28, 2015, http://search.ebscohost.com/login.aspx?direct=true&db=aph &AN=89086995&site=ehost-live&scope=site.

7. "ASP," Tech Terms, accessed October 11, 2014, http://www.techterms.com/definition/ asp.

8. Brian Westover, "How to Clone a Hard Drive," *PC Magazine*, July 9, 2013, http://www .pcmag.com/article2/0,2817,2421302,00.asp.

9. "Cloud Computing," Tech Terms, accessed October 11, 2014, http://www.techterms .com/definition/cloud_computing.

10. "What Is Assistive Technology and How Is It Used in Schools?" South Carolina As- sistive Technology Program, last modified June 13, 2013, accessed January 25, 2015, http:// www.sc.edu/scatp/cdrom/atused.html.

11. "Assistive Technology: What You Need to Know," Library Accessibility and Assistive Technology, last modified 2010, accessed April 28, 2015, http://www.ala.org/ascla/sites/ala .org.ascla/files/content/asclaprotools/accessibilitytipsheets/tipsheets/11-Assistive_Technol .pdf.

12. "How Firewalls Work," Boston University Information Services & Technology, accessed October 11, 2014, http://www.bu.edu/tech/services/security/resources/host-based/intro/.

13. "Children's Internet Protection Act," Federal Communications Commission—Chil- dren's Internet Protection Act, last modified July 2014, accessed October 11, 2014, http:// www.fcc.gov/guides/childrens-internet-protection-act.

14. "Types of Broadband Connections," Federal Communications Commission—Broad- band.gov, last modified 2014, accessed October 11, 2014, http://www.broadband.gov/ broadband_types.html.

15. Ibid.

16. Kathryn Zickuhr et al., "How Americans Value Public Libraries in Their Communities," Pew Research Center, last modified December 13, 2013, accessed October 11, 2014, http://libraries.pewinternet.org/files/legacy-pdf/PIP_Libraries%20in%20communities.pdf.

17. B. Sheckley et al., "Trio: An Emerging Model of Adult Professional Development," *Proceedings of the 49th Annual Adult Education Research Conference*, June 2008.

REFERENCES, SUGGESTED READINGS, AND WEBSITES

American Library Association. "ALA Library Fact Sheet 26." Internet Access and Digital Holdings in Libraries. Last modified 2015. Accessed April 28, 2015. http://www.ala.org/tools/libfactsheets/alalibraryfactsheet26.

"ASP." Tech Terms. Accessed October 11, 2014. http://www.techterms.com/definition/asp.

Association of Specialized and Cooperative Agencies—American Library Association. "Assistive Technology: What You Need to Know." Library Accessibility and Assistive Technology. Last modified 2010. Accessed April 28, 2015. http://www.ala.org/ascla/sites/ala.org.ascla/files/content/asclaprotools/accessibilitytipsheets/tipsheets/11-Assistive_Technol.pdf.

Breeding, Marshall. "Investing in the Future." *Library Journal* 134, no. 6 (2009). https://web.a.ebscohost.com/ehost/pdfviewer/pdfviewer?vid=7&sid=8b7ff5b9-5715-4258-ab56-21d1960c249b%40sessionmgr4005&hid=4106.

"Children's Internet Protection Act." Federal Communications Commission—Children's Internet Protection Act. Last modified July 2014. Accessed October 11, 2014. http://www.fcc.gov/guides/childrens-internet-protection-act.

"Cloud Computing." Tech Terms. Accessed October 11, 2014. http://www.techterms.com/definition/cloud_computing.

Corrado, Edward, and Heather Moulaison. "The Library Cloud." *Library Journal* 137, no. 4 (March 1, 2012). Accessed February 17, 2015. http://search.ebscohost.com/login.aspx?direct=true&db=aph&AN=71940731&site=ehost-live&scope=site.

"How Firewalls Work." Boston University Information Services & Technology. Accessed October 11, 2014. http://www.bu.edu/tech/services/security/resources/host-based/intro/.

Rayward, W. Boyd. "A History of Computer Applications." *IEEE Annals of the History of Computing*, 2002, 1–12. http://people.lis.illinois.edu/~wrayward/HistComputerApsinLibsAnnls.pdf.

"SaaS." Tech Terms. Accessed October 11, 2014. http://www.techterms.com/definition/saas.

Sheckley, B., M. Kehrhahn, S. Bell, and R. Grenier. "Trio: An Emerging Model of Adult Professional Development." *Proceedings of the 49th Annual Adult Education Research Conference*, June 2008.

Straszheim, Deborah. "Groton Schools' New Business Manager Wasting No Time Saving District Money." *The Day* (New London, CT), February 16, 2015, sec. A. http://www.theday.com/local/20150216/groton-schools-new-business-manager-wasting-no-time.

TechDictionary.com. "TechDictionary." TechDictionary. Last modified 2015. Accessed November 7, 2014. http://www.techdictionary.com.

TechSoup Global. "Buying and Deploying Technology." TechSoup for Libraries. Last modified 2015. Accessed February 17, 2015. https://www.techsoupforlibraries.org/cookbook-3/buying-and-deploying-technology/buying-refurbished-computers.

TechTerms.com. "TechTerms." TechTerms.com. Last modified 2015. Accessed November 9, 2014. http://www.techterms.com/definition/.

Thompson, Susan. "Student Use of Library Computers: Are Desktop Computers Still Relevant in Today's Libraries." *Information Technology and Libraries* 31, no. 4 (December 2012): 20–33. Accessed April 28, 2015. http://search.ebscohost.com/login.aspx?direct=true&db=aph&AN=89086995&site=ehost-live&scope=site.

"Types of Broadband Connections." Federal Communications Commission—Broadband. gov. Last modified 2014. Accessed October 11, 2014. http://www.broadband.gov/broad band_types.html.

University Center for Excellence. "What Is Assistive Technology and How Is It Used in Schools?" South Carolina Assistive Technology Program. Last modified June 13, 2013. Accessed January 25, 2015. http://www.sc.edu/scatp/cdrom/atused.html.

University of Chicago. "Computer Leasing." University of Chicago IT Services. Last modified 2015. Accessed February 16, 2015. https://itservices.uchicago.edu/services/computer-leasing.

Webopedia.com. "Webopedia." Webopedia. Last modified 2015. Accessed November 12, 2014. http://www.webopedia.com/.

Westover, Brian. "How to Clone a Hard Drive." *PC Magazine*, July 9, 2013. http://www.pc mag.com/article2/0,2817,2421302,00.asp.

Zickuhr, Kathryn, Lee Rainie, Kristen Purcell, and Mauve Duggan. "How Americans Value Public Libraries in Their Communities." Pew Research Center. Last modified December 13, 2013. Accessed October 11, 2014. http://libraries.pewinternet.org/files/legacy-pdf/PIP_Libraries percent20in percent20communities.pdf.

Zickuhr, Kathryn, Lee Rainie, and Kristen Purcell. "Library Services in the Digital Age." Pew Research Center. Last modified January 22, 2013. Accessed October 11, 2014. http://librar ies.pewinternet.org/2013/01/22/library-services/.

PART III

New Directions

CHAPTER 12

Current and Future Trends

Library Support Staff (LSS) know the general trends and developments in technology applications for library functions and services. (ALA-LSSC Technology Competency #1)

LSS demonstrate flexibility in adapting to new technology. (ALA-LSSC Technology Competency #5)

Topics Covered in This Chapter:

- Creativity and Collaboration
  - Makerspaces
  - Online Makerspaces
- Mobile Access to Information
  - Underserved Populations
  - Privacy Concerns
  - QR Code Generator
- Electronic Publishing and Digital Storytelling
  - Electronic Publishing
  - Digital Storytelling
- Automation, Drones, and Robotics
  - Automation
  - Drones
  - Robots
- Social Media and Networking
- Library Support Staff and the Future

Key Terms:

3-D Printing: Three-dimensional printing is a manufacturing process whereby an object is built of very thin plastic or other material. The process begins at the base of the design and layers the object upwards until completed. The 3-D printer is attached to a computer where a design of a digital model was created with special software. Libraries are acquiring 3-D printers so that patrons can learn about this technology as they use it to create and build innovative concepts. Library staff who are trained to use 3-D printers can help and support the learning and skills patrons acquire using 3-D printers.

Cloud Computing: The Internet is referred to as the cloud. Librarians use the Internet to transfer data over the Internet to servers not in the library for back-up and storage of data. Cloud computing replaces the need to keep and store data on your hard drive. Cloud computing removes the daily necessity of library staff backing up data or the concern of data integrity if there is an emergency. Library staff should know about the servers their library uses, how often data is backed up, and other policies that control the storage, accessibility, and privacy of their data, especially for circulation, cataloging, and e-mail.

RSS Feed: RSS stands for Really Simple Syndication. RSS is a way to have news and other regular web content delivered to your own personal wire service. RSS channels web content to your website, blog, e-mail, or other web service. Library websites often have RSS feeds of news or other wire services that patrons would have interest in. Library staff can direct patrons to the library RSS feed or help patrons set up their own feeds. Most website providers include an RSS option.

SaaS: SaaS stands for Software as a Service. These are computer programs and applications running on a server outside of the library. The host service provider maintains the software and makes it seamless for the library staff and patrons to use. An example of SaaS is the online catalog hosted by a contract vendor or provider. Some libraries also use SaaS for their office software or accounting systems. Library staff do not have to be concerned about upgrades or software problems as part of the SaaS is maintenance and troubleshooting.

Creative suggestions abound about what a library could look like in five, ten, or even twenty-five years from now. There is no definitive answer to describe the futuristic library. In this chapter we will have fun exploring trends that will *most likely* influence future library services. We can be sure libraries will continue to find ways to use new technologies for services, and library staff will continue to need to be trained and competent users of digital resources and technology to support new services.

Who are the present and future users of libraries? Public libraries are free and open to everyone, but some people frequent them more than others. According to the report "The Next Library and People Who Will Use It"[1] from the Pew Research

Center, 30 percent of respondents said they are high users, 39 percent are medium users, 17 percent consider themselves low users, and 14 percent said they do not use the library at all. Users were almost equally divided by their gender; however, a significant predictor of use is educational level. The higher the educational level, the more people use their libraries. Library staff provide programming and services for those who frequent the library, but we must also reach out to the underserved who do not.

In this chapter we will look at influences and trends which predict the future of libraries. Demographics and patterns of users will undoubtedly change. In my crystal ball I predict future library trends and services will attract patrons if they are embedded in technology which spurs creativity and collaboration, provides access to information in multiple and mobile ways, encourages independent publishing and digital storytelling, enhances automation of services, employs robotics, drones, or other highly technical devices, and, of course, capitalizes on social networking and instant communications.

CREATIVITY AND COLLABORATION

In 1999, when we were designing a new library, the architect didn't believe I wanted a highly visible, glass-walled project "mudroom" where students would have the freedom to make and create in unstructured ways. We set up our project room near the entrance of the library with scissors, old magazines, poster board, laminators, string, yarn, glue, and various odds and ends. Large workspace tables are utilized daily, and over time technology was acquired. The project room is a space where interesting and varied hands-on activities take place. For example, an archeology class spends the first half of the semester on site locating and excavating buried objects on sites around town. Owners of colonial period homes and other places of interest give permission for digs to take place. The second half of the semester the teacher and students bring crates and buckets of artifacts encrusted in dirt that are cleaned, tagged, and identified. We acquired a Scalar Scope on a Rope[2] that, connected to a computer, allows one to take a magnified JPEG digital image of the object being examined. Collaboratively, students with the help of their teacher and library staff, spend weeks researching information about the artifacts and completing detailed journals about their research.

Makerspaces

Our project room was a precursor to what are now known as makerspaces. Makerspaces (or hackerspaces) are places in libraries where patrons can model and configure their innovative ideas by building or creating objects from materials and technology. Everyone is welcome to collaborate and share ideas in an unstructured, open setting. Hackforge,[3] a hacker/makerspace at the Windsor Public Library in Ontario, aims to be as inclusive as possible. Less than 25 percent of computer programmers are female. Hackforge encourages women to participate because "technology, especially computer code, is defining the structure of our lives in the twenty-first century. It's dangerous to exclude people from that process."[4] Hackforge library

Figure 12.1.   HATCH Makerspace. *Watertown Free Public Library, Watertown, MA*

staff provide the space and tools for programmers and nonprogrammers of differing ages and genders to collaborate and learn from each other. Hackforge aligns with the library's mission,[5] which includes lifelong learning, community, and teamwork.

HATCH[6] is a makerspace of the Watertown Free Public Library in Massachusetts located in a nearby shopping mall (see figure 12.1). The mall gave a free lease of one year to the library. Recently a visitor there saw how well outsourcing HATCH worked as many shoppers stopped in to see what it was all about. There were several stations for collaborative creativity: a **3-D** printing station, an electrical or circuitry area, computers for programming, a sewing station, and abundance of cardboard, just to name a few of the makerspaces. Staffed by volunteers, a professional architect guided me through my tour.

There was a lot going on at HATCH on the Friday afternoon we visited (see figure 12.2). The volunteer staff were key to establishing an environment of learning, innovation, and collaboration. Teens were at the sewing station while younger children were exploring mechanical devices and circuits.

3-D printers are important tools for makerspaces. 3-D printing was very expensive fairly recently and was strictly for manufacturing sites. A 3-D printer is connected to a computer with computer-aided design software such as CAD. The design that is created can be "printed" into plastic objects (see figure 12.3). The plastic can be the shell or full core. Parts can be movable in full or partial scale. Today the cost of 3-D printers has become affordable for most libraries, and they are seen as essential tools for creative thinking and innovation.

Figure 12.2. Exploring the Public Workshops at HATCH. *Watertown Free Public Library, Watertown, MA*

Figure 12.3. 3-D Printer and Objects Printed. *Watertown Free Public Library, Watertown, MA*

Online Makerspaces

Some libraries provide online makerspaces. Edmonton Public Library in Canada[7] has been experimenting with makerspaces both in their building and online. They found teens are interested in creating projects together online but prefer to post and communicate with each other through social networking such as Facebook. New York Public Library (NYPL)[8] has a makerspace site that you must check out called Stereogranimator. In this site you can create 3-D images from the NYPL stereograph collections and share and refine your work with others online. A future trend that I predict we will see is other libraries and museums around the world also providing online collaboration and tools. Being able to critically look at and manipulate fine art and photographs spurs our thinking about the information and aesthetics of imagery. Library staff can promote online makerspaces by making available tutorials, editing tools, public domain images, and creating social network forums on the library website for people to tinker, share their work, and communicate new ideas.

What role can library support staff have with makerspaces? These areas almost run themselves, but they do need someone on staff who is interested in fostering creativity and is supportive of the idea of a mudroom. It is helpful if the makerspace is in a room not too removed from the main center of the library so that occasional supervision can take place. It will also need periodic straightening and cleaning. Most importantly, library support staff can be enthusiastic about the collaboration and learning that can take place and encourage youth and adults to experiment and try their ideas in conceptual ways. Library staff can have as much fun as the patrons when they learn how to use a 3-D printer (it really is easy!), scanner, cutters, or basic design software. Begin small and build a community of users who will return with friends. Makerspaces are an exciting service of any library (see table 12.1).

MOBILE ACCESS TO INFORMATION

More and more cell phones are smartphones. Smartphones are computers with Internet access and program applications. Oh yes, they are also used to make telephone calls and text messages either by service providers or through a wireless Internet network. Tablets have similar functions as smart phones. Libraries are experimenting with mobile devices and services to support information needs of patrons, wherever they may be. Using the ever-growing capabilities of these mobile devices, libraries can offer quick access to main features of their websites and catalogs to people on the go such as book reserves, reference services, e-books, e-journals, live streaming and/or on demand video, audio, and multimedia content. Mobile devices

Table 12.1. Makerspaces Resources

MakerSpace	http://makerspace.com/
The Maker's Manual	http://www.psfk.com/report/makers-manual
The Most Interesting Makerspaces in America	http://makezine.com/magazine/make-40/most
Make Magazine	-interesting-makerspaces-in-america/

EXAMPLES OF MOBILE LIBRARY APPS

Destiny Quest Mobile App brings our school library to the mobile device you use the most.

AccessMyLibrary app provides access to your library's Gale online resources—anytime, anywhere!

With EBSCO Ultra Online Mobile, all smartphones and tablets are auto-detected and redirected to the EBSCO mobile website.

World Book Mobile allows users to have access to the entire World Book Student database in the palm of their hand.

Encyclopaedia Brittanica Mobile allows users to have access to the entire Encyclopaedia Brittanica in a mobile site.

Overdrive App lets you download e-books and audio books from our library directly to your favorite mobile or e-book device.

ABC-CLIO Mobile is optimized for viewing e-book content on your smartphone.

Libguides Mobile with pathfinders for your class projects comes in a convenient mobile site.

EasyBib App generates citations for your bibliographies and "works cited" pages just by scanning the book barcode.

---

provide tremendous flexibility for those who wish to take advantage of library services. By going mobile, a library offers patrons flexible 24/7 service.

Businesses have created applications of their products so that patrons can access online catalogs and download journal articles and other content that are presentable to read on a small screen. Library staff work with vendors to include in contracts to manage digital rights and content licensing for mobile devices. For example, where once articles could only be downloaded in the library setting, with appropriate licensing agreements, patrons may download content and back it up in storage of their smartphone clouds with rights of ownership and use.

Underserved Populations

The proliferation of mobile devices and services provides access to digital information services. With the continued adoption of mobile devices, traditionally underserved populations can have access to library services. According to the Pew Research Center[9] as of January 2014:

- 90 percent of American adults have a cell phone.
- 58 percent of American adults have a smartphone.
- 98 percent of Americans ages eighteen to twenty-nine own cell phones.
- 84 percent of Americans with household income of less than $30,000 own cell phones.

As cell phones become more affordable and are upgraded to smartphones, the public will have greater access to library resources through mobile devices. Library staff can help patrons maximize use of their smartphones by helping individuals and demonstrating to groups of patrons how to upload library and vendor apps, digital content from library databases, or download e-books. When patrons learn how easy it is to use their smartphone for library services and digital resources, they may more frequently use library services and change from never or slightly using their library to becoming regular users because of their mobile devices.

Privacy Concerns

We grapple with Internet privacy concerns. Our mobile devices have global positioning tracking software that can locate the holder any place in the world. Personal data and information we use on our phone is automatically backed up to the cloud of servers for convenience . . . but also outside of control. As library staff promote the use of mobile devices, they should also alert patrons to these potential privacy concerns.

1. Library staff uphold the American Library Association "Library Bill of Rights" that guarantees patrons free access to information and freedom of inquiry. When privacy is not guaranteed, patrons' First Amendment freedoms of speech rights are compromised. Library staff guard patrons' privacy by deleting circulation records once items are returned. However, records of smartphone activities may be stored on the cloud and thus compromise patrons' right to privacy. Library staff should be aware of this and work with vendors to see if permanent storage of patrons' library use can be avoided.
2. Patrons may use mobile devices on unsecured networks that track what they do. Not all wireless networks have a high level of security or confidentiality.
3. Patrons' reading habits may be tracked by e-book providers, including their searches, thus compromising their First Amendment rights to privacy.
4. Mobile devices can collect and transmit data to third-party vendors and others about the content users downloaded and interacted with—even track the location of where the user has been!

There is no doubt that smartphones and future devices have become a part of our lives. In almost any setting, I can observe people accessing their phones. Library staff should become familiar with vendor products and work to guarantee that products have a high level of reliability but also security built into them.

QR Code Generator

A great way for library staff to help patrons find digital resources using their mobile devices is to generate QR codes for specific URLs of websites and digital content. An example of a QR code is shown in figure 12.4 and is embedded with information of a specific URL.

Smartphones have QR code readers that can interpret the graphic and instantly upload the website link. Library staff can create QR codes on posters or pamphlets that will direct people to specific digital resources.

How do you make a QR code? Faster than I can write these instructions, you can create one (see textbox)!

We have only scratched the surface with what library staff can do to promote library services through mobile devices. We can create our own library mobile apps[10] to have chat, forums, RSS feeds, guest books, surveys, etc., by using various free or small cost products such as Winksite (http://www.winksite.com). Many other library website or digital products offer app building. Librarians endorse such ready-made apps as this list of the "45 Most Exciting Apps for Librarians"[11] that promote better reading choices for patrons, help with organization such as note taking or citing sources, and provide basic reference sources.

We know that people have rapidly become reliant on their smartphones and that they are never more than a few inches away from their grasp. The challenge for library staff is to create and promote library digital resources that will enhance our knowledge and skills as lifelong learners. A patron no longer has to enter our libraries when he or she has a mobile device to use many of our important resources.

Figure 12.4. QR Code

PRACTICE: MAKE A QR CODE

1. Go to a free QR code generator such as https://www.the-qrcode-generator.com/.
2. Select the link for the type of information you wish the QR code to represent. This could be text, URL, phone number, contact information, or text message.
3. Type or copy the information in the appropriate box.
4. As you type a QR code is generated. You can save, share, resize, or print it.

ELECTRONIC PUBLISHING AND DIGITAL STORYTELLING

Both electronic publishing and digital storytelling are future trends which encourage patrons to share their ideas, experiences, or knowledge with others. Libraries can support these efforts with enthusiastic and knowledgeable staff who understand simple file formats and file management. Libraries will need to have policies in place which are specific to acceptable use that align with expected library behavior. They may also want to have an editorial policy if the library name is associated with the electronically published piece.

Electronic Publishing

Traditional publishing is a very selective process that is juried and takes time. A trend I predict that libraries will fully develop in the future is online or electronic publishing. Large universities that are academic publishers are already moving toward e-publishing. For example, Purdue University Libraries[12] in Indiana offers electronic publishing services for faculty, staff, and students to disseminate their work. In addition to providing editing and other help, the library helps manage digital sales through Ingram CoreSource, which serves over 160 electronic information providers including amazon.com, bn.com, and Apple, while partnering primarily with Project Muse and ebrary to serve libraries. Open Access publications are distributed through the Purdue e-Pubs platform.[13]

Electronic publishing shortens the time from what is normally one year to publish a book. In today's world where there is need, particularly in the sciences, medicine, and technology for information to be rapidly shared, electronic publishing makes sense. Public and school library staff can also help patrons electronically publish their writing. Recently I assigned my digital resources class to make a small e-book. Students could elect to self-publish their book on Amazon. One student electronically published a book about work and money management for young people and had a few sales on Amazon within the week.

It makes sense that if library staff encourage patrons to create multimedia and other works that they should offer electronic self-publishing services. Electronic publishing enables libraries to produce content, either on site or through an established press or open source,[14] so that patrons can share their ideas and concepts with people outside of the library community.

Library staff can begin to learn about electronic publishing by experimenting in the following ways.

- Read information about self-publishing from sites such as Amazon, CreateSpace.com, and other commercial sites. Try self-publishing a short piece of your own writing such as a children's story on these sites.
- Write a pilot or trial short story, poem, instructional bulletin, or other item and save it in .pdf, .text, .html, and .doc file formats so that you can experiment with different file types. Ask for a folder of storage space on the library server or cloud to keep your pilot or trial work in. Upload the file in .pdf format to different e-readers to see how it presents to different device functions. With help of the library webmaster, link the html or the doc file to a hidden page or a personal website.

The more you experiment with electronic publishing, the more familiar and comfortable you will be with it. Finally, when you are ready to share with others, demonstrate your work and ask to work with others to formulate a plan to create an electronic publishing center in your library that includes not only the equipment needed but also user policies, budget, and staff allocations. Like the makerspace, patrons will be interested in your concepts and appreciate the opportunity to become published authors!

Offering electronic publishing as a library service will enhance the purpose and thus the future of libraries. As academic libraries have discovered, there is a real need to disseminate information and libraries can become electronic publishers in their communities!

Digital Storytelling

Storytelling has been around since the beginning of mankind. Through story we have passed along culture, knowledge, and experiences—in essence our past or who we are is our story. History or his-story is making sense of our past. Storytelling is who we are and what we do. It is a perfect correlation that libraries promote digital storytelling in ways that help people share their personal narratives with others and pass on their life experiences.

Libraries have been recording personal narratives for decades in the form of interviews. The Library of Congress American Memories is rich with recorded tapes of people from the past who had unique life experiences such as the *Slave Narratives* from the Federal Writers' Project of 1936–1938, which contains more than 2,300 first-person accounts of slavery. Some of these narratives have been converted to digital audio files but they do not contain visual images. Digital storytellers use multimedia to tell their stories[15] because so much information about one's life experiences about time, place, and the impact of culture and events is conveyed in images. Multimedia can be in the form of video, still images, slide shows, or even pop-up books. Digital stories are accessed via the computer and are enhanced with visual images that support the personal narrative.

Libraries may promote digital storytelling to preserve community memories. My own local public library is currently interviewing shipyard workers of the World

War II era about their work in order to capture primary source or firsthand accounts and memories of building submarines. Digital interviews coupled with multimedia images of the submarines, World War II, and other related events create digital storytelling. Similar to a TV documentary, the combination of multimedia with voice makes the story a powerful experience for others.

My own experience with digital storytelling comes from being part of a team that collaborated on the creation of digital yearbooks. Media of school events were combined with students telling their stories of their years as high school students. Digital storytelling does not take many resources from the library. Library staff can lead a community project in digital storytelling by determining the following with others.

- *What* is the desired focus or content of the digital stories? Are they to share and collect local history about an important event? Are they to add to a genealogy collection?
- *Who* will be interviewed? Are there selection criteria that determine the personal narratives you want to capture?
- *Where* will the digital stories be produced? Will you take people on site or will you have them come to the library?
- *When* is the time period of the digital stories? Are you seeking a particular era, such as World War II?
- *How* will you produce the digital story? Will you use the assistance of staff that have training or do you need to acquire software and training in order to do the project? (See table 12.2 for some apps or software suggestions.)

For schools, digital storytelling is an excellent way library staff can support students' English Language Arts skills. Digital storytelling requires students to acquire and practice multiple skills such as planning, organization, writing, reading, research, speaking, and performance to tell a personal narrative. Students also will acquire digital media and other technology skills to make a digital story.

While using a digital camera is all one needs to create a digital story, there are some software applications library staff may want to consider purchasing to help create professional works (see table 12.2). Most of these applications are intuitive and are meant for the general user, requiring very little training or practice.

Following the lead of the Library of Congress and academic libraries, school and public libraries can serve their communities today and in the future by offering digital storytelling services to capture important personal narratives embedded with visual images.

AUTOMATION, DRONES, AND ROBOTS

The way work is done in libraries is changing with technology. Advances in integrated library systems (ILS) are allowing patrons more control of their circulation activity. When patrons take responsibility for routine tasks, library staff can use their time to perform a higher level of customer service, training, or programming. The

Table 12.2. Examples of Digital Storytelling Applications*

iMovie	iMovie is a good choice for Mac users who want to create digital stories. This digital movie creation and editing program supports the use of full-motion video clips.
Photo Story 3	Photo Story 3 is a free, easy-to-use software application from Microsoft that lets you create slideshows using your own digital photos and images you download from the web or scan from old photographs, documents, books, magazines, or newspapers.
PhotoShop Elements	Adobe Photoshop Elements contain an easy-to-use slide show creation module that works very much like Photo Story 3, allowing you to create slide shows that can contain zooms and pans, recorded narration, and added text and transitions, such as fade in and out. Photoshop Elements also allow you to add video clips to the slide show.
ShowMe Interactive Whiteboard	Turn your iPad into your personal interactive whiteboard!
ZooBurst	ZooBurst is a digital storytelling tool that lets anyone easily create his or her own 3-D pop-up books.
MapSkip	With MapSkip we can create a weave of stories about the places in our lives. Users are invited to create a free account and to mark up places in Google Maps with their own stories and photos.

*These applications are examples of software that currently exist. In the future there will be other products or enhanced upgrades to today's versions.

future holds possibilities for more mechanization so that library staff can perform skills of a higher order.

Automation

What once was unthinkable, today patrons manage their accounts by placing holds and renewing their materials from home, they self-checkout books and DVDs, and perform other tasks that once were the work only of library circulation staffs. The heart of automation in libraries is the ILS that integrates modules of circulation, cataloging, serials, reserves, and other functions. But libraries today and in the future handle more than books. The online catalog that only displays the print collections does a disservice to patrons who seek a federated or complete search of digital and print resources on a topic. Resources are often ignored or unknown because they are not searchable from the main catalog. People may not know of the databases available to them because articles and documents from them do not appear in the library catalog. One stop shopping (or indexing) is desirable and needed in our future.

The landscape of ILS is changing. ILS will be different than what most libraries experience today whereby online catalogs are for the tangible, physical items circulated by the library. ILS are becoming *library service platforms*.[16] Another term library staff should know is **SaaS** or Software as a Service. SaaS is a type of library service platform whch manages a wide variety of library software by one provider. SaaS is a real boost for small to medium size libraries that do not have on site their own IT team. According to the Sirsi/Dynix website, their SaaS guarantees libraries:

- full range of software solutions hosted for all types and sizes of libraries;
- on-demand system capacity and all-inclusive resources to meet scaling needs;
- 24 × 7 × 365 support coverage with built-in disaster recovery;
- rapid implementation and on-demand upgrades; and
- reduced total cost of software/hardware ownership.

With Software as a Service, not only may libraries see cost savings but, more importantly, different technologies, such as e-mail, website management, security software, editing software, printing applications, etc. are now handled by the provider. By outsourcing the management of the many different library software and applications, staff can direct their attention to patrons' services and not focus their time on routine—or complex—technology issues.

Both ILS and library service platforms have some overlap. These two categories also have significant areas of overlap in functionality, and some products embrace characteristics of both.[17] Why should you be interested in these future changes in library automation? An important reason is library service platforms have the potential to map Marc metadata structures into a linked data model.[18] As we learned earlier in this book, libraries and museums have distinct systems of classification and cataloging (MARC and metadata, such as Dublin Core). When these systems are mapped and linked using library service platforms, information will be able to be found about any library resources whether it be from traditional collections, digital resources and databases, or artifacts. The Library of Congress is exploring ways to map the two systems for a more effective way of searching books and artifacts that appears to be one catalog to the user.

Drones

We have become used to instant deliveries and having devices do work for us. What once seemed like science fiction—small flying objects that discern and land deliveries to a specific location—drones today are becoming mainstream. Drones are unmanned small flying aircraft that have proven effective for reconnaissance and warfare. They are also used for peaceful operations that include agriculture, such as herding cattle, counting wildlife, or applying pesticides. Drones have become popular in the film industry for close-ups or daring scenes in the creation of movies or advertisements in ways that traditional aircraft would be unsafe or cannot be used. The possibility of a drone landing at my house became more than science fiction when Amazon recently laid out a plan to use drones to deliver goods to customers.

In the future of libraries drones may have an important place. According to the American Library Association,[19] Google's Project Loon is experimenting with providing Internet access in remote areas by drones. Drones in the future may be used to bring into our library communities services for those who live in remote locations. Most libraries struggle to find efficient and expedient ways to move interlibrary loan materials. Drones could be employed to deliver library resources to individuals, but they may be of particular use to deliver to isolated, homebound, or people affected by disasters. Research could be shared or collaborations be made via video-equipped drones. Additionally, video content made by drones for communities could be collected and managed by libraries.[20]

Robots

Personally, I consider my robot vacuum that cleans my floors each day one of the best inventions! This robot saves me hours of time and does the job just as good—if not better, than me. In the future we will expect to see more and more functions taken over by robotic devices in our personal lives as well as in our libraries. Already robots are being used in large library depositories, such as at the closed shelves of the University of Chicago Mansueto Library, to retrieve and deliver books. It is within our grasp to imagine robots performing not only cleaning and other maintenance tasks in future libraries, but also shelving and handling materials. Collaborative robots called CoBots help with fetching activities and can be programmed to perform specific tasks.[21]

Robots will also be used to help people learn. At Westport Public Library[22] two humanoid robots have been acquired for its makerspace so that people can learn robotics first-hand from interactions. Their primary purpose is to teach the kind of coding and computer programming skills required to animate robots by having people be able to experiment first-hand with artificial intelligence. The library staff held competitive programming challenges requiring contestants to have the robots recite a poem, give a speech, and do a dance, among other things.

While I cannot predict all of the future ways robots and robotics will enhance library services, I do know that by looking at trends around us in manufacturing, government, and education, robotics will play a strong role in relieving humans from routine tasks and be useful educational tools for lifelong and career changing learning.

SOCIAL MEDIA AND NETWORKING

Libraries have done an excellent job of using social media to promote their programs and services. It is hard to find a library website that does not connect with their patrons through one or more of these popular social networks: Facebook, Twitter, Pinterest, Yelp, Tumblr, Flickr, Google, and other sites. Libraries use social media today to communicate and market services to their communities of patrons and to outreach to those who may not be regular library users. Communications could be about new services, programs, events, collaborations, calendars, and postings of exciting images of recent events or newsworthy occasions. Like mobile devices, social networking has become a mainstay in our lives and has been adapted by people of all ages and socioeconomic backgrounds. For many, social media has replaced newspapers and other traditional ways of obtaining news.

It is presumptuous for me to be able to predict how social media will be used five, ten, or even twenty-five years from now when just a few years ago it did not exist. However, trends predict[23]:

- social media will be used to facilitate mobile payments via debit and credit;
- there will be a proliferation of new or niche social media sites;

- shopping will be brokered through social media;
- devices will be interconnected with social media; and
- privacy will be assured on social media.

Libraries can capitalize on each of these trends. For example, mobile payments and shopping sites could be tailored for libraries for fine collection or fundraising. People could be better connected to library services and catalogs. Table 12.3 shows a few of the new social media sites that libraries may also consider using.

Libraries have always valued and upheld patron privacy, so as social media sites do this better, it may be more appropriate for some of the library functions, such as circulation of materials. As proven effective, social media will continue to be a way for libraries to creatively communicate and market their services to the community.

LIBRARY SUPPORT STAFF AND THE FUTURE

Thinking about the future of libraries unleashes hundreds of possibilities! Undoubtedly there will be changes not only in libraries services and functions, but the work we do will evolve to be more highly technical yet customer friendly. My local public library board has been observing the trend of circulation of books is down yet use of digital resources, community programs, and the number of people who use the library each month continue to increase. The work of library staff is changing as well. In the article "The Librarian in 2020 | Reinventing Libraries,"[24] the authors suggest the following new job titles for library staff.

- The *embedded librarian* is responsible for physically and virtually traveling around all communities to catalog all pieces of the environment. This position is vital for ensuring that all people can use embedded or wearable technology to get instant information about everything in their surroundings.
- The *content packaging librarian* is responsible for making dynamic connections among library and community information so that users can easily find data that relates to particular topics and can lead to other beneficial information.
- The *robotic maintenance engineer* is responsible for ensuring that all public-assistant and stack robots are in good working order.
- The *lifestyle design librarian* is responsible for leading a team of librarians who specialize in individualized and customized assistance for public members navigating learning, career transitions, health, and other specific needs.

Table 12.3. Examples of New Social Media Sites

Snapchat	Snap a photo or a video, add a caption, and send it to a friend. They'll view it, laugh, and then the snap disappears from your history.
Yik Yak	Get a live feed of what everyone's saying around you.
Telegram	Telegram seamlessly syncs across all of your devices and can be used on desktops, tablets, and phones alike. You can send an unlimited amount of messages, photos, videos, and files of any type (.doc, .zip, .pdf, etc.).
Ello	Built by a group of artists and programmers as a private, advertisement-free social network, there is now a public version for everyone to use.

- The *cloud engineer* is responsible for providing system requirements for the development of the cloud-based library's data warehouses worldwide, increasing capacity and accessibility of information for the public.

My recommendation for you is to be curious and imaginative with new digital resources and technology. Like our patrons who use our makerspaces, experiment and try out new devices, databases, and e-book platforms. Create digital resources by scanning unique documents and imaging important artifacts. Learn from and with others as you experiment with technology. Finally, seek news about technology for all institutions, including libraries from the following and other places.

- *American Library Association*: *The Center for the Future of Libraries* identifies trends relevant to libraries and librarianship. This trend library is available to help libraries and librarians understand how trends are developing and why they matter. Each trend is updated as new reports and articles are made available. New trends will be added as they are developed.
- *9to5Mac*: Dedicated to all things Mac, you will find all kinds of Apple related news, from iOS to MacOS or iPhones to Macbooks.
- *9to5Google*: This blog is similar to 9to5Mac except it covers Google products as its name suggests.
- *RSS Feeds*: Alerts you to newsworthy technology posts.
- *Twitter*: Subscribe to technology tweets.
- *Newspaper Technology Columns* such as:
  ○ The *New York Times'* David Pogue's technology column and posts,
  ○ The *Wall Street Journal's* Walt Mossberg's Personal Technology columns.

CHAPTER SUMMARY

As I stated at the beginning of this chapter, I have no special view of the future. In this chapter we did explore trends with technology and digital resources which have the potential to change library services and the skills and roles library support staff will have in the future. If you have a curiosity about how technology can improve and enhance library services and functions, you are in the right place to be a part of the future of libraries. Library support staff who know the general trends and developments in technology applications for library functions and services will demonstrate flexibility in adapting to new technology to enhance the missions of libraries to improve the community and promote lifelong learning. It is surely an exciting time to be library support staff!

DISCUSSION QUESTIONS AND ACTIVITIES

Discussion Questions

1. How do makerspaces and 3-D printing potentially affect and support learning?

2. Why have makerspaces and 3-D printing become popular in libraries? Why are libraries appropriate places for these activities?
3. What are QR codes and how can library staff creatively use them to help patrons with information or other services?
4. What is electronic publishing and how can LSS support patrons who may want to use it?
5. Discuss the social media sites you think are best suited for libraries to use. How did you make your choices?
6. What do you think the future is for libraries and digital resources? What digital services do you predict libraries will use ten or twenty years from now? How will they change libraries from how we know them today?

Activities

Activity 1: QR Codes in the Library
Here are just a few ways QR codes can be used in the library:

1. QR code books to websites that provide background information.
2. QR code items of local interest or history. Link explanatory websites.
3. QR code technology and equipment with web tutorials or instructions.

Look around your library and make a list of other ways to use QR codes.

Activity 2: Enhance your new books through QR codes
This is an activity I did with students which they thoroughly enjoyed!

1. Be sure your smartphone, mobile device, or tablet has a QR code reader app. The app is free from the iTunes store and there are many sites for free downloads for android smartphones.
2. Select several new books that you would like to bring to the attention of patrons. My example will be a new biography on Jacqueline Kennedy Onassis.
3. Research websites that provide information about the time period, events, or topics of the books.
4. Make a list of the websites. Select one or two websites that best provide background information for each book. In my example, I find websites on the biography of Jacqueline Kennedy Onassis, post-traumatic stress syndrome (PTSS), and the John F. Kennedy assassination.
5. Generate QR codes for each website using QR Code Generator or other free downloads.
6. Make an attractive display that encourages people to use the QR codes to help them select a new book.

NOTES

1. Lee Rainie, "The Next Library and the People Who Will Use It," Pew Research Center—Internet, Science & Tech, last modified 2014, accessed January 27, 2015, http://www.pewin ternet.org/2014/11/13/the-next-library-and-the-people-who-will-use-it/.

2. "Scope-On-A-Rope," Scalar Scopes: Advanced Digital & Video Microscopes, last modified 2015, accessed January 27, 2015, http://www.scalarscopes.com/vl7ex/vl7exmain.htm.

3. Luke Simco, "Hackforge Unveiled in Windsor Library," *Metro*, last modified May 28, 2013, accessed January 27, 2015, http://metronews.ca/news/windsor/687053/hackforge -unveiled-in-windsor-library/.

4. Ibid.

5. "Our Mission," Windsor Public Library, Ontario, Canada, last modified 2013, accessed January 27, 2015, http://www.windsorpubliclibrary.com/?page_id=129.

6. *HATCH: It's a Public Workshop and It's Free* (Watertown, MA: Watertown Free Public Library, 2015).

7. Pilar Martinez, "Bigger Than Our Buildings: Transforming Spaces and Services at EPL," *Feliciter* 60, no. 6 (December 2014), accessed January 28, 2015, http://search.ebscohost.com/login.aspx?direct=true&db=aph&AN=100262029&site=ehost-live&scope=site.

8. "Stereogranimator Welcome!," New York Public Library Labs, last modified 2015, accessed January 28, 2015, http://stereo.nypl.org/.

9. "Mobile Technology Fact Sheet," Pew Research Center—Internet, Science & Technology, last modified January 2014, accessed January 27, 2015, http://www.pewinternet.org/fact-sheets/mobile-technology-fact-sheet/.

10. "Seven Tools to Create a Mobile Library Website (without Technical Knowledge)," Seven Tools to Create a Mobile Library Website, last modified October 12, 2011, accessed January 27, 2015, http://infopeople.org/sites/all/files/webinar/2011/10-12-2011/7_Tools _to_Create_a_Mobile_Library_Website.pdf.

11. "45 Most Exciting Apps for Librarians," LibraryScienceList.com, last modified June 15, 2014, accessed January 27, 2015, http://librarysciencelist.com/25-most-popular-apps-used -by-librarians/.

12. "Purdue University Libraries Publishing Division," Purdue University Libraries, last modified 2015, accessed January 27, 2015, https://www.lib.purdue.edu/publishing.

13. Ibid.

14. Gary Price, "Library Futures and Trends: First Ever 'Horizon Report For Libraries' Released by New Media Consortium," Infodocket, last modified August 2014, accessed January 27, 2015, http://www.infodocket.com/2014/08/20/library-futures-first-ever-horizon-report-for-libraries-released-today-by-new-media-consortium/.

15. Suzana Sukovic, "iTell: Transliteracy and Digital Storytelling," *Australian Academic & Research Libraries* 45, no. 3 (September 2014), accessed January 27, 2015, http://search .ebscohost.com/login.aspx?direct=true&db=aph&AN=98376518&site=ehost-live&scope=site.

16. Marshall Breeding, "Competition and Strategic Cooperation," Library Systems Report 2014, last modified April 15, 2014, accessed January 28, 2015, http://www.americanlibrar iesmagazine.org/article/library-systems-report-2014.

17. Ibid.

18. Marshall Breeding, "Library Technology: The Next Generation," *Computers in Libraries* 33, no. 8 (October 2013), http://search.ebscohost.com/login.aspx?direct=true&db=aph&AN =91561536&site=ehost-live&scope=site.

19. "Trends," Library of the Future: Center for the Future of Libraries, last modified 2015, accessed January 28, 2015, http://0-www.ala.org.librarycatalogs.nnu.edu/transforminglibrar ies/future/trends.

20. Ibid.

21. Ibid

22. Loretta Waldman, "Coming Soon to the Library: Humanoid Robots," *Wall Street Journal* (New York, NY), September 29, 2014, accessed January 28, 2015, http://www.wsj.com/articles/coming-soon-to-the-library-humanoid-robots-1412015687.

23. Ryan Holmes, "5 Trends That Will Change How You Use Social Media in 2015," *Time*, November 18, 2014, accessed January 29, 2015, http://search.ebscohost.com/login.aspx?dir ect=true&db=aph&AN=99506280&site=ehost-live&scope=site.

24. Stacey Aldrich and Jarrid Keller, "The Librarian in 2020 | Reinventing Libraries," *Wall Street Journal* (New York, NY), October 10, 2013, accessed January 28, 2015, http:// lj.libraryjournal.com/2013/10/future-of-libraries/the-librarian-in-2020-reinventing-librar ies/#_.

REFERENCES, SUGGESTED READINGS, AND WEBSITES

Aldrich, Stacey, and Jarrid Keller. "The Librarian in 2020 | Reinventing Libraries." *The Wall Street Journal* (New York, NY), October 10, 2013. Accessed January 28, 2015. http://lj.libraryjournal .com/2013/10/future-of-libraries/the-librarian-in-2020-reinventing-libraries/#_.

American Library Association. "Trends." Library of the Future: Center for the Future of Librar- ies. Last modified 2015. Accessed January 28, 2015. http://0-www.ala.org.librarycatalogs. nnu.edu/transforminglibraries/future/trends.

Breeding, Marshall. "Competition and Strategic Cooperation." Library Systems Report 2014. Last modified April 15, 2014. Accessed January 28, 2015. http://www.americanlibraries magazine.org/article/library-systems-report-2014.

———. "Library Technology: The Next Generation." *Computers in Libraries* 33, no. 8 (October 2013): 16–18. http://search.ebscohost.com/login.aspx?direct=true&db=aph&AN=915615 36&site=ehost-live&scope=site.

Google. "Drone." Google Images. Last modified 2015. Accessed January 28, 2015. https:// www.google.com/search?q=drone+public+domain+image&biw=1024&bih=615&tbm=isc h&tbo=u&source=univ&sa=X&ei=rnPJVNOwLYzGsQT9l4DYDg&ved=0CDIQ7Ak.

HATCH: It's a Public Workshop and It's Free. Watertown, MA: Watertown Free Public Library, 2015.

Holmes, Ryan. "5 Trends That Will Change How You Use Social Media in 2015." *Time*, No- vember 18, 2014. Accessed January 29, 2015. http://search.ebscohost.com/login.aspx?dire ct=true&db=aph&AN=99506280&site=ehost-live&scope=site.

Infopeople.org. "Seven Tools to Create a Mobile Library Website (without Technical Knowledge)." Seven Tools to Create a Mobile Library Website. Last modified Oc- tober 12, 2011. Accessed January 27, 2015. http://infopeople.org/sites/all/files/webi nar/2011/10-12-2011/7_Tools_to_Create_a_Mobile_Library_Website.pdf.

LibraryScienceList.com. "45 Most Exciting Apps for Librarians." LibraryScienceList.com. Last modified June 15, 2014. Accessed January 27, 2015. http://librarysciencelist .com/25-most-popular-apps-used-by-librarians/.

Martinez, Pilar. "Bigger Than Our Buildings: Transforming Spaces and Services at EPL." *Fe- liciter* 60, no. 6 (December 2014): 32–34. Accessed January 28, 2015. http://search.ebsco host.com/login.aspx?direct=true&db=aph&AN=100262029&site=ehost-live&scope=site.

New York Public Library. "Stereogranimator Welcome!" New York Public Library Labs. Last modified 2015. Accessed January 28, 2015. http://stereo.nypl.org/.

Pera, Mariam. "Midwinter Preview." *American Libraries* 46, no. 1/2 (January/February 2015): 70–76. Accessed January 27, 2015. http://search.ebscohost.com/login.aspx?direct=true&d b=aph&AN=100161162&site=ehost-live&scope=site.

Pew Research Center. "Mobile Technology Fact Sheet." Pew Research Center—Internet, Sci- ence &Technology. Last modified January 2014. Accessed January 27, 2015. http://www .pewinternet.org/fact-sheets/mobile-technology-fact-sheet/.

Price, Gary. "Library Futures and Trends: First Ever 'Horizon Report For Libraries' Released by New Media Consortium." Infodocket. Last modified August 2014. Accessed January 27,

2015. http://www.infodocket.com/2014/08/20/library-futures-first-ever-horizon-report
-for-libraries-released-today-by-new-media-consortium/.

Purdue University. "Purdue University Libraries Publishing Division." Purdue University Libraries. Last modified 2015. Accessed January 27, 2015. https://www.lib.purdue.edu/publishing.

Rainie, Lee. "The Next Library and the People Who Will Use It." Pew Research Center—Internet, Science & Tech. Last modified 2014. Accessed January 27, 2015. http://www.pewinternet.org/2014/11/13/the-next-library-and-the-people-who-will-use-it/.

Scalar. "Scope-On-A-Rope." Scalar Scopes: Advanced Digital & Video Microscopes. Last modified 2015. Accessed January 27, 2015. http://www.scalarscopes.com/vl7ex/vl7exmain.htm.

Simco, Luke. "Hackforge Unveiled in Windsor Library." *Metro*. Last modified May 28, 2013. Accessed January 27, 2015. http://metronews.ca/news/windsor/687053/hackforge-unveiled-in-windsor-library/.

Sukovic, Suzana. "iTell: Transliteracy and Digital Storytelling." *Australian Academic & Research Libraries* 45, no. 3 (September 2014): 205–29. Accessed January 27, 2015. http://search.ebscohost.com/login.aspx?direct=true&db=aph&AN=98376518&site=ehost-live&scope=site.

Waldman, Loretta. "Coming Soon to the Library: Humanoid Robots." *Wall Street Journal* (New York, NY), September 29, 2014. Accessed January 28, 2015. http://www.wsj.com/articles/coming-soon-to-the-library-humanoid-robots-1412015687.

Windsor Public Library. "Our Mission." Windsor Public Library, Ontario, Canada. Last modified 2013. Accessed January 27, 2015. http://www.windsorpubliclibrary.com/?page_id=129.

Zak, Elizabeth. "Do You Believe in Magic? Exploring the Conceptualization of Augmented Reality and Its Implications for the User in the Field of Library and Information Science." *Information Technology & Libraries* 33, no. 4 (December 2014): 23–50. Accessed January 27, 2015. http://search.ebscohost.com/login.aspx?direct=true&db=aph&AN=100227707&site=ehost-live&scope=site.

Glossary

3-D Printing: Three-dimensional printing is a manufacturing process whereby an object is built of very thin plastic or other material. The process begins at the base of the design and layers the object upwards until completed. The 3-D printer is attached to a computer where a design of a digital model was created with special software. Libraries are acquiring 3-D printers so that patrons can learn about this technology as they use it to create and build innovative concepts. Library staff who are trained to use 3-D printers can help and support the learning and skills patrons acquire using 3-D printers.

Algorithms: These are formulas created by search engine companies that determine how certain web pages show up in the results list. Results may be based on such things as the number and quality of other websites that are linked to a page, how many times key words appear on the page, or the quality of the sites that appear within the page. Library staff can recommend search engines to patrons with confidence when they know how result lists are determined.

Analog: Tape was the type of media libraries circulated for many years. Examples are audio and video cassettes, VHS tapes, 16 mm film, and phonograph records. Recorded in a continuous line with a beginning and end, to search a certain frame or location, one had to play or fast forward from the beginning of the tape. Libraries preserve important analog collections or convert them to digital.

Application Software: Programs installed on computers that are designed for staff and patrons to perform specific tasks or functions.

Apps: A common abbreviation for computer software applications. Examples of application software used by library staff and patrons are database programs, word processors, spreadsheets, online catalogs, social media, quick access newspapers, journals, magazines, and many other programs used for education, literacy, or research.

Archive: This term has two meanings for library staff. As a verb, it is the act of acquiring, preserving, and maintaining special resources or materials that have a high value to researchers and others. As a noun, it is a special location in a library where the unique materials are preserved and housed with restricted access.

Libraries are increasingly scanning archived materials in large numbers for Internet patron access.

Artifacts: These are two- or three-dimensional objects that have artistic, cultural, personal, or historic value. Libraries and museums preserve these objects in special collections for future generations with care because of their irreplaceable value. Most are original to the time period or event and are not circulated. Libraries today can create and share online digital collections of images of valuable objects from their special collections.

Authentication: This is the method of identification needed to access an online digital library or a database that is agreed upon by the library and the data provider. The proof for access could be such things as the patron barcode, unique username and/or password, or using an authorized library computer.

Boolean Operators: Words added to the search that limit or expand the results. The words AND, OR, and NOT are common. For example, "AND" actually limits the search results because at least two words—this AND that—must be present in the web page. Library staff perform or assist with more effective searches when they use operators.

Census: A survey typically conducted by the state or federal government which gathers information about people. The survey typically provides descriptive demographic data about each household and its members. Library staff who know how to find census data can help patrons research social issues, the economy, health, and many other aspects of life and culture.

Cloud Computing: The Internet is referred to as the cloud. Librarians use the Internet to transfer data over the Internet to servers not in the library for back-up and storage of data. Cloud computing replaces the need to keep and store data on your hard drive. Cloud computing removes the daily necessity of library staff backing up data or the concern of data integrity if there is an emergency. Library staff should know about the servers their library uses, how often data is backed up, and other policies that control the storage, accessibility, and privacy of their data, especially for circulation, cataloging, and e-mail.

Database Providers: Companies that market, demonstrate, negotiate, sell, and distribute their own or other publishers' online information. The provider may offer training, marketing, and other support to library staff so that they become familiar users.

Digital: This standard of today's technology uses binary code to create, store, and process data. Computers read data that is either expressed as "on"(1) or "off"(0). Alphabets and numbers are converted into binary code. Searching and other functions are much more efficient with digital than analog. Understanding how digital works is important for library staff who work with it every day.

Digital Collections: These are files of data whose content has a common theme, subject, time period, or other logical grouping. Types of data in digital collections can be text, sound, images, video, or combinations of each. Library staff create digital collections for preserving and sharing local history, genealogy, research, special interests, or programs.

Digital Copyright Protection: Federal law that gives control to the creator of a digital content the right to limit the number of copies and the sales of the work. In order for a work to be copyrighted, it must meet three criteria: it must be tangible or fixed (not an unwritten idea), original, and minimally creative. Library staff should learn the law and report any abuse they see of it to their supervisor.

Digitization: Digitization is the process of scanning and converting text and pictures into a digital format. Library staff can learn how to digitize text, pictures, photographs, and other physical items in order to share them with patrons in an online format.

Directory: A list of websites organized around a subject or theme for the purpose of guiding searchers to recommended sites. Library staff use authoritative national and state directories to help patrons find information. Library staff may also create their own directories of valid websites for research, local history, reading selection, or other topics that are important to patrons.

Dynamic IP Range: Consecutive numbers randomly assigned to library computers which make database searching faster because devices on the library network are preregistered with the provider to be legitimate users.

Electronic Resources: This is another name for digital resources. E-book comes from the term "electronic book." Library staff will find the term "electronic" or "electronic resources" in some of our literature or on library products.

Encryption Code: Instructions in the code of the e-book that cripple or make it no longer usable upon expiration of the loan time. Library staff can show patrons how to renew a library e-book to avoid it becoming encrypted before they are finished reading. E-book circulation is controlled by the computer instructions embedded in the e-book code.

Enumeration District: A census taker is also called an enumerator, someone who counts or quantifies information. His or her assigned geographic area, which could be as small as a city block or as large as a county, is called an enumeration district (ED). Census data is collected and displayed by ED. Library staff should become familiar with how to identify enumeration districts to effectively help patrons search the US Censuses online.

E-Rate: Implemented in 1997, the E-Rate Universal Service Fund provides discounted rates for Internet service for schools and libraries. The amount or percentage of the subsidy increases with the town poverty level.

Fair Use: Educators and students may use copyrighted material for their teaching and learning without seeking permission from the author for a one-time, spontaneous occasion. A small portion of a copyrighted work may be used without permission but never for commercial gain. Libraries receive special consideration because they promote and advance learning, a goal of the US Copyright Act. Library staff should know the basics of fair use. If they are uncertain as to the law, they should seek guidance from their supervisors before making digital copies.

Federated Search: This type of search cross-indexes multiple subscriptions simultaneously. The results are viewed in one screen even though the results come from different databases. Library staff should be familiar with federated searching because it is an efficient way to search many products at once.

File Extension: Appearing at the end of a computer file name, this three- or four-letter code represents the software application of the file. Common e-book file extensions are .doc for Word files, .azw for Kindle, .html for web hypertext, and .pdf for Adobe. Library staff help patrons download e-books to e-readers with knowledge of the how extensions work.

Filters: These are software applications and/or hardware solutions that block inappropriate or damaging Internet content from being viewed or downloaded on users' computers. Library staff are required by federal law to protect patrons under age eighteen from inappropriate Internet sites by equipping library computers and Wi-Fi with such solutions.

Grants: These are funds provided by others to pay for materials, equipment, labor, or other supports to advance the work of an important project. The library commits to mutually agreed upon goals, conditions, and activities with the funding agency.

HTML: Hypertext Mark-up Language is the computer code most commonly used to create websites. This code permits the linking of text or images to internal and external web pages. Many library digital resources, such as websites, articles, e-books, and documents can contain hyperlinks because they are written in html format.

In-Kind Contributions: Grants often fund part of a project and require the applicant to contribute the rest. The share or match required by the library for a grant could be things the library already has in place like staff time and skills, existing equipment, or materials. The library may have to do fundraising to acquire their amount of the project. Each grant will stipulate whether there is any matching effort required. Library staff can help with reaching the required match by providing their own expertise or skills for a project or outside activities like training volunteers and fundraising.

Information and Communications Technology (ICT): ICT is an acronym used to identify the many technologies for accessing information and communicating with others. ICT used in libraries are the online catalog, subscription databases, special collections, digital media, sound recordings, and digital images. Library staff use ICT to communicate information about programs, materials, and events to patrons and each other via e-mail, the library website, and social media.

Internet Protocol (IP): In order to access the Internet network, a computer must be uniquely identified by its IP address. Libraries share their computers and wireless IP addresses with Internet and database providers for authorized patron use within the library.

JPEG: An abbreviation for *Joint Photographic Experts Group*, and pronounced *jay-peg*. This file format compresses a color image to about 5 percent of its normal size with only slight loss of quality. Because the JPEG file size is so small, download speed is faster and less storage space is needed. JPEG is the accepted file format for Internet images.

Lexile Score: A measure of the reading level or difficulty of a text. Aligned to grade level, the scores indicate the reader's knowledge of vocabulary and ability to comprehend the text. Many items in subscription databases have Lexile scores. Library staff who are knowledgeable about Lexile can help patrons select appropriate reading level materials.

License Agreement: This is a contract between the library and the database company provider that specifies how long and under what conditions library patrons may use the subscription database or resource. Sometimes one license agreement is negotiated between a provider and multiple libraries for consortium or discount pricing.

Literacy: The ability and skills of a person to read, write, and perform mathematics. The term also defines having knowledge and expertise in a particular field of study.

LSTA Grants: The Library Services and Technology Act supports over 2,500 competitive grants each year that are administered through all of the fifty state libraries administration services. Grants are used to support statewide initiatives and services or cooperative agreements among public, academic, research, school, or special libraries serving the needs of all people. LSTA grants favor library projects that will benefit a large community for shared resources.

Makerspaces: Makerspaces are collaborative, hands-on learning places where people gather together to share ideas and create prototypes with tools and equipment. These can be such things as 3-D printers and media equipment, sewing machines, art supplies, and electronics and circuits. Popular in libraries these spaces bring community members of all ages together.

Memoir: This is a first-person account of the author about how his or her life was impacted by a change in attitude, beliefs, or even a philosophical enlightenment. While autobiographies typically chronicle an author's lifespan, a memoir focuses on what made the author have significant emotional or mindset changes. Library staff create or support the making of digital collections of memoirs for the library collection. Memoirs can be of elderly who saw or participated in events, people who contributed to town government, or others whose stories and perspectives are important to preserve.

Metadata: In cataloging, these are additional elements or pieces of information data that describe an object beyond its basic description. Examples of the elements are the names of those who contributed to the creation or preservation of the object or what materials the object is made of. Library staff use these additional elements in descriptive cataloging for artifacts and objects. Library staff apply metadata elements to conduct more effective searching of digital objects of online museum and library collections.

Metatag: This is a top line of computer code on a web page for inputting searchable subjects which will enhance the ranking of the page. These lines of code influence search engine results by matching the user's search terms with the subjects found in these lines of code. Library programmers can influence the ranking of their websites using metatags.

Network Infrastructure: The equipment, wiring, software, and other resources needed to move data to and from outside providers of services like the Internet or subscription databases to the patron user. Networks and equipment vary in size according to the location, size, and needs of the library. Library staff who are familiar with key component equipment can communicate with and support ICT staff for quick resolution of problems.

Nonlinear Text: Words or sentences that are not in consecutive order nor follow a left-to-right, line-by-line arrangement. Nonlinear text may be words in any vertical or horizontal manner and may not appear connected to each other.

OCR: This is an acronym for optical character recognition. The software converts scanned documents into word processing text that can be edited and changed on a computer. Library staff who are familiar with OCR can scan paper documents for later editing with a word processing program.

Open Source: This is software that has been developed by programmers that is free and without license or copyright. It is available for anyone to download and use. The software is often a collaborative effort among many contributors who improve the application. Libraries often have substantial technology cost savings when they use open source; however, they may also take a risk because the products often lack formal vendor or other technical support.

Outsource: Work or products the library contracts to have done by an outside company for cost savings or efficiency.

Peer Review: Before a scholarly article is accepted for publication by a journal, experts in the same subject (peers) read the article for accuracy, originality, depth of knowledge, etc., to validate its content. Library staff can guide patrons to authoritative research with confidence when they select *peer review* or *scholarly* as an advanced search limiter.

Portal Interface: This is a starting point or gateway for searchers to locate a large number of websites on a topic at once. Library staff who are familiar with specific portals can help patrons find information from many sources simultaneously on a topic or theme.

Preservation: The action or process of keeping an item from harm or decay so that it is maintained in its original state. There are many ways to maintain library artifacts beginning with climate control, secure handling, and protective covering. Library staff can locate artifacts within the library and research the correct archival supplies that can help maintain original integrity. Libraries often are the keepers of local history and artifacts. The act is to maintain something in its original state. Library staff often accept unique or important items into the library collections to maintain and keep for future generations.

Public Domain: In relation to copyright law, this term refers to *everyone*. Works that are not copyrighted have unrestricted use by all with no obligation to seek permission or compensate to use the work commercially or otherwise. After a set period of time all copyrights expire and the works become available for anyone to use freely. Library staff learn the basics of the law to know how to evaluate if a library material is in the public domain. Libraries are obligated to uphold copyright laws and allow only permissible uses of materials, including digital resources.

Refurbished Computers: These are used computers that have key component parts such as hard drives wiped clean or replaced. Faster memory and processors may be substituted, and new and updated operating systems or software added. Libraries can acquire these computers for normally half the cost for their online catalog stations or other functions that do not require high end computing.

Remote Access: This is the ability for a patron to externally access and use a library subscription database from outside of the library. The patron gains access typically with their barcode or a password.

RSS Feed: RSS stands for Really Simple Syndication. RSS is a way to have news and other regular web content delivered to your own personal wire service. RSS channels web content to your website, blog, e-mail, or other web service. Library websites often have RSS feeds of news or other wire services that patrons would have interest in. Library staff can direct patrons to the library RSS feed or help patrons set up their own feeds. Most website providers include an RSS option.

SaaS: Saas stands for Software as a Service. These are computer programs and applications running on a server outside of the library. The host service provider maintains the software and makes it seamless for the library staff and patrons to use. An example of SaaS is the online catalog hosted by a contract vendor or provider. Some libraries also use SaaS for their office software or accounting systems. Library staff do not have to be concerned about upgrades or software problems as part of the SaaS is maintenance and troubleshooting.

Scan: The act of creating file images using imaging technology. Libraries offer scanning technology to patrons to make digital copies of print documents. Library staff may use scanning technology to preserve documents, post copies of print items online, or communicate or archive other important information. Most scanners convert images of the page to the PDF computer file format that is efficient in storage space and commonly accepted for personal and business use.

Search Query: These are the actual words typed into the blank box of a search engine to locate information on the Internet. How the query is constructed determines the results. Library staff can suggest ways to improve a patron's search by using different combinations of shortcuts, words, and operator options to find desirable results.

Simulations: These staged experiences imitate a true process or an action. The viewer may be asked to assume a role, make a choice, or participate in other ways so that they feel they are contributing to the process or action. In science, we may observe a multimedia presentation which simulates a reaction or phenomena. Libraries may use simulation software for educational programs or even to attract teens such as Wii sports or other gaming software.

Simultaneous Use: More than one patron may access a subscription database at the same time. Depending on the license agreement between the library and the database provider, the number of users at the same time may be unlimited or restricted to a specific number such as five or ten.

Spider: Not the arachnid, this type of spider, also called a web crawler, is a program created by search engine companies to scan through all Internet web pages. Searching for key words, images, and other information, these programs search uncountable Internet sites to identify pages searchers would like to find. The selected websites are then referenced in the search engine index for quick retrieval.

Streaming: This is the process of data being transferred over the Internet at a very high speed. The database provider sends sound and media data in a continuous steady flow rather than in bunches or packets that can be "jerky." Patrons prefer streaming video because the flow of movement is smooth and more true to watching a film on television or in the movies. Libraries should seek streaming video whenever possible for patron satisfaction.

Subscription Databases: These are collections of searchable and authoritative documents, articles, images, sound, media, websites, or other information formats clustered around a broad theme or subject. With editorial review for inclusion of materials, library staff and patrons can rely on information from databases that is likely more reliable and authoritative than that of the free Internet.

Tablet: This is a light and compact computer that has a built-in screen. The keyboard is typically a touch pad from the screen. Many patrons bring their own tablets into the libraries and use the library Wi-Fi to access the Internet. These devices also serve as e-book reader devices for many of the different types of e-book file types, particularly .html and .pdf.

Technology Standards: Clear expectations of outcomes that define what students should know how to do with technology and be able to using technology to support their learning. Standards set goals for student achievement.

Troubleshooting: This term describes being able to quickly diagnose and solve a technology problem. Many problems arise with library technology because of the heavy use many patrons give the equipment each day.

URL: This is the abbreviation for the term Uniform Resource Locator, the global address of documents and other resources found in servers on the World Wide Web. Because it would be impossible to remember all of the different numbered addresses of servers, the numbers have been converted into names such as www .mylibrary.com that are uniform for locating a web page. Librarians use URLs in their work as they recommend websites to patrons or retrieve information from reliable sources.

Virtual Library: This is another name for multiple online digital collections. Library staff should be familiar with this term as some people or places prefer to use it to describe their digital resources collections.

Index

About the Author

Marie Keen Shaw is the program coordinator for the Library Technical Assistant certificate program at Three Rivers Community College in Norwich, Connecticut, where she has also been an adjunct professor since 1999. She teaches digital resources, cataloging and classification, reference services, and management strategies. She currently serves on boards of the Connecticut Digital Library, the Connecticut Library Consortium, and the Groton Public Library. Marie received her doctorate of education from the University of Connecticut in educational leadership and adult learning, a sixth-year degree from Southern Connecticut State University in educational leadership, and her MS from Purdue University in library and information science and educational media. A retired certified high school library media specialist and curriculum instructional leader, she chaired numerous district curriculum, library, and technology committees. She has been a speaker at state library and educational media conferences in Rhode Island, Illinois, and Connecticut and is a past president of Libraries Online. Shaw is the author of the book *Block Scheduling and Its Impact on the School Library Media Center* and her doctoral dissertation "Teacher's Learning of Technology: Key Factors and Process."